# PARTY & OPPOSITION
# OPPOSITION

## Congressional Challengers in American Politics

# PARTY &
# OPPOSITION

## Congressional Challengers in American Politics

### Jeff Fishel

INDIANA UNIVERSITY

*With a Foreword by*
ALLARD K. LOWENSTEIN

DAVID McKAY COMPANY, INC.
*New York*

*for Ivan J. Kubanis* (1921–1965),
who first taught me
the distinction between science
and politics as vocations;
*and for Lynn,*
who helped make my choice survive.

**PARTY AND OPPOSITION**
*Congressional Challengers in*
*American Politics*

DESIGNED BY ANGELA FOOTE

LIBRARY OF CONGRESS CATALOG CARD NUMBER: 72-92656

MANUFACTURED IN THE UNITED STATES OF AMERICA

# Preface

To the extent such phrases have any meaning, the 1960s were an Age of Opposition. "Another book," said one younger veteran of this decade, "on a disappearing institution." I skipped asking him which part of the title he had in mind. The irony remains.[1]

American parties have acquired the annoying historical habit of outliving most of those who are convinced of their imminent demise. How they have done so reinforces a permanent tension in the ebb and flow of political opposition and institutional response.

This book is a collective political biography about one form of opposition. It begins with 390 congressional challengers who moved to oppose a similar number of incumbents in the 1964 election and ends with 41 congressmen who survived six years of repeated attempts to send them back from whence they came. Facing up to *their* opposition in 1972 is a problem all must confront. Most who emerged victorious during the preceding three campaigns will win, but some will not. Were it otherwise, neither parties nor opposition would be worth writing about, at least in any sense that distinguishes democratic from other types of political systems.

While many of the 1964 challengers have long since returned to political obscurity, some have begun to have significant national impact: John J. Gilligan, now governor of Ohio, a former English professor who overcame the legacy of the Tafts and the reality

1. The 1960s may well become known as the Age of Age Designations. They have variously been labeled the Age of Rubbish (Richard Hofstadter), the Age of Outrageous Paradox (Emmett Hughes), the Age of Protest (Walt Anderson), and a host of other "Ages" too numerous to mention.

of Frank Lausche, both remarkable political feats; John Conyers (D.-Mich.), an organizer of the increasingly influential Black Caucus; Howard "Bo" Calloway, first Republican to win a Georgia gubernatorial race since Reconstruction, only to be denied the office by Lester Maddox when the state legislature decided the final outcome; Patsy Mink (D.-Hawaii), an early and articulate advocate of women's rights and ethnic pluralism; John Tunney, the only freshman member of the 89th Congress who successfully moved on to the Senate; Edwin Reinecke, now lieutenant governor of California; William R. Anderson (D.-Tenn.), first skipper of the *Nautilus*, unimpeachable member of "the establishment," who stunned Tennesseans with his eloquent defense of the Berrigans.

Others, equally skilled but less well known, are now working their way up the more normal routes of power in the House. What of the rest—those who couldn't quite overcome the electoral realities of most congressional campaigns? Popular and scholarly opinion has not been exceptionally kind to this cadre of highly active citizens. The two most frequently heard stereotypes are attorneys on the make and party dullards. This study proposes some alternative images.

I came to the book along a typical intellectual path, believing the British Labour and Conservative parties models of intelligent and meaningful organization—"Opposition," in Allen Potter's phrase, "with a capital 'O.'" Such comparisons have always been misleading. France, not Great Britain, seems the more likely analogue.

Woodrow Wilson and an army of subsequent Wilsons, some more radical, some less, have persistently sought to impose the British model on the American political system. The product, had they succeeded, would still have been forced to confront the sociology governing political behavior in this society. Reversing Christopher Lasch's comment on Mailer, the result surely seems predictable: a Rocky Mountain tough in the guise of a Boston Brahmin. Toughs, now as in the past, are rarely comprehensible in the reform salons of intellectuals. So it is with Congress and the two parties that dominate it.

Like many others, I have spent a substantial part of the past seven years signing petitions; teaching and learning in countless "teach-ins"; marching down Pennsylvania Avenue or up the Mall and across Memorial Bridge to "confront" the Pentagon; joining caucuses for "new" political sciences, "new" Democratic parties, "new" universities; assisting in various minor ways the data needs of a string of coalitions for change (Now! and Always!); admiring and defending (most of) the political mobilization of blacks, Chicanos, American Indians, women, students; and not admiring but defending (some of) the counterresurgence of cops, hardhats, middle Americans, "silent majorities," and others. But where does political science, *as science*, fit into the transformations spawned by demands for and resistance to political change?

Given my own values, it is clear that scientific political analysis has too frequently been used as an indiscriminate defense of the status quo, whether it involved strategic misplanning in Vietnam, or sweeping generalizations about "real majorities," working class "authoritarianism," or the "anti-politics of the young." Political change and institutional responsiveness are complex phenomena. Specifying the costs, as well as the benefits, of how Congress and the major parties attempt to deal with these twin problems can generate a more fruitful dialogue between change-oriented activists and political science. Value neutrality strikes me as impossible, uncritical commitment unhealthy.

Karl Deutsch and Sheldon Wolin offer alternative professional visions to the fetish of instant relevance. While not incompatible, they move one toward decisions of emphasis. The inadequacies of my own professional values, closer to Deutsch than Wolin, will be readily apparent in the book that follows. I still believe the behavioral persuasion (post and otherwise) will more likely increase our ability to deal with some of the structural defects of American society than other currently popular alternatives. But C. Wright Mills, not a squad of "system engineers," is the more convincing model for a critical and applied behavioral science.[2] In any event, I hope both scholars and practitioners will find something of use in this analysis.

The research upon which the book is based was originally begun as a dissertation involving a comparative study of American congressional and West German Bundestag candidates. For a variety of reasons, the German data have been excluded and the American portion substantially expanded. The logic of building on the earlier data base dictated that the national focus be reduced, a decision I hope others more generously endowed (with talent, money, and time) will not be forced to duplicate. Earlier and shorter versions of chapters 3 and 4 have been published in the

2. Out of fashion because of the date, although still useful is Mills' *The Sociological Imagination* (New York: Oxford University Press, 1959).

*Journal of Politics* and the *American Political Science Review.* I am grateful to the editors for permitting me to incorporate them.

One naturally accumulates debts over time that no amount of reciprocity can repay. Mine are legion:

The Falk Foundation, through the Political Behavior Archives at the University of California, Los Angeles, and The Brookings Institution in Washington, D.C., provided institutional support for different phases of the project.

Harry M. Scoble and Dwaine Marvick, friends, teachers, mentors; each, reflecting quite different styles, a master craftsman; without their encouragement, criticism, and direction, this book could never have been written.

Robert R. Alford, Michael B. Conant, Earl H. DeLong, Ivo Feierabend, Harold H. Haak, Henry L. Janssen, Richard P. Longaker, L. Vincent Padgett, and Austin Ranney, all of whom prevented me from retreating back to journalism.

My former colleagues at American University and San Francisco State College helped me over a number of obstacles, intellectual and otherwise. I would be remiss in not singling some out. Coralie Bryant, Frederic S. Burin, Robert E. Cleary, A. Lee Fritschler, Ralph M. Goldman, Jerome J. Hanus, Louis Loeb, Martin Meadows, Sandra S. Powell, Bernard H. Ross, Charles L. Ruttenberg, and Morley Segal are particularly guilty on this score.

William R. Keech and Allan Kornberg read the entire manuscript and gave me the benefit of their highly constructive and acute critical faculties.

Edward Artinian has been a patient but persistent editor for David McKay Company.

Thomas M. Rees, whose urbane wit and sophisticated reform battle plans from inside Congress made the House of Representatives more comprehensible for both the Fishels.

Allard K. Lowenstein, tireless challenger and incurable optimist, who proved that even Texas mountains (if not Brooklyn molehills) could be moved.

And finally, Lynn, occasional conspirator with Rees and Lowenstein, who surmounted the abstractions of academia and made a sizable intellectual contribution to this book.

Regrettably, none can share responsibility for the remaining deficiencies.

Nashville, Indiana

# Foreword by
# Allard K. Lowenstein

Many political institutions sacrifice efficiency for democracy, or democracy for efficiency. Congress sacrifices both to achieve neither. This book suggests why that is so and presents some interesting ideas about how to improve the situation.

Not all Jeff Fishel's proposals will please the advocates of conventional reforms, for this book is not a retelling of old tales or a reiterating of old conclusions. Rather, it is a fresh and unpredictable effort to harness facts in a way that will guide tactics toward achievable goals. As such, it reads challengingly and merits the attention of anyone concerned about those problems of congressional effectiveness and structure that have become so crucial to the future of the Republic.

Max Weber once observed that politics "is a strong and slow boring of hard boards. It takes both passion and perspective. Certainly all historical experience confirms the truth that man would not have obtained the possible unless time and time again he had reached for the impossible." Professor Fishel understands this and helps us to understand which is which and where to reach.

I once remarked that not even societies that worship their ancestors automatically make them chairmen of all their committees. Yet the average age of committee chairmen in the House of Representatives is several years older than the compulsory retirement age for other government employees. Quite apart from abstract questions of democratic principle, it should be clear by now that this situation is not helpful to a form of government that is supposed to be based on a balance of energy, responsibility, and power between coequal branches. So Professor Fishel's book is especially timely now that the effort to change antiquated procedures is at higher priority than at any time in recent memory. He provides information and insights that can be valuable in that effort, and even manages to show that the House of Representatives has, on occasion, been innovative and a force for change in social and economic policy. Additionally, he shows that congressional challengers—both within the House and outside it—who worked for much-needed change did not necessarily suffer at the polls because they had not compromised basic beliefs. Cynics will profit from a careful reading of his documentation of a fact that is generally ignored or discounted by politicians and pundits alike—that although political virtue is no guarantor of electoral success, neither is political vice.

The notion that adherence to conviction is likely to be fatal can make decent men timid and timid men venal. In fact, election is a goal so embedded in the folkways of Congress that many members have lost sight of why they are, or are not, elected or reelected. It is no surprise that this retards their ability to function as independent legislators and to resist domination by misguided presidents. Professor Fishel demonstrates that it has proved politically naive when relating to their constituents.

This book challenges many other conventional assumptions as well. It is well documented, forthright, and fair. I think people who have grown accustomed to viewing themselves as a kind of permanent opposition will benefit from paying close attention to many of Professor Fishel's arguments. Far too often, high-minded reformers, as well as some self-styled "revolutionaries," prove on inspection to be just another brand of political elitists, naive about what's what, almost irrelevant to efforts to change what they do not like. Realists who understand that basic changes are desperately needed—people who want to see America moving toward social justice and who believe that effective democratic institutions are the best way to get there—will value this book. It relates the impact of individuals on institutions to the context in which each interact, focusing on roles that have too long been obscure. As the title of his book suggests, Professor Fishel undertook a large and important task. We are fortunate that he chose this task; and we are fortunate that it is he who undertook it.

# Contents

# Tables

# 1

# OPPOSITION AND CONGRESSIONAL CAMPAIGNS

*College professors and philosophers who go up in a balloon to think are always discussin' the question: "Why reform administrations never succeed themselves!" The reason is plain to anybody who has learned the a,b,c, of politics . . . a reformer can't last. They're mornin' glories—look lovely in the mornin' but are all withered up by night.–(Plunkitt, 1898)*

Among the persistent themes in Western political thought, the recruitment and performance of political leaders has been central for all normative and empirical theorists.

"Who cares 'Who Governs'?" a sardonic remark with an obvious reference, begs a number of critical questions. Taken seriously, such a perspective virtually eliminates one of the two major components in democratic theories of representation. Whether viewed as vanguards or rulers, elites or decision makers, the history of things political is saturated with a concern for this question.

Social scientists have generated an enormous array of social background, attitudinal, and behavioral data on American public figures. Increasingly, research has moved beyond description and microexplanation in efforts to link such data with the functioning (or malfunctioning) of powerful political structures.[1]

1. Reviews of emerging trends in contemporary research can be found in *Political Decision-Makers*, ed. Dwaine Marvick (Glencoe, Ill.: Free Press, 1961); Wendell Bell, Richard J. Hill, and Charles R. Wright, *Public Leadership* (San Francisco: Chandler, 1961); Carl Beck, James M. Malloy, and William R. Campbell, *A Survey of Elite Studies* (Washington, D.C.: Special Operations Research Office, 1965); Lewis J. Edinger et al., *Political Leadership in Industrialized Society* (New

1

Congress, perhaps more than any other institution, has been a major focus for this interest. Understandably, political scientists have usually begun with the members of Congress (or a party, bureaucracy, court, etc.) and then traced back through time to the sources and causes of their selection. Very often this leads to describing and explaining the behavior of those who already occupy positions of power without considering the process by which some are admitted and others rejected.[2] The emphasis is on the *legislative* rather than the *electoral* arena.

From the viewpoint of understanding the ability of parties to mobilize and organize effective opposition to existing alternatives in Congress (personnel and policy), this emphasis is clearly deficient. A broader perspective should focus on candidates in both arenas, outside and inside the House or Senate. Assessing the impact of prelegislative factors on the subsequent behavior of the few who become representatives provides one powerful mechanism for connecting the process of recruitment with the performance of legislatures.

Moreover, theories of representation that are not linked to those who are defeated, in addition to the successful, will always convey distorted images of democratic government. For better or worse, political systems are as distinguished by who they reject as who they accept in the collective decisions that endow some with leadership roles.

---

York: Wiley, 1967), pp. 1–21; Andrew S. McFarland, *Power and Leadership in Pluralist Systems* (Stanford: Stanford University Press, 1969); Peter Bachrach and Morton S. Baratz, *Power and Poverty: Theory and Practice* (New York: Oxford University Press, 1970); and Kenneth Prewitt, *The Recruitment of Citizen Politicians* (Indianapolis: Bobbs-Merrill, 1971). For a historical survey of the importance attached to the recruitment of leaders in political philosophy, from Plato to Rousseau, see David Schwartz, "Political Recruitment: An Essay in Theory and Research" (Ph.D. dissertation, Massachusetts Institute of Technology, 1965). A sustained critique of elite studies, cross-national and otherwise, is Dankwart A. Rustow, "The Study of Elites: Who's Who, When, and How," *World Politics* (July 1966): 690–717. Robert L. Peabody provides a systematic and incisive review of research on Congress in his introductory chapter to Ralph K. Huitt and Robert L. Peabody, *Congress: Two Decades of Analysis* (New York: Harper, 1969). An earlier literature review, which includes data and studies from the state legislative milieu is Heinz Eulau and Katherine Hinckley, "Legislative Institutions and Processes," *Political Science Annual*, vol. 1, ed. James A. Robinson (Indianapolis: Bobbs-Merrill, 1966).

2. Herbert Jacob, "Initial Recruitment of Elected Officials in the U.S.—A Model," *Journal of Politics* (1962): 708; and Rufus Browning, "The Interaction of Personality and Political System in Decisions to Run for Office," *Journal of Social Issues* (July 1968): 93–110.

Congress is not highly regarded by those who value rapid and massive transformations in personnel. Every two years a sizable number of congressional challengers surface who collectively stand about one in five chances of success. While most are defeated, some are victorious, thus beginning the long climb to positions of potential national power. What follows, if anything, for who does what, and who gets what, in the American political struggle?

This book considers the role of challengers in linking elections, parties, and opposition to congressional representation. Two broad questions structure the analysis: (1) What incentives do major parties provide to build stable opposition roles in the political environment *outside* Congress? (2) Can the few challengers who win have any significant impact on public policy, or on the way citizens are represented inside Congress?

## Framework

Reflecting on the diversity of those comprising the membership in any modern legislative body, T. V. Smith, philosopher-cum-legislator from Chicago in the 1930s, once declared:

> Lean men there are as legislators, and fat men; tall men and short men, bald men and Beaux Brummels, old men and young men, sober men and smiling men, modest men and mere men, rich men and poor men, college bred and corn-fed; men there are, indeed, of every sort and condition. . . . Seek the representatives out one by one. Hunt for their common quality in statistical tables. Still it seems that age cannot wither nor custom stale their infinite variety.[3]

Without detracting from Smith's poetic description nor the accuracy of his conclusion, it can be argued that the burden of considerable research has been directed toward showing the substantial restrictions within which the "infinite" takes place.[4]

3. T. V. Smith, *The Legislative Way of Life* (Chicago: University of Chicago Press, 1940), p. 33.
4. The standard source on U.S. senators is Donald R. Matthews, *U.S. Senators and Their World* (New York: Vintage, 1960), chapter 2. See also Andrew Hacker, "The Elected and the Annointed," *American Political Science Review* 55 (1961): 539–49. No published analysis of the social background of representatives has appeared since Madge M. McKinney's, "The Personnel of the Seventy-Seventh Congress," *American Political Science Review* 26 (March 1942). The Legislative Reference Service of the Library of Congress does compile data on occupation and education for each session, as does *Congressional Quarterly.* One of the major his-

Congressional recruitment involves more than simply isolating the social groups from which members are drawn, however. Lester G. Seligman, in a seminal article, distinguishes two phases in the recruitment process: certification—the social and political parameters that result in eligibility; and selection—which includes the actual choice of candidates. For Seligman, as for others, the political party is the primary instrument for screening and selection "because a party that cannot attract and then nominate candidates surrenders its elementary opportunity for power."[5] Exercising power is quite different from the opportunity to do so; all contemporary power theorists insist on the importance of this distinction.

Congressional races provide potential leaders high opportunity for assuming powerful roles, but a low probability of ever being able to capitalize on them. Certainly the low turnover rate (not exceeding 26 percent since 1932) would seem to discourage ambitious American politicians from challenging incumbents. Although there are nonelectoral benefits associated with standing for Congress, any serious hope of wining must be balanced against one fact: only rarely are more than 15 percent of those incumbents who actively seek reelection ever defeated. And the nonelectoral side payments (advancing one's business career, for example) are among the most exaggerated political boodle in American politics.[6]

---

torical projects now underway at the Inter-University Consortium for Political Research involves codifying biographical information for all House members from the Continental Congresses through the twentieth century. An early analysis (1940) of state legislators can be found in Charles Hyneman, "Who Makes Our Laws," reprinted in *Legislative Behavior*, ed. John Wahlke and Heinz Eulau (Glencoe, Ill.: Free Press, 1959), pp. 254–64. For recent data, see John Wahlke et al., *The Legislative System* (New York: Wiley, 1962), particularly pp. 486–92; and Malcolm E. Jewell and Samuel C. Patterson, *The Legislative Process in the United States* (New York: Random House, 1966), chap. 5.

5. "Political Recruitment and Party Structure: A Case Study," *American Political Science Review* (1961): 77.

6. The costs of political defeat, financial and otherwise, are consistently underestimated in popular and scholarly literature. Three recent empirical studies, one of challengers in 1962, another of Wisconsin politicians, and a third focusing on congressional candidates in the San Francisco Bay area, provide a more balanced perspective on this problem: Robert Huckshorn and Robert Spencer, *The Politics of Defeat* (Amherst: University of Massachussets Press, 1971); John W. Kingdon, *Candidates for Public Office* (New York: Random House, 1968); and David Leuthold, *Electioneering in a Democracy* (New York: Wiley, 1968).

If the drive for power is the most compelling incentive in recruiting party candidates, how, one might ask, does either organization ever attract opposition in districts other than those which are most marginal? Various studies over the past fifteen years have provided an alternative image of the incentive systems which sustain both major parties. Although power-oriented, each party is simultaneously held together by a complex set of multiple incentives.[7] Five seem germane in examining the opposition roles undertaken by congressional challengers:[8]

1. *Representational incentives:* Alternative avenues for representation by candidates from social groups usually associated with the party of the incumbent. Here the out-party can provide a mechanism for nominating group members who typically constitute a small portion of that party's electoral base; e.g., black Republicans.

2. *Open career incentives:* The major American party organizations are frequently characterized as open and fluid for a variety of political entrepreneurs. Some candidates are committed professionals in the normal career sense, others are amateurs. How receptive to this vocational pluralism are the parties at the congressional level?

3. *Ideological incentives:* American parties may suffer relative to their European counterparts, but they can provide candidates an opportunity for articulating programmatic alternatives about the current and future course of national policy. Do candidates formulate meaningful alternatives?

4. *Strategic incentives:* Campaign resources—money, manpower, information—are scarce commodities in politics. Both parties share their limited capability in this regard with other groups. Given this reality, what can they offer candidates?

5. *Power incentives:* The low probability of success for most

7. Samuel J. Eldersveld's study is still the most thorough documentation of multifunctionality. *Political Parties: A Behavioral Analysis* (Chicago: Rand McNally, 1964), pp. 333–410.

8. These have been abducted from a variety of sources. For a review of theoretical problems, and some alternatives to the ones I'm using, see Peter B. Clark and James Q. Wilson, "Incentive Systems: A Theory of Organization," *Administrative Science Quarterly* (September 1961): 129–66.

candidates makes this a marginal but still potent utility which is monopolized by the major parties. How do candidates exploit this incentive when they are successful?

"Third" parties have made considerable contribution to the scope and vitality of political opposition in the United States. They have suffered, relative to the dominant organizations, because they have rarely provided a continuing mix of each of the above. To be sure, repeated electoral failure tends to bias the kind, amount, and duration of all other incentives parties can provide. The process is circular and probably mutually reinforcing.

Historical transformations in the parties' social bases, in critical issues, and in organizational alternatives have consistently challenged the survival of American parties.[9] In different periods, quite distinctive incentives have probably assumed ascendancy over others. Still, I would contend that the major parties have retained their dominance because each has pursued a strategy of offering increments of *all* five to potential recruits.

Incrementalism has costs, here as in other areas of American life. This seems particularly true when applied to the way each party has focused (or not focused) opposition roles in national elections. It is difficult not to agree with Robert Dahl when he suggests "that a distinctive, persistent, unified [large and party-based] opposition scarcely exists . . . to say where the government begins and 'the opposition' ends is an exercise in metaphysics."[10] But some parties have more on which to capitalize than others. Examining the scope and impact of this wherewithal constitutes the major analytical task of the book.

The relationship of congressional campaigns to *effective*[11]

9. Three historical interpretations which make these themes central are Walter Dean Burnham, *Critical Elections and the Mainsprings of American Politics* (New York: Norton, 1970); Everett C. Ladd, *American Political Parties: Social Change and Political Response* (New York: Norton, 1970); and Michael Rogin, *The Intellectuals and McCarthy: The Radical Spectre* (Boston: MIT Press, 1966).

10. Robert A. Dahl, ed., *Political Oppositions in Western Democracies* (New Haven: Yale University Press, 1966), p. 34.

11. I'm using "effective" in a straightforward manner, meaning that opposition candidates can at least occasionally threaten incumbents by gaining in excess of 40 percent of the vote. Richard Hofstadter makes a similar argument for parties generally, although he adds to this definition a policy-oriented stipulation involving the political feasibility of proposed programs. While this may be useful for Hofstadter, it would unnecessarily complicate this definition. See his *The Idea of a*

electoral opposition is paradoxical. On the one hand, individual challengers typically cannot change through their campaign efforts the voting behavior of more than 5 to 8 percent of the electorate. Since the more important determinants of victory involve the relative ratios of district party strength and other characteristics of the constituency, changing the current shape of party dominance in Congress will be subject to alteration in these deeper, less transient factors. The probability of massive (30 percent plus) incumbent defeats during any single campaign is remote.[12]

On the other hand, electoral opposition will badly atrophy unless parties are capable of supplying other incentives in the hope candidates can eventually capitalize on whatever long-run shifts might be occurring in the district. The tension between short-run costs and long-run gains is a permanent aspect of any strategy of political change.

Obviously, changing the voting intentions of 5 to 8 percent of a congressional electorate can make a critical difference; strategic intelligence, backed by necessary resources, is important for this "floating" vote.[13] Concentrating on this minority makes sense only if challengers enter the campaign relatively secure about the other 45 percent. Proportionately few do.

By focusing on both components of the recruitment process—inside and outside Congress—candidacy becomes a vehicle for responding to a variety of political needs. Important questions

*Party System: The Rise of Legitimate Opposition in the United States, 1780–1840* (Berkeley: University of California Press, 1970), pp. 4–5.

12. There is little reason to believe that patterns established in the 1940s and '50s have changed over the last decade. The best source for the period 1952–62 is Charles O. Jones, "Interparty Competition for Congressional Seats," *Western Political Quarterly* (1964): 461–76.

13. A net change of 38 seats in 1964 had significant policy consequences, as my analysis later documents. If Republicans had made a net gain of 40 during 1972, they would have captured control of the House. The impact of different campaign activities, a subject of considerable dispute, has been examined quasiexperimentally off and on over the years. A good summary, with data based on varying kinds of offices, can be found in William Crotty, "Party Effort and Its Impact on the Vote," *American Political Science Review* (June 1971): 439–51. The most widely publicized mobilization of resources of recent vintage was undertaken by the Movement for a New Congress and the Universities Anti-War Fund in the 1970 congressional elections. Preliminary evaluation can be found in William T. Murphy, "Student Power in the 1970 Elections: A Preliminary Assessment," *P.S.* (Winter 1971): 27–32.

about the candidates' electoral strategies, bases of support, programmatic preferences, or behavior as congressmen, cannot be reduced to simple formulas of "moving to the center" or "winning at all costs." Parties may very well be losing some of their historic functions,[14] but the recruitment of opposition candidates, from president to county commissioner, is still central in their continuing survival.

## Themes

The analysis that follows is aimed at a variety of audiences: specialists in the theory and research of leadership recruitment; students of party organization and behavior, or of Congress and the distinctive role of the House of Representatives in the policy-making process; those concerned with the way campaign resources are developed and utilized in House elections; and, one hopes, sophisticated laymen who are interested generally in the conduct and impact of congressional elections.

Accordingly, different chapters will vary in their appeal, depending on the reader's general interest and background.

The five major incentives discussed earlier—social representation, open career possibilities, ideological articulation, strategic needs, and options for using power and representing different interests—provide the organizing framework for each chapter.

Chapter 2, a congressional "land and people" background analysis, raises questions about the social composition of challengers and incumbents. The social parameters of eligibility are considered, exploring the degree to which opposition candidates are using parties as alternative routes of social representation. Do the kind of candidates who move to oppose incumbents undermine the dominance of white middle-class males in both the parties and Congress? Answer: a little bit, but not much.

Unless the reader is particularly concerned with recruitment theory and its implications for leadership opportunity, chapter 3 on ambition in politics can most profitably be scanned. Theories of ambition and power motivation are discussed, a measure of career commitment developed, and a variety of questions empirically

14. Anthony King, "Political Parties in Western Democracies," *Polity* (Winter 1969): 111–41.

analyzed: What social and political background factors are associated with varying degrees of a commitment to a career in politics? What effects flow from different socialization patterns? Is candidacy a direct extension of coming from politically active families, or does it represent a new shift to a different frame of reference? Do different kinds of career paths—through party or public officeholding—typify the way candidates are churned up for Congress? Are candidates who consider themselves amateurs less likely to win? Are there any differences in policy orientation among careerists and amateurs? How does electoral defeat or success structure the openness of parties to candidates with varying levels of political ambition?

Candidates for Congress are frequently condemned for being "Tweedledum and Tweedledee" on the broad issues that have confronted the United States over the past ten years. But are they? If so, is it meaningful to consider these candidates as an "opposition" in congressional campaigns? If not, does it have any impact on their ability to win? On what ultimately happens in Congress if they succeed? Chapter 4 focuses on the programmatic orientation of challengers. What are the major policy differences between candidates of the two parties? What factors are associated with undercutting these differences? Intensifying them? How do these affect the choices provided voters? Is the legislative productivity of Congress affected by what these men and women believe *before* they enter the House?

Chapter 5 concentrates on that perennial problem of all candidates: finding and using the necessary campaign resources to compete. Incumbents typically enter a congressional race with a substantial advantage over their challengers. How do challengers attempt to counterbalance this strategic problem? What kinds of resources are sought? Where used? With what effect? How do challengers perceive the small bounty distributed by local and national party organizations? Is there significant variation by types of districts? If so, does it make any difference on the types of candidates who do compete? Or on the eventual outcome of congressional elections?

Fortune, skill, circumstance; all converge to reduce the possibility of winning for most challengers. Chapter 6 examines the behavior of the few who first won in 1964. While the next chapter concentrates on their fortunes during the 1965–70 period, this chapter focuses on their initial experience as freshmen in the House. How do they relate to early problems of adaptation? What are their perceptions of the strengths and weaknesses of legislative life generally in Congress? In committees? How do they cope with the trials and tribulations of being freshmen in a body universally known for its emphasis on seniority? Are congressmen ambitious for careers outside the House different from those more content to work their way up the usual inside ladder? How do they evaluate the responsiveness of the House and its capabilities for internal reform? Did these freshmen have any effect on the legislative output of the "Great Society"? This section sketches the impact of membership turnover on institutional policy making.

The 89th Congress (1965–66) is frequently regarded as a watershed in the dominant shape of coalitional politics stemming from the New Deal. Three major events subsequently reopened fundamental questions about the responsiveness of American institutions: the Watts insurrection and its consequences on the mobilization of blacks, other minorities, and the counterresponse of various whites since Watts; the Vietnam war; and six years of unprecedented student political activism. How did those members from the "Class of 89" who were reelected in 1966 and 1968 respond to the demands and issues of the 1960s? Their behavior on four critical issues—student protest legislation, crime, attempts to restrict the range of antiwar demonstrations, and the Nixon Administration's Vietnam policies—are examined in chapter 7. What impact have these issues had on their political fortunes and careers? What conclusions might be drawn about the flexibility and/or rigidity of Congress in a period of intense crisis?

Electoral opposition, like Congress, should begin at the grass roots of American political life. The final chapter examines and proposes some changes in the way political resources are distributed and used in congressional campaigns. A brief summary is presented, speculating on the implications for parties, opposition, and congressional response. Although my own values usually find me drifting along with the reformers of political science, certain contradictions in many of the standard proposals seem inescapable. Facing up to some of these, I believe, will provide a more realistic estimate of the possibilities *and* limitations of electorally based opposition in the United States.

# Background

Popular and scholarly commentary on the 1964 national election has been varied and substantial.[15] The nomination of Barry Goldwater and the subsequent massiveness of his defeat emphasized some enduring and curious aspects in the character of the two-party struggle. Gloomy predictions of the "end" of the Republican party were commonplace, postcampaign recriminations were bitter.[16] The Republicans had indeed nominated "a choice," the campaign had received enormous attention here and abroad, but the "silent majority" was neither silent nor a majority.

Lyndon Johnson polled over 60 percent of the total vote and the Democrats managed a net gain of 38 seats in the House. The latter is modest by comparison with Johnson's performance or the 1936 presidential landslide when Republicans in the House were reduced to 89 members. If, as Milton Cummings points out,[17] the outcome of these contests had mirrored the presidential vote in each district, the Democratic-Republican ratio would have stood at 375–60, not 295–140. In 1966 the Republicans were able to recoup their losses (plus nine) when they scored a 47 net-seat gain. The average off-year switch since 1950 has been 25. Obviously, the 1964 interment had been premature.

The 89th Congress, organized by a huge Democratic majority (295) in 1965–66, is widely considered to have been the most innovative Congress since World War II. Eight years and "two, three, many Columbias" later, Republicans had regained the presidency and the party ratio in the House stood uncannily near the early 1964 figure: 254–178 with 3 vacancies in 1972.

How atypical were these 1964 challengers and the few who have consistently been reelected to the House since that first winning campaign? Other than to note that *all* social science is bound

15. Among which are Philip Converse et al., "Electoral Myth and Reality: The 1964 Election," *American Political Science Review* 69 (June 1965): 321–36; Karl Lamb and Paul Smith, *Campaign Decision-Making* (Belmont: Wadsworth, 1968); John H. Kessel, *The Goldwater Coalition* (Indianapolis: Bobbs-Merrill, 1969); Milton Cummings, ed., *The National Elections of 1964* (Washington, D.C.: Brookings, 1966); and Theodore H. White, *The Making of the President, 1964* (New York: Atheneum, 1965).

16. As they usually are for the losing party. But the Republican aftermath was particularly intense. See Lamb and Smith, *Campaign Decision-Making*, pp. 2–13, for a concise review.

17. Cummings, *National Elections of 1964*, p. 229.

by time and space, is there any reason to believe the 1964 congressional races attracted an exceptionally distinctive group of candidates? Or that those who have survived the past six years are an idiosyncratic group of congressmen? Until the necessary comparative research is undertaken neither question can be adequately answered. Various factors argue against this kind of bias, however.

First, as noted above, the Johnson landslide was not fully paralleled in the House; turnover was slightly *under* the twenty-year average preceding the 1964 election. Goldwater activists were probably most heavily engaged at the presidential level, but there is a possibility of disproportionate influence in each of the congressional districts as well. Such a possibility would impose greater limitations on these data than would be the case in a "normal" presidential year. Normality is a slippery concept. Other data, derived from 1956 and 1968,[18] suggest the "normal" ideological position of most Republican activists would predispose them toward nominating a Goldwater-type candidate even when they were selecting an Eisenhower or Nixon. Studies of this campaign have not indicated that Goldwater's "comprehensive planning" extended deeply into each congressional district. The geographical dispersion of American party organizations, combined with the diffusion of campaign resources, deters groups from mounting a centralized, nationally directed congressional blitz.

. Second, while many issues have obviously changed over the last decade, highly active "liberal" Democrats and "conservative" Republicans are still not too difficult to spot. Considerable attention is later devoted to examining continuities and change in the policy response of challengers first elected in 1964, and who survived through 1970. All were first inducted on the terms of the Great Society.

Important features affecting congressional elections have remained constant: small turnover, scarce campaign resources, relatively low levels of voter participation, relatively stable partisan identification, simple majority electoral laws, a growing but

18. Compare Herbert McClosky et al., "Issue Conflict and Consensus . . . ," *American Political Science Review* (June 1960): 406–29; with John Soule and James Clarke, "Issue Conflict and Consensus: A Comparative Study of Delegates to the 1968 Convention," *Journal of Politics* (February 1971): 72–92, and David Nexon, "Asymmetry in the Political System: Occasional Activists in the Republican and Democratic Parties," *American Political Science Review* (September 1971): 704–16.

still small southern Republican threat. Others have changed: a new addition to the franchise via the eighteen-year-old vote, new issues, the potential impact of the black vote in both the North and South; new campaign finance laws; and, Barry Goldwater is back in the Senate.[19]

Still, the 1964 election was unique in certain respects, as are the congressmen who have survived since then, and this should not be ignored.

Three phases of data collection, involving different but complementary techniques, were employed for the study. Most of the data were generated through a questionnaire mailed to all challengers, and timed to reach them two days after the election in November 1964.[20] Three waves of questionnaires netted a 70 percent response rate, certainly high enough to treat these data with some confidence. A second research phase was undertaken using open-ended and structured interviews with the 83 winners. Of these, 69 were completed during the latter part of 1965 and throughout 1966. Documentary sources such as the *Congressional Record* and periodic reinterviews with various members and others provide the major data and evidence for the later period.

A variety of techniques have been used to increase the reliability and validity of all the data examined in this book. The methodologically conscious reader is referred to an appendix where some of the problems are treated in detail.

19. Nor did most of his strong supporters in the House—contrary to popular impression—go under in the 1964 deluge. Two recent studies have convincingly demonstrated that conservative Republicans do seem to suffer electorally, relative to their moderate colleagues. The same is not true for liberal and moderate Democrats. See Robert Schoenberger, "Campaign Strategy and Party Loyalty," *American Political Science Review* (June 1969): 515–29; and Robert S. Erikson, "The Electoral Impact of Congressional Roll-Call Voting," *American Political Science Review* (December 1971): 1018–33. Different findings and measures are reported in Harry Phillips, "The Relationship Between Party Regularity on Roll Call Votes and Subsequent Re-Election Attempts" (Ph.D. dissertation, Indiana University, 1972).

20. Democrats nominated a candidate in every district but the first of Massachusetts. This is where Republican Silvio Conte had consistently won both nominations, the Democratic on the basis of primary write-in campaigns. Conte has sometimes found himself in an uncomfortable position because of this. In 1968, Republican pressure forced him to file an affidavit "disavowing" his write-in victory in the Democratic primary, but he waited until it was too late for the Democrats to place anyone else on the ballot. Republicans nominated 388 candidates in 1964. Almost all the vacancies were in the South. Occasionally, they also failed to nominate a candidate in the North or West, e.g., against Philip Burton in San Francisco.

# 2

# SOCIAL
# REPRESENTATION

Few myths die harder than
the persistent belief that a political career is socially analogous to
organized crime—open and fluid, providing the scions of ethnic
minorities, the working class, and the lumpen bourgeois an equal if
alternate channel for social mobility in American society.

Fiorello LaGuardia and Richard Daley notwithstanding, the
existence of rather sharp differences in the social status of political
leaders and the electorate is certainly one of the most consistently
well-documented propositions of empirical social science.[1]

Neither the House of Representatives nor the Senate is nu-
merically a social microcosm of their respective electorates. Researchers have long disputed the utility of such findings for making
inferences about the attitudes and behavior of these legislators.
Exhaustive information about leaders' occupations, religion, class
origins, demographic background, etc. have been compiled on the
assumption that such knowledge would help predict and explain

1. Two caveats should be mentioned. First, the social science stereotype for the
politically active in American society, a middle-class male WASP, is a statement
based on statistical proportions which vary substantially as one considers different
geographical and ecological areas, different political institutions or different societies, so that the relationship between social status and political activity is not a
simple linear development. For some data on American party activists which contradicts the stereotype, see Samuel J. Eldersveld, *Political Parties* (Chicago: Rand
McNally, 1964), pp. 47–72. Second, there still remain large deficiencies in reliable

the behavior of individuals occupying these roles. The problem, widely noted, has been demonstrating that these common environmental factors do in fact lead to significant similarities or differences in behavior. But as Reinhard Bendix and Seymour Lipset argued fifteen years ago, the proof that leaders always act in their self-interest, as determined by their class and status roles, is never provided; it is simply inferred from the statuses occupied.

Testing the impact of different background variables is a highly useful exercise. It avoids, however, some alternative perspectives on how one treats the political significance of social exclusion—as the Democratic party and other organizations have learned since 1968. Group representation is not simply a matter of competing belief systems.[2] Ronald Dellums and Philip Burton may not look very different on anyone's measure of liberalism, but they represent very different ways of responding to the needs of black Americans. Public leaders, confronted by the demands of newly mobilized minorities and women, are slowly, perhaps painfully, beginning to understand this. Nor is it a very new lesson. William F. Whyte thirty years ago eloquently and forcefully condemned the Brahmin settlement houses in the Italian communities of Boston for similar reasons.

## Old Problems and Persistent Demands

Historically, the conflict between "standing for" and "standing from" different groups evolved out of three different perspectives on the relationship of social class and political behavior.

Some,[3] following Aristotle, have seen middle-class dominance as a powerful guarantee that the "virtues of civility," moder-

---

and comparable data about the social background of leaders in important and powerful political organizations such as various civil rights, black power and ethnic solidarity groups, trade unions, deviant symbolic crusade movements (the Yippies?), as well as inadequacies in usable cross-national material, despite the now fashionable tendency to dismiss social background studies as mere "fact snuffling."

2. The most sophisticated treatment of different themes in this regard is Hanna Pitkin, *The Concept of Representation* (Berkeley: University of California Press, 1967).

3. Among others, see Alfred de Grazia, *Public and Republic* (New York: Knopf, 1951), pp. 146–234; William Kornhauser, *The Politics of Mass Society* (Glencoe, Ill.: Free Press, 1959), pp. 29–30; S. M. Lipset, *Political Man* (New York: Doubleday, 1960), pp. 45–74; and Richard Hofstadter, *The Age of Reform* (New York: Doubleday, 1958).

ation, tolerance, pluralism would forestall the rapid rise to power of mass-based authoritarian and/or totalitarian movements. Others, following Marx,[4] have interpreted such findings as additional proof that parliamentary institutions are no more than vehicles where the wealthy and privileged make sure *they* get the most of what there is to get. Yet another group has viewed the socially unrepresentative character of these institutions as irrelevant; neither providing sufficient protection against antidemocratic behavior[5] nor serving as singleminded representatives for "their" best "interests."[6]

Despite the long-standing controversy over consequences, theorists interested in representation and recruitment would hardly dismiss the social background of leadership as being unimportant. Rather it seems useful to conceive of political opportunity structures[7] as being national in scope so that societies can be compared, as well as specialized along regional, institutional, and functional lines. Thus, the relatively large number of working-class deputies

4. This is not to suggest that Marxists monopolize modern criticism; quite the contrary. Many twentieth-century liberals share Marx's critical attitude toward legislative institutions, although not necessarily because the institutions are socially unrepresentative. See, for example, James MacGregor Burns, *The Deadlock of Democracy* (Englewood Cliffs, N.J.: Prentice-Hall, 1963), pp. 257–67. Nor is it true that Marx was responsible for formulating the notion that Western political institutions were creatures of, and responsible to, the "interests" of the economic elite. Early attacks by Jeffersonians on the Federalists, and later the populist/progressive movements, were suffused with "antielite" components. Interestingly, however, the Jeffersonians viewed legislatures as instruments par excellence for representing the interests of "the people" against the power of the landed and corporate rich. On the whole, contemporary ruling-elite theorists, like C. Wright Mills, ignore Congress or simply assert that legislators, regardless of social background, are errand boys for the economic elite: Mills, *The Power Elite* (New York: Oxford University Press, 1956), pp. 242–75.

5. Nelson W. Polsby, "Toward an Explanation of McCarthyism," *Political Studies* (October 1960): 250–71; Peter Bachrach, *The Theory of Democratic Elitism* (Boston: Little, Brown, 1964), pp. 26–65; and Michael Rogin, *The Intellectuals and McCarthy* (Boston: MIT Press, 1967), pp. 9–32, 261–83.

6. A recent pluralist exposition can be found in Robert A. Dahl, *Pluralist Democracy in the United States* (Chicago: Rand McNally, 1969.)

7. The term was employed by Joseph Schlesinger in a more limited fashion than used here, since he excludes most social background data (except age) and focuses on prior officeholding and office turnover as operational measures of the "shape" and "size" of political opportunity structures. As used in this study, political opportunity structures will refer to the configuration of social and political parameters which shape the recruitment process. Cf. Schlesinger, *Ambition and Politics* (Chicago: Rand McNally, 1966), pp. 20–21.

in the French Chamber is simultaneously a characteristic of the national opportunity structure of France, and a function of the manner in which the French Communist party has channeled political opportunity. Moreover, while American parties tend to draw activists from generally similar social strata, each characteristically has a unique base, corresponding roughly to its source of votes in the electorate. Although small in number, Democrats more often than Republicans tend to attract a greater proportion of their recruits from the young, the working class, and from ethnic and religious minorities with proportions depending on the region and ecology of the areas involved.

Two sets of questions are still relevant when background data is being used for legislative candidates, independent of any inferences one might wish to make about the behavior of those individuals. The first relates to the electoral role of the party; the second to the social consequences of different recruitment strategies. Together these constitute one of the broad representational functions supposedly performed by parties in democratic societies. Few would deny that the structure of political opportunity, and hence the potential for power, is fundamentally influenced by the manner in which certain groups are given or denied access to the arena. And this holds regardless of the association (or lack thereof) between group background and behavior.

The power-oriented, vote-seeking image of both American parties emphasizes tactics which presumably widen, not restrict, their organizational appeal as an electoral unit.[8] Ethnic, religious and, more recently, racial[9] balancing is a phenomena to which American political leaders have always given prominent consid-

8. The conditions under which this tendency is either submerged or suspended in the United States, and the consequences, are traced for the Republicans in 1964 by Philip Converse, Aage R. Clausen, and Warren E. Miller, "Electoral Myth and Reality: The 1964 Elections," *American Political Science Review* 59 (June 1965): 321–36.

9. Despite the occasional emergence of a prominent Republican black leader such as James Farmer as a congressional candidate, it is not clear that the traditional methods parties have used for (or been used by) minorities will not sometimes be counterproductive, e.g., the frequent scorn many blacks attach to balancing as becoming "ITT or General Motors' nigger." Yet the struggle that took place prior to the 1972 national conventions, which centered on the difference between token and major representation, was consistent with historical tendencies.

eration; one would expect congressional challengers socially to "mirror" the opposition, or at least depart significantly from their party's normal constituency base.[10]

Second, one might predict that a kind of "social ladder" process is operating on the structure of recruitment so that challengers reflect an openness in the character of access not evident by looking only at the established (incumbent) leadership in each party; i.e., greater proportions would be younger, black, female, socially mobile, urban-born, and drawn from ethnic and religious minorities.[11]

Chapter 2 is therefore devoted to two aspects of the congressional recruitment process in the United States—the social parameters of candidacy and the political consequences these parameters suggest for the role of opposition.

The initial section describes and analyzes some background data for challengers, concentrating on differences between Republicans and Democrats, incumbents and nonincumbents. Attention is then directed to a comparative examination of winners and losers, showing how electoral outcomes affect party cleavages, both within and between the two major parties.

## Social Parameters

*Origins*

Twelve years ago, Donald R. Matthews and other students of legislative behavior could convincingly argue that the "typical" American legislator had probably grown up in a rural or small town environment and that ". . . the most consistently overrepresented birth places ranged in size from 2,500 to 5,000 inhabitants."[12] More recently, two observers, after noting the preponderance of small-town origins for state legislators, suggested that at the "national level an even higher proportion of legislators appear to have had rural and small town origins," a claim based

10. A pattern, for example, that was found to be characteristic of Pennsylvania candidates. See Frank Sorauf, *Party and Representation* (New York: Atherton, 1963) pp. 63–94.

11. An argument suggested by Donald Matthews for the character of all levels of political office in the United States in his *U.S. Senators and Their World* (New York: Vintage, 1960), p. 19.

12. Ibid., p. 16.

primarily on Matthews' findings.[13] But the great shifts of population during this century are beginning to be reflected in a very different representational base than was true twenty years ago. Leroy Rieselbach has convincingly shown that "rural and small town" legislators are no longer overrepresented in the House of Representatives.[14] Indeed, they may be slightly underrepresented. My data on challengers are consistent with this finding. Not only were challengers competing in different sorts of districts, but 55 percent grew up in cities of 25,000 or more[15] while a comparable figure for incumbents[16] was 50 percent. Nor are these groups concentrated in the small-to-medium-size cities: 61 percent of those challengers who grew up in towns of 25,000 or more were raised in large metropolitan centers of more than 250,000 (28 percent of the total), and 42 percent of the incumbent population who spent their youth in cities greater than 25,000 did so in the large metropolitan areas (21 percent of the sample). Predictably, a slightly greater proportion of challengers than incumbents grew up in cities of 250,000 or more. The same figures indicate that if there ever was any difference between Democrats and

13. Malcolm E. Jewell and Samuel C. Patterson, *The Legislative Process in the United States* (New York: Random House, 1966), pp. 101–2.

14. In his "Congressmen as 'Small Town Boys,' " *Midwest Journal of Political Science* (1970): 321–30.

15. Some caution is necessary. Matthews designated "small cities and towns" as those places with populations between 2,500 and 100,000; "large" cities as those with populations over 100,000; and rural areas as those places with less than 2,500. Although he does not present his data in such fashion that exact recalculation could be undertaken, it would be impossible for more than 15 percent of the senators he studied to have been born in areas larger than 100,000 persons. Of the two groups of candidates considered here, 50 percent of the nonincumbents and 33 percent of the incumbents "grew up in" communities larger than 100,000 which, of course, suggests an additional problem, i.e., the different manner in which scholars use ecological origins. Matthews employed birthplace and this observer's data is based on responses to a question asking where they were raised. Although the latter method has problems, it seems more reliable as an indicator of early exposure since most political scientists are interested in inferring attitudes or mental sets from the environment in which individuals actually mature. On the other hand, Jewell and Patterson present data from John Wahlke et al., *The Legislative System* (New York: Wiley, 1963). Wahlke and his colleagues asked legislators if they grew up "in a city, small town, farm, or a combination" but did not specify any size for these subjective categories. Thus the Wahlke data and that offered above are not comparable. The evidence presented for congressional candidates, after all the necessary qualifications, do show that the widespread image of American candidates as corn-fed and small-town is simply no longer true for a majority of challengers.

16. The incumbent data is based on the original sample and thus is open to an unknown amount of error. It is presented for illustrative purposes only.

Table 2.1

A Social Profile of Candidates for the House of Representatives, 1964, by Incumbency, Party, and Electoral Outcome (*In Percent*)

| Attribute | Incumbents[a] | Non-incumbents | Nonincumbent Democrats | Nonincumbent Republicans | Nonincumbents Democrats WINNERS | Democrats LOSERS | Republicans WINNERS | Republicans LOSERS |
|---|---|---|---|---|---|---|---|---|
| **Size community candidate grew up in[b]** | | | | | | | | |
| farm | 15 | 14 | 13 | 14 | 9 | 15 | 27 | 13 |
| under 26,000 | 35 | 31 | 34 | 30 | 35 | 33 | 55 | 28 |
| 26,000–50,000 | 6 | 8 | 7 | 8 | 2 | 11 | — | 8 |
| 51,000–99,000 | 20 | 6 | 5 | 6 | 11 | 1 | — | 7 |
| 100,000–249,000 | 20 | 12 | 12 | 12 | 13 | 12 | 18 | 13 |
| 250,000 plus | 21 | 28 | 28 | 29 | 30 | 26 | — | 29 |
| n.a. | — | 1 | 1 | 1 | — | 2 | — | 2 |
| **Age** | | | | | | | | |
| 21–29 | — | 3 | 3 | 4 | 2 | 4 | — | 5 |
| 30–39 | 10 | 32 | 35 | 30 | 33 | 37 | 38 | 29 |
| 40–49 | 32 | 40 | 38 | 43 | 41 | 38 | 55 | 42 |
| 50–59 | 31 | 16 | 18 | 15 | 22 | 15 | 9 | 15 |
| 60 and over | 25 | 6 | 4 | 9 | 2 | 6 | — | 8 |
| *Median age* | *53* | *44* | *44* | *43* | *45* | *42* | *44* | *43* |

| | | | | | | | | |
|---|---|---|---|---|---|---|---|---|
| **Sex** | | | | | | | | |
| male | 97 | 99 | 97 | 100 | 98 | 97 | 100 | 100 |
| female | 3 | 1 | 3 | — | 2 | 3 | — | — |
| **Race and ethnicity[c]** | | | | | | | | |
| white | 98 | 98 | 99 | 98 | 98 | 99 | 100 | 96 |
| black | 2(6) | 2(6) | —(1) | 2(5) | 1 | — | — | 4 |
| Spanish surname | —(2) | —(2) | 1(2) | —(—) | 1 | 1 | — | — |
| **Religion** | | | | | | | | |
| Protestant | 75 | 61 | 48 | 69 | 49 | 46 | 81 | 69 |
| Catholic | 21 | 26 | 30 | 22 | 20 | 35 | 9 | 23 |
| Jewish | 3 | 5 | 7 | 4 | 7 | 7 | — | 3 |
| other Protestant[d] | 1 | 5 | 7 | 4 | 15 | 4 | 10 | 4 |
| no preference | — | 1 | 2 | 1 | — | 4 | — | 1 |
| n.a. | — | 2 | 5 | — | 9 | 1 | — | — |
| **Education** | | | | | | | | |
| post-graduate[e] | 59 | 59 | 69 | 50 | 70 | 68 | 64 | 49 |
| college graduate | 16 | 23 | 13 | 32 | 11 | 15 | 27 | 32 |
| some college | 12 | 13 | 11 | 14 | 9 | 13 | 9 | 14 |
| less | 11 | 4 | 6 | 3 | 10 | 7 | — | 5 |
| **Occupation[f]** | | | | | | | | |
| professional [law] | 56 [49] | 45 [35] | 49 [39] | 43 [30] | 54 [38] | 44 [34] | 55 [32] | 42 [29] |
| teachers, writers, ministers | 6 | 12 | 14 | 8 | 13 | 16 | — | 8 |
| business executives | 11 | 18 | 13 | 22 | 15 | 12 | 27 | 21 |
| business sales | 9 | 17 | 11 | 20 | 4 | 15 | 18 | 20 |

| Attribute | Incumbents[a] | Non-incumbents | Nonincumbent Democrats | Nonincumbent Republicans | Nonincumbents Democrats WINNERS | Nonincumbents Democrats LOSERS | Nonincumbents Republicans WINNERS | Nonincumbents Republicans LOSERS |
|---|---|---|---|---|---|---|---|---|
| other nonmanual | 17 | 8 | 10 | 7 | 9 | 11 | — | 7 |
| skilled worker | 1 | 1 | 2 | — | 2 | 2 | — | — |
| Father's occupation | | | | | | | | |
| professional | — | 22 | 23 | 24 | 26 | 21 | 31 | 20 |
| proprietors, managers, officials | — | 33 | 31 | 35 | 35 | 26 | 50 | 34 |
| farmers | — | 13 | 16 | 10 | 14 | 17 | 6 | 10 |
| clerical | — | 2 | 3 | 1 | — | 4 | — | 1 |
| craftsmen, foremen | — | 16 | 14 | 18 | 15 | 16 | 6 | 19 |
| unskilled labor | — | 10 | 10 | 10 | 7 | 14 | 6 | 12 |
| n.a. | — | 4 | 3 | 3 | 3 | 4 | — | 4 |
| | (435) | (303) | (145) | (158) | (63) | (82) | (16) | (142) |

Note that totals will not always add to 100% due to rounding.

[a] Data for members of the House in the 88th Congress were obtained from the following sources: for age, sex and religion. *Congressional Quarterly*, 13 January 1964; for occupation. "Occupational Composition of Post-War Congresses." *Legislative Reference Service Special Report* (June 1966); for education. Carl F. Hawver. "The Congressman's Conception of His Role: The Use of Public Opinion Polls by Members of the House of Representatives" (Ph.D. dissertation. The American University, 1963). Data on community size is from the survey and open to an *unknown* amount of error.

[b] Reliable data for father's occupation were not available.

[c] The number of black and Spanish-surname leaders who were candidates are in parentheses.

[d] Includes Unitarians. Universalists and Mormons.

[e] The data for representatives includes all those who obtained a professional degree, regardless of previous college preparation. On the other hand, coding for nonincumbents permitted discrimination between those with no college, but who had obtained a professional degree and those with some college and a professional degree. Those with no college and a professional degree are included in the "less" category and constitute only one percent of the candidates with a professional degree; those with some college and professional training were included among the post graduate category.

[f] See Fishel. "Parties, Candidates, and Recruitment: West Germany and the United States" (Ph.D. dissertation, UCLA. 1970).

Republicans, it had disappeared among nonincumbent candidates in 1964. Both parties attracted candidates with roughly comparable origins. While it is not true that the "typical" legislator is now from a large metropolis, it does appear that the general shift of population from rural to metropolitan areas is increasingly being reflected in the origins of candidates for the House of Representatives.

## Age

Information on age level, an important background factor in the recruitment process, is also presented in table 2.1. Joseph Schlesinger has shown that the bulk of new entrants to the House in the 85th Congress tended to cluster in the 30–45 age group[17] and the data for challengers presented here does nothing to contravene that finding: 72 percent of the candidates were between the ages of 30 and 49 years; 32 percent were under 40; three percent under 30. The median age for challengers was 44, while the median for representatives, understandably older, was 53. Although no evidence exists on candidates to state legislatures, a comparison of figures for incumbents in the House and in the four state legislatures studied by John Wahlke and his colleagues[18] indicates that the median age for congressmen tends to be about ten years older than for their counterparts in the states. If a similar spread exists for nonincumbent candidates, one would expect the median age for state assembly aspirants to fall somewhere in the mid-thirties. Among others, Harvey Lehman,[19] David Walker,[20] and Schlesinger[21] have all argued that age in recruitment is a factor that affects both the ideological and professional outlook of politicians, that youthful candidates are more often the selection of forces of protest and unrest, and, in Schlesinger's opinion, ". . . the younger a man is when he enter politics, the greater the range of his ambition and the likelihood of his developing a career commitment to politics."[22] Whether a candidate "generational

17. Schlesinger, *Ambition and Politics*, p. 177.
18. Wahlke et al., *Legislative System*, p. 491.
19. Harvey Lehman, *Age and Achievement* (Princeton: Princeton University Press, 1953).
20. David B. Walker, "The Age Factor in the 1958 Congressional Elections," *Midwest Journal of Political Science* (February 1960): 1–26.
21. Schlesinger, *Ambition and Politics*, pp. 172–93.
22. Ibid., p. 176.

gap" exists—a major question about which little systematic evidence has been collected—will be directly examined later in this book. Whatever the consequences, neither party is in danger of being captured by opposition candidates under thirty-five.

## Sex

The absence of a statistically large number of women in public and private positions of power hardly needs documenting.[23] These data show little evidence that either party is challenging male dominance in Congress by nominating substantial numbers of women. Indeed, there were slightly *fewer* women among the ranks of challengers than among incumbents; only 3 percent of the House and 1 percent of the challengers were women. Nor has six years of political agitation greatly changed this picture. In 1970, 5 percent of major party challengers were women; 3 percent of the House. Despite the "stepped-up [sic] campaign to attract women to public positions of power," existing structural and psychological barriers to their entry are still overwhelming.[24]

## Race and Ethnicity

The McGovern-Fraser Commission has made the recruitment of women, blacks, and ethnic minorities central in the 1972 Democratic presidential nomination conventions. Watts and the events following 1965 may have been a watershed in black protest but the results on changing significantly the dominant makeup of Congress, and of their opposition opponents, have been quite limited. Although the number of blacks in the House doubled between 1965 and 1970, they still constitute under 3 percent of the total membership. Moreover, the few represented in 1964 among the Republican candidates, competing typically against black Democratic incumbents, were subjected to even harsher treatment than usual because of Goldwater's candidacy. One wrote that some of his workers were severely beaten when they attempted to distribute campaign literature which unfortunately carried Goldwater's name in small print at the bottom of

23. The most comprehensive existing study of women in legislatures is still Emmy E. Warner, "Women in Congress: 1917–1964," *Western Political Quarterly* (March 1966): 16–31.

24. Warner shows a steady increase in the number of women who are legislators, growing from 234 in 1945 to 351 in 1964. This still constitutes less than 5 percent of the total state legislature membership.

some flyers. The political deprivations affecting the Spanish-speaking community in the United States are even sharper if these data are used. Only two incumbents and two challengers—all Democrats—were Latinos.

## Religion

Data on the religious preference of candidates is also shown in table 2.1. It seems clear that both parties—but particularly the GOP—are beginning to nominate a significant number of Catholics. Although the differences between incumbents and nonincumbents are small, challengers had 5 percent more Catholics in their ranks than was true for the House membership. Thirty percent of the Democratic and 22 percent of the Republican nonincumbent candidates (a large group for the traditional party of the Protestants), were Catholic. Consistent with the tendency to nominate more candidates from other minority religious groups,[25] the slight increase of Jews among the nonincumbents is predictable. Although small in proportion, both parties had a larger number of nonincumbent candidates who were Jewish than was true for the House. Only two nominees, on the other hand, claimed to be agnostics or atheists.

## Education, Occupation, and Social Mobility

### Education

Reported formal education sustains the fact that American congressmen, and their opponents for office, are among the highest educated groups in the United States. Amomg challengers, 82 percent claimed a college degree and 59 percent possessed a college degree and postgraduate training, mainly of course in law. For the House in the 88th Congress, 75 percent were college graduates and 59 percent had some kind of postgraduate training.

25. The proportion who were Catholic is certainly important when compared with the regligious affiliation of Republican members in the House: of members who were Catholic, 86 percent were Democrats; of members who were Republican, 11 percent were Catholic. Although Republicans clearly seek to countervail the presumed electoral potency of Catholic affiliation in northeastern industrial districts, the fact that *both* parties had larger proportions of Catholic and Jewish candidates among their nominees can be interpreted as stressing the relevance *and* irrelevance of religion and legislative candidacy, paradoxical as that may appear.

The social-ladder hypothesis receives some support[26] if these data are compared with educational data for state legislators. Of ten states surveyed by Jewell and Patterson,[27] New Jersey had the *highest* proportion of college-educated legislators in its ranks (63 percent) and the average for all ten was closer to 50 percent, one-third less than was true for congressional candidates. Nationally, assuming that membership in the Senate carries higher status than in the House, one would expect senators to have higher levels of education. There were no differences between the formal education of the two groups, however. Like their counterparts in the Senate, a greater proportion of challenging Democrats than Republicans tend to have postgraduate training; but, contrary to expectation, this is only partially due to a greater proportion of attorneys among Democrats (see table 2.1). Rather, it seems a function of the ability of the Democratic party to attract a larger number of the intelligentsia and professionals and fewer businessmen.[28]

## Occupation

For over twenty years, lawyers have been the single most dominant profession in both houses of the national legislature. Matthews found that 58 percent of those serving in the U.S. Senate had gone to law school, and data for various sessions of the House since 1938 have shown the distribution of attorneys hovering around 50 percent.[29] Thus, the occupational data for challengers are striking because they show a marked decline in the proportion of attorneys among the candidates, 35 percent, and an increase in other professional categories. Included among the candidates were a sprinkling of the vast occupational variety that characterizes the *nonmanual* working force in the United

26. Level of education is at best a crude indicator of status. A better operational measure would be the quality of the degree-granting institution and not simply the level attained.

27. Jewell and Patterson, *Legislative Process*, p. 101.

28. Among Republican candidates, 42 percent were in business careers while the figure for Democrats was 24 percent. On the other hand, 73 percent of the Democratic candidates were professionals of some kind while this was true for 58 percent of the GOP hopefuls.

29. Source: "Occupational Composition of Congress" (special report of the Legislative Reference Service, 1965). Earlier sessions are covered in Madge McKinney, "The Personnel of the 77th Congress," *American Political Science Review* (March 1942): 68.

States: a mortician, veterinarian, justice of the peace, artist, three bank presidents, musician, architect, two dentists, and three physicians. But the concentration of skills in positions that have traditionally been associated with standing for office in America— attorneys, business officials, and salesmen—is still unmistakable.

Despite the dwindling proportion of lawyers, professionals of all categories, excluding business groups, still constitute 57 percent. Differences between Republicans and Democrats in this regard are about what one would expect: a slightly smaller proportion of professionals and intellectuals are represented among the GOP. The larger proportion of attorneys found in senatorial Democratic ranks, however, does not hold true for this group of candidates. Approximately one-third of the nominees from each party were attorneys, a significant difference from the data reported by Matthews for U.S. senators.[30] And, again, while miniscule in proportion, one machinist, one production worker, one truck driver, and one bartender were found among Democratic ranks while no Republican candidate reported a traditional working-class occupation.

The shape of the opportunity structure in the United States is certainly skewed toward those occupational groups who attract members deft at symbolic manipulation, but it does not follow, as some have feared, that attorney-legislators monopolize these skills.

## Social Mobility

Even if challengers tend to hold high status roles in private life, what of their origins? Do most come from more humble social backgrounds? The data presented on intergenerational mobility in table 2.1 are subject to varying interpretations, but two points seem clear. First, a majority (55 percent) are products of middle-class families, but the 26 percent drawn from working-class backgrounds is a higher figure than Lloyd Warner found[31] for either business executives (15 percent) or higher civil servants (20 percent) and four times higher than noted by Matthews for senators.

Alternatively, the distribution of occupational backgrounds

30. Among senators, Matthews found that 63 percent of the Democrats and 45 percent of the Republicans possessed legal training. Matthews, *U.S. Senators*, p. 35.
31. W. Lloyd Warner et al., *The American Federal Executive* (New Haven: Yale University Press, 1963), pp. 29–36.

for the fathers of these candidates is about the same as was found in the Wahlke et al. four-state legislative study, except that fewer congressional aspirants had farmer-fathers. The decreasing salience of farm backgrounds is further underscored by the fact that only 13 percent of the candidates—compared to 34 percent for United States senators and 25 percent for state legislators—had fathers who were farmers. Unfortunately, comparable data could not be located for House incumbents.

The mobility of nonincumbent candidates, with higher levels of education but similar class origins to state legislators, is about the same as Lipset and Bendix reported for the adult male population circa 1959.[32] The few differences, contrary to what one might expect, in the percentage of socially mobile in either party tends to favor the Republican party, who more frequently nominated upwardly mobile challengers. While not particularly illuminating as a comparative base, it is apparent that candidates are no more, but no less, likely to be socially mobile—measured in terms of manual-nonmanual intergenerational movement—than American adult males among the population at large.

## Winners, Losers, and Social Representation

Looking at the differences between losers and winners within the two parties uncovers one important finding: challengers from social minorities in the Republican party were almost without exception among the losers.

All the blacks, all the educators, all those under thirty, most of the upwardly mobile, almost all the Catholics, and all the Jewish candidates went down to defeat. To be sure, the 1964 election wasn't exactly a big Republican event. But the absence of these groups in significant numbers among GOP winners cannot be discounted as purely a function of that election, nor of the relatively large number of southern victories which gave the Republicans some historic firsts. It is precisely in those districts where Republican nonincumbents tend most frequently to mirror socially their Democratic incumbent opponents that they stand, statistically, the least chance of winning. The unusually bad Republican year of 1964 does not affect that problem. Only four of the sixteen GOP

32. S. M. Lipset and Reinhard Bendix, *Social Mobility in Industrial Society* (Berkeley: University of California Press, 1959), p. 20.

winners included above (the actual figure was five of nineteen) were from the Deep South.

Rather, it may suggest that the electoral system partially reinforces those social cleavages which since the depression have divided the two parties, even though these divisions are not reflected among leaders in the same degree as among followers.

These findings should not be surprising, given the stability of the vote in most congressional districts, but they underscore the problems often implied in campaign strategies which insist that "social broadening" will surely reap large electoral gains for parties competing in districts normally dominated by the opposition.

Moreover, particularly for House candidates, differences between the parties as reflected in the social backgrounds of winners and losers should not be overstressed. While small cracks in the wall of middle-class white Protestant dominance of leadership roles do appear among challengers, these are openings of degree, not preludes to a flood. The data surveyed here show that parties are providing only the slightest hint of serving as alternative modes for social mobility—at least if congressional candidacy is a primary vehicle.

An important question, one to which this study now turns, is whether or not these middle-class choruses are in fact singing the same song.

# 3

# AMBITION

"Ambition," writes Joseph Schlesinger, "lies at the heart of politics... the central assumption of ambition theory is that a politician's behavior is a response to his office goals." But the structure of motivation and the shape of opportunity have been extremely difficult to link empirically.

Some years ago Harold Lasswell ridiculed the notion of a "regimented" escalator carrying politicians in an orderly and inevitable fashion from the lowest to the highest positions of power in the United States. Various structural and motivational factors operate against a conception which posits rigid career ladders in the political fortunes of American elective leaders.

Yet Lasswell and others would certainly agree that "... political careers may be subjectively conceived as real and because they are so conceived, have real consequences for the taking of political roles and behavior."[2] This premise constitutes the base for most recent theories of political recruitment and has provided a common focus for a small but growing body of empirical research.[3]

1. Joseph A. Schlesinger, *Ambition and Politics* (Chicago: Rand McNally, 1966), pp. 5–6.
2. John Wahlke et al., *The Legislative System* (New York: Wiley, 1964), p. 74.
3. In addition to the state legislative project of John Wahlke and his colleagues, see Gordon S. Black, "A Theory of Professionalization in Politics," *American Political Science Review* (September 1970): 865–78; Kenneth Prewitt, *The Recruitment of Citizen Politicians* (Indianapolis: Bobbs-Merrill, 1970); Rufus Browning, "The Inter-Action of Personality and Political System in Decisions to Run for

By almost any standards, the opportunity structure of the House of Representatives is restricted;[4] few elective institutions in American political life have achieved the degree of stability which since the depression has characterized membership in the House.

Given the limited opportunity structure, why do candidates participate? To what extent does challenging an incumbent open up the possibility of building a career in politics? How important is this in the calculations candidates make when they move toward opposition roles in congressional campaigns?

The durability of American party organizations is often considered dependent on their ability to encourage motivational diversity among the ranks of the most highly active. Indeed this diversity is frequently cited as one of the most important distinguishing characteristics of the major parties.[5] Tensions stemming from this diversity, particularly between "amateurs" and "professionals," are thought to be central in explaining conflict over goals, strategies, and payoffs in party work.[6] The 1968 McCarthy campaign and the attendant journalistic commentary on the resur-

---

Office," *Journal of Social Issues* (July 1968): 93–110, and his "Hypotheses about Political Recruitment: A Partially Data-Based Computer Simulations," in *Simulation in the Study of Politics*, ed. William Coplin (Chicago: Markham, 1968); Alan Fiellin, "Recruitment and Legislative Role Conceptions: A Conceptual Scheme and Case Study," *Western Political Quarterly* (June 1967): 271–88; Leo M. Snowiss, "Congressional Recruitment and Representation," *American Political Science Review* (September 1966): 627–40; or James Barber, *The Lawmakers* (New Haven Yale University Press, 1965). Earlier recruitment research also pegged much of their work on this assumption: Lester G. Seligman, "Recruitment in Politics," *PROD* 1(1958): 14–17, and his "Party Structure and Legislative Recruitment," *American Political Science Review* 55 (September 1961): 77–86, Herbert Jacob, "Initial Recruitment of Elected Officials in the U.S.—A Model," *Journal of Politics* (1962): 708–9; and Frank Sorauf's analysis of legislative recruitment in Pennsylvania, *Party and Representation* (New York: Atherton, 1963). A useful inventory can be found in Heinz Eulau and Katherine Hinckley, "Legislative Institutions and Processes," in *Political Science Annual, Vol. 1*, ed. James Robinson (Indianapolis: Bobbs-Merrill, 1966), pp. 85–191.

4. This can be deceptive, depending on comparative benchmarks. Internally (compared to American state legislatures) the House is quite restricted; externally (compared to the British House of Commons or the West German Bundestag, for example) the U.S. House is less so, as the three have approximately equal turnover rates. See Austin Ranney's estimates in his *Pathways to Parliament* (Madison: University of Wisconsin Press, 1965), p. 5.

5. Eldersveld, *Political Parties—A Behavioral Analysis* (Chicago: Rand, McNally, 1964), pp. 272–303.

6. James Q. Wilson, *The Amateur Democrat* (Chicago: University of Chicago Press, 1960), chap. 1.

gence of the amateur in American politics once again focused
interest on the problems endemic to organizations which invite participation by others than careerists. Yet the organizational survival
of responsive parties presupposes that such conflict be a permanent
part of their incentive systems. Professional cadres of party candidates, unresponsive to less involved aspirants, would rapidly
dissolve one of the greatest organizational strengths of both parties.
The major analytical question of this chapter focuses on one broad
question: do parties provide open and plural career incentives for
candidates seeking public office? As Kenneth Prewitt argues, ambition theory adds another dimension to research on leadership and
representation by holding that expectations of the future shape current behavior. Such expectations should fundamentally affect the
behavior of candidates and the style of party opposition in
congressional campaigns.[7]

This chapter seeks to (1) develop an operational measure
which distinguishes various levels of political careerism and examine data showing how widely such attitudes are distributed; (2)
examine the configuration of variables which tend to produce different types of career commitment among candidates; and, (3)
test the extent to which three important consequences—ideological, partisan, strategic—follow from differences in these orientations. A final section summarizes the findings and suggests some
broader implications for parties, candidates, and opposition.

## Some Theoretical Problems

Traditionally, political scientists have focused on candidacy as
a type of penultimate activity in a hierarchy of political involvement which begins with exposure to political stimuli and moves
upward through party activity, contributions, and so forth to holding office. Thus, Lester Milbrath places it among the "gladiatorial"
activities characteristic of an extremely small political stratum.[8]
Considerable attention has subsequently been devoted to understanding the political, psychological, and social determinants of
various forms and levels of political involvement.[9] Although Mil-

7. Prewitt, *Recruitment of Citizen Politicians.*
8. In his *Political Participation* (Chicago: Rand McNally, 1965), particularly
pp. 5–38.
9. The excessive stress on participation as an individual act, thus being empirically grounded in variables such as political efficacy, is stressed in Robert Alford and Harry M. Scoble, "Sources of Local Political Involvement," *American
Political Science Review* (December 1968): 1192–1207.

brath is ambivalent on this point, gladiatorial activities are often viewed as an extension of other lower-level activity, albeit involving an increasing commitment of time and resources.

Alternatively, those following Lasswell's early psychoanalytic efforts have begun with an identifiable political strata, developed and utilized personality typologies, and argued that political candidacy is best seen, not as an extension of regular activity, but as a major shift to a new frame of reference. Here the critical problem is to isolate a configuration of personality variables (self-esteem, distinctive concerns with power and achievement, etc.) which explain why this new shift takes place.[10] While different schools emphasize different aspects of this process, all insist on the primacy of personality factors in the decision making of prospective candidates.

The link between motivation and personality, however, confronts some rather stiff conceptual and empirical obstacles.[11] Personality-oriented research shares the defects and strengths of clinical psychology (from which it is derived); heavy emphasis is placed on the interviewer's interpretive ability; the kind of inferences made from data are usually related to the analyst's training in one of the various schools of personality theory; conflicts over explanation(s) or interpretation are difficult to resolve by recourse to mutually accepted canons of evidence; similar behavior can be explained by contradictory formulations; or contradictory behavior can be explained by a single formulation so inclusive that actual behavior is irrelevant; generalization is quite difficult.[12]

Among the advantages, depth analysis permits exploration of the complexity, subtlety, and ambiguity characteristic of most politicians; explanations are usually less simplistic or mechanistic; and considerable insight should flow from analyzing the "whole" or "total field" of an individual rather than isolated aspects of motivation and behavior. But research of this type has long been under pressure to develop more rigorous measuring instruments which can operationally relate needs to purposive behavior. The

10. Barber, *Lawmakers*, pp. 221–15.

11. Despite the heroic efforts of Fred I. Greenstein, "The Impact of Personality on Politics: An Attempt to Clear Away the Underbrush," *American Political Science Review* (September 1967): 629–43.

12. Similar themes are developed in the context of criticizing Lucian Pye's personality-based work on political development in Robert T. Holt and John E. Turner, *The Political Basis of Economic Development* (Princeton, N.J.: Van Nostrand, 1966), pp. 24–34.

work of James Barber on Connecticut legislators, based heavily on clinical-type biographies, is probably the best recent example of the strengths and weaknesses of this approach.[13]

Some of these problems are reduced, but not eliminated, in the research of Rufus Browning and others on power motivation[14] and political recruitment, using standardized TATs. Applying the well-known affiliation, achievement, and power motivation tests to a small number of politicos, Browning has been able to explore and systematically test some recruitment hypotheses derived from personality theory. The subjects have been few, the application limited, the generalizability of the findings difficult. As he concedes, "efforts to ascertain the personality correlates of politicians' behavior have met with indifferent success."[15]

His framework is still a sophisticated and parsimonious model of the recruitment process—office seeking, office accepting, and officeholding—with computer simulation potential. Whether scholars can ever overcome resistance by leaders other than "locals" in order to test the model in a national environment is problematic. Administering TATs to congressmen (or other nationally prominent leaders), no matter how much the instrument is disguised as a test of creativity, confronts formidable problems.

The primary advantage of Browning's research (contrasted with Barber and others who rely on less structured methods) is that in principle it permits application of a more or less validated test which can generate quantitative data relating personality to behavior. Hence a set of precise, testable propositions, replicable under various conditions and by various researchers, is possible. The major deficiency stems from data collection problems associated with this technique.

These difficulties are reduced if one begins from a slightly different theoretical position, making no assumptions about the underlying forces of motivation, and adopts less sophisticated measuring instruments.

The approach proposed here is both consistent with theories of ambition and power motivation, while divergent in some important respects from each. Rather than asking why persons similarly situated in the social structure do or do not become candi-

13. Barber, *Lawmakers*.
14. Browning and Jacob, "Power Motivation and the Political Personality."
15. Browning, "Interaction of Personality," p. 7.

dates (Browning's major interest), this research begins once that decision has been made and seeks to describe the distribution of careerist attitudes and examine the consequences.

Comparatively, such a strategy leads to two major payoffs. First, a critical component of ambition theory (itself a theory of motivation) will be examined against a background of different social and political factors. Unlike Schlesinger, who must infer a complex set of attitudes from aggregate data on career paths, the analysis here is based on a direct operational measure of this complex set. Second, opting for a standardized measure of political ambition overcomes the considerable restrictions imposed on data-gathering activities geared to projective interviews. Finally, linking ambition to the function and operation of parties is one way political scientists can move beyond the disciplinary limitations of motivational psychology.

It may be, as James C. Davies has written, that "... along the path of motivational investigation lies madness." But the broad proposition entertained here—that challengers strongly oriented toward a career in politics will emerge from different environments and will respond to their current and future environments in different fashion from those not so oriented—makes no claim about the underlying causes of such motivation. Self-actualizing or displacing, inner-directed or other-directed, power-oriented or affiliative, the focus is on the consequences once a goal has been established and the configurative pattern in which this type of goal-directed behavior surfaces.

## Careerists, Transitionals, Amateurs

Congressional challengers, like other American politicians, are certainly a multivalued, psychologically diverse lot. Although they are not a social microcosm of the population at large, it does not follow that politicians are ideologically or psychologically monolithic. But then neither are they simply random figures floating on unpredictable political tides. The electoral and party arenas provide socializing structures, independent of the legislature, in which a candidate's professional orientation to politics is tested, revised, constricted, or expanded.

While survey instruments of the kind used here do not allow one to develop complex motivational profiles of these candidates,

two questions, when combined, seem operationally to tap some
major elements in these profiles. Eight standard "motivational"
items were included in the questionnaire,[16] two of which seem
theoretically and empirically useful for rank-ordering and classifying candidates: the individual's estimate of candidacy as a vehicle
for building a future in politics and his orientation toward politics
as a normal part of his life style. The index developed for this chapter does not assume that candidacy is at the apex on a gradient of
political activity, nor that standing for office constitutes the same
level of involvement for all candidates. Rather it provides a direct
test of ambition while anchoring it in a measure of the day-to-day
salience of politics for each candidate.[17]

This seems essential for distinguishing between candidates
whose ambition is not matched by stable socialization in political
roles or those with low levels of ambition but for whom seeking
election is simply an expression of a continuing involvement in
party activity. The latter, generally local party activists, do not
perceive candidacy as a strategic mechanism for advancing their
ambition, while the former's ambition is undiluted by the responsibilities and frustrations of a more complete immersion in politics.
Still, because their perceptions are subject to change, given a
change in their strategic situation (low ambition types winning;
high ambition types assuming increasing responsibility in the local party organization), these candidates seem prone to a tentativeness about political opportunity; hence their "transitional"
character. The logic of the index is presented in table 3.1, and the
classification in table 3.2.

Consistent with most simple measures, the index of political
commitment discriminates fairly well between high and low, presenting the toughest problem in the middle range. When the six

16. The concept "motivation" will be used throughout this study as an individual's justification for strategies of action—"in order to"—rather than in the psychoanalytic sense of "because of." This avoids a number of pitfalls; mainly, as Richard Snyder argued some years ago, the assumption that social science can only deal
with motivation if it can reconstruct individual acts sequentially, beginning with
childhood. See his now classic "The Decision-Making Approach," in *Approaches to
the Study of Politics*, ed. Roland A. Young (Evanston: Northwestern University Press,
1957), particularly pp. 30–33.

17. Barber's original index is somewhat similar to this, although it does not provide a direct test of ambition (other than the desire to stand for reelection), and the
test of political involvement—amount of legislative floor activity—is confined to
candidate's "lawmaker" roles.

## Table 3.1

### Index of Political Commitment,
### Congressional Challengers

| Politics as Way of Life | Opportunity to Build a Future in Politics[a] | | |
|---|---|---|---|
| | VERY IMPORTANT | SOMEWHAT IMPORTANT | NOT VERY IMPORTANT |
| Very important | 1 | 2 | 4 |
| Somewhat important | 2 | 3 | 5 |
| Not very important | 4 | 5 | 6 |

[a] The question asked candidates to rank various factors in relation to their decision to run for office. The exact wording: "The following reasons are often given in explaining why persons become candidates for public office. How important in your own case, do you consider each of the following?"

## Table 3.2

### Levels of Political Commitment, by Party and
### Electoral Outcome, Congressional Challengers
### (In Percent)

| Index of Political Commitment | Democrats | Republicans | Democrats | | Republicans | |
|---|---|---|---|---|---|---|
| | | | WINNERS | LOSERS | WINNERS | LOSERS |
| Careerists | | | | | | |
| 1 | 26 | 14 | 26 | 25 | 18 | 14 |
| 2 | 18 | 12 | 25 | 12 | 18 | 11 |
| subtotals | 44 | 26 | 51 | 37 | 36 | 25 |
| Transitionals | | | | | | |
| 3 | 19 | 15 | 12 | 23 | 25 | 14 |
| 4 . | 9 | 7 | 3 | 12 | 6 | 7 |
| subtotals | 28 | 22 | 15 | 35 | 31 | 21 |
| Amateurs | | | | | | |
| 5 | 16 | 20 | 20 | 13 | 18 | 20 |
| 6 | 7 | 26 | 6 | 9 | 12 | 28 |
| subtotals | 23 | 46 | 26 | 22 | 30 | 48 |
| Unclassifiable | 5 | 6 | 7 | 6 | 3 | 6 |
| N = | (145) | (158) | (63) | (82) | (16) | (142) |

possible scores are collapsed into three types, this seems less intractable. Moreover, the analytical types generated through collapsing —Careerists, Transitionals, and Amateurs—conform readily to other typologies in recruitment and permit simpler and clearer exposition.

Consider the data in table 3.2. Democratic challengers quite clearly were much more likely to perceive candidacy as a stepping stone in the process of building a career in politics: 44 percent of the Democrats compared to 36 percent of the Republicans are Careerists, about equal proportions from each party conform to the Transitional mode, but nearly one-half (46 percent) of the GOP challengers (as compared to 23 percent of the Democrats) were Amateurs. Comparatively, differences between winners and losers are in the predictable direction, but it is equally significant that Republican winners were no more likely than Democratic losers to be Careerists. Among winners approximately equal proportions (one-fourth) in both parties were Amateurs.

Because the differences between Democratic and Republican challengers cannot be explained by the higher social status of Republicans, nor a greater degree of social mobility among Democrats (the standard "alternative mobility" explanation), one is left with an unfashionably simple conclusion: Democrats, as Democrats, are just more professionalized (or potentially professionalizable) than Republicans.[18] That larger proportions of Democratic candidates would have different expectations about office-based careers in politics, and hence would see the struggle for office differently, also squares with Schlesinger's characterization of the relationship between opportunity and party systems. Using two indicators, age at arrival and amount of prior public office, he was able to classify the Republican opportunity structure as "hierar-

18. Candidacy as a vehicle for status-striving behavior among Democrats, status-affirming activity among Republicans, is still a possibility since I have no evidence on how candidates perceive the status (or value) of their nonpolitical careers. The gross data showing little intergenerational class movement for either group, unlike the findings of Marvick and Nixon for local party activists, are not however consistent with a status-striving hypothesis. See Dwaine Marvick and Charles Nixon, "Recruitment Contrasts on Rival Campaign Groups," in *Political Decision-Makers*, ed. Dwaine Marvick (Glencoe, Ill.: Free Press, 1961), pp. 206–7. A study that found some evidence that political activism may be a function of "occupational marginality" (and hence status-striving) is presented in Lewis Bowman and G. R. Boynton, "Recruitment Patterns Among Local Party Activists," *American Political Science Review* (September 1966): 667–77.

chical" (older) and based on nonlegislative offices (external); the Democratic as "open" (younger) and office-based (internal).[19]

Most certainly the simple effect of electoral success strongly influences postures toward the political environment, but the fact that substantial movement in the opposite direction also occurred underscores the importance of more stable, less situationally based drives among American politicians. And this despite the severe structural restrictions imposed on the possibility of success for these challengers.

## Sources of Motivational Diversity

So much evidence has accumulated on the socializing role of families in the developmental profiles of the politically active, transitional, and apathetic in the United States that it seems useful to place this research in context. Demonstrating that politicians emerge more frequently from politicized family groups than non-politicians (or, among citizens, the active more frequently than the inactive) provides little knowledge about the different styles, commitment, and attitudes of politicians, most of whom presumably grow up in politically engaged families.[20] Nor has empirical research of this kind systematically examined the rather stable and proportionately large numbers who do not conform to the finding. Although most social scientists consider it bad form to linger too long with "deviant" cases (for good epistemological reasons), our understanding of the subtle admixture of various socializing agents would certainly be improved by more intensive research on counterinstances.

From the viewpoint of this chapter, however, the first problem is of greater significance. All studies of legislative recruitment have documented the salience of "political families" for some candidates.[21] Neither the work on ambition or power motivation has made clear how salient, and with what variation, parental

19. Joseph Schlesinger, "Political Careers and Party Leadership," in *Political Leadership in Industrialized Society*, ed. Lewis Edinger (New York: Wiley, 1967), pp. 266–94.

20. A similar point is made for research on nonleaders by Richard Dawson and Kenneth Prewitt in their survey of the subfield and literature, *Political Socialization* (Boston: Little, Brown, 1969), pp. 202–3.

21. This aspect is given particular emphasis in Wahlke et al., *Legislative System*, pp. 82–84, although the authors also stress the importance of other factors.

political activity is for the development of a discrete set of attitudes about the career in politics. The relationship between patterns of family involvement and different types of political commitment would logically be a plausible explanation for motivational diversity among congressional challengers. Some evidence on this score, derived from two widely-used measures of family political roles, is presented in tables 3.3 and 3.4.

## Table 3.3

### Parental Political Activity[a] and Types of Political Commitment, Congressional Challengers
#### (*In Percent*)

| *Political Commitment* | *Democrats* | | *Republicans* | |
| --- | --- | --- | --- | --- |
| | HIGH PARENTAL ACTIVITY | LOW PARENTAL ACTIVITY | HIGH PARENTAL ACTIVITY | LOW PARENTAL ACTIVITY |
| Careerists | 52 | 38 | 34 | 21 |
| Transitionals | 33 | 21 | 23 | 23 |
| Amateurs | 11 | 34 | 38 | 53 |
| n.a. | 4 | 6 | 3 | 3 |
| *N* = | (67) | (78) | (58) | (100) |

[a] The political activity of parents is estimated from responses to the following: "How active was your father and/or mother in political affairs when you were growing up: very, somewhat, or not very active?" Candidates who placed their parents in the very or somewhat active categories were classified as "high" parental activity; those who indicated their parents were not very active were classified as "low" parental activity.

First it should be stressed that majorities in each party *did not* mature in families where one or both parents were deeply involved in politics. Quite the contrary: 58 percent of the Democrats and 61 percent of the Republicans considered their parents (jointly or individually) "not very active" in political affairs. A forced-choice question of this nature, leaving to each candidate the definition of what constitutes "very," "somewhat," or "not very active," is obviously a restricted measure of familial political activity, but the responses do raise some questions about the nuclear family as a dominant primary socializing group for candidates.

The problem here is whether candidates from active families differ substantially from those who were not so engaged; data provided in table 3.3 imply a cautious affirmative. Among Demo-

Table 3.4

Intergenerational Partisan Stability and Change
in Relation to Types of Political Commitment,
Congressional Challengers
(*In Percent*)

| | *Father's Partisan Identification* | | | | | |
|---|---|---|---|---|---|---|
| | *Democrats* | | | *Republicans* | | |
| *Political Commitment* | STABLE DEMOCRAT | INDE-PENDENT[a] | STABLE REPUBLICAN | STABLE DEMOCRAT | INDE-PENDENT | STABLE REPUBLICAN |
| Careerists | 50 | 32 | 44 | 31 | 38 | 23 |
| Transitionals | 26 | 28 | 36 | 14 | 14 | 31 |
| Amateurs | 21 | 31 | 17 | 50 | 48 | 44 |
| n.a. | 3 | 9 | 3 | 5 | — | 2 |
| *N* = | (83) | (22) | (32) | (44) | (21) | (83) |

[a] Three Democratic and two Republican challengers indicated their father's identification varied over the years; they are included with the "independent" group.

crats, for example, 52 percent of those from active families were psychologically oriented to politics as Careerists, 33 percent as Transitionals, while only 11 percent perceived candidacy in distinctly Amateur's terms. Thus, nine out of ten of those Democratic candidates growing up in active families were likely to consider candidacy as something more than civic obligation.

Conversely, three times as many of those Democrats from inactive families, 34 percent, were Amateurs, although 38 percent could nevertheless be classified as Careerists and 21 percent as Transitionals.

The Republicans present a similar picture, since differences between those from highly active and generally inactive families are about the same as for their Democratic counterparts. But, the substantially larger number of Amateurs within Republican ranks, despite variation in family political activity, reinforces the argument advanced earlier: independent of developmental factors, party appears to be a powerful, perhaps continuing, mid-life socializing agent in the career perspectives of congressional challengers. This interpretation is sustained by a variety of other studies that emphasize socialization as a continuing process in which early family experience plays an important but functionally limited role.[22] More precisely, empirical research has demonstrated that family is a major influence in shaping partisan orientation, but the effect on other attitudes (ideology, intense ambition, etc.) is far from uniform.

Republican and Democratic candidates did tend to retain their father's partisan identification (56 and 60 percent respectively) although the stability of father-to-son partisanship was less than is estimated for the national electorate (64 to 70 percent), but substantially more than Scoble found for activists in the NCEC, a large nonpartisan, indeed antiparty, interest group (35 percent).[23]

As in the SRC's studies of the electorate,[24] intergenerational shifts among candidates seem to more often benefit the GOP. It is important to emphasize, however, that this small pro-Republican shift does not appear to be a function of mobility; rather it stems from the proliferation of southern Republican candidates, most of whom had Democratic fathers. One-half of the GOP's sixteen winners in 1964 were sons of Democrats, but five of the eight were contesting in the South.

Still, the significant question is whether shifting partisan identification has any substantial bearing on the candidate's political commitment. As the data in table 3.4 show, the consequences of this process are mixed and somewhat ambivalent. Two tendencies seem to be operating on Democratic challengers. Candidates growing up in families in which the father was either a Democrat *or* Republican, but not an Independent, are much more likely to be ambitious for, and active in, politics as a career. Partisanship generally, rather than commitment to either of the two parties, is important here. This theme is caught in the remarks of a southwestern Democrat, a Careerist and the scion of a Republican family:

I had been thinking about it for a long long time although
you can't say I actually planned it. You might say I was born

22. See Allan Kornberg's study of Canadian MPs, *Canadian Legislative Behavior* (New York: Holt, 1968), p. 50, and the citations listed therein.

23. Harry M. Scoble, "Political Money: A Study of Contributors to the National Committee for an Effective Congress," *Midwest Journal of Political Science* (August 1963): 229–53.

24. Angus Campbell, Philip Converse, et al., *The American Voter* (New York: Wiley, 1960), pp. 117–68. More recent evidence suggests this is no longer benefiting Republicans. See E. C. Ladd, *American Political Parties* (New York: Norton, 1970).

> to politics. My father had been very active, as had my grand-
> father. They were both Republicans. In fact, so was every-
> body in the family . . . when I became a Democrat, my father
> raised hell for a little while, but it subsided because we were
> one of the first settlers in the area and the name is associated
> with community activity. So it was expected, even if they had
> to live with the fact that I was going to do it as a Democrat.

On the other hand, many if not a majority of the stable identifiers are reflected in the response from a midwestern Democrat
and Transitional politician:

> I don't come from a family who were in politics, like many
> of the members have. But they were always interested in na-
> tional affairs, and my family were strong Democrats in Re-
> publican country. . . . I can still remember discussions when I
> was in elementary school. . . .

Among Democratic candidates whose fathers were Indepen-
dents, on the other hand, substantially fewer were Careerists and
considerably more, 31 percent, were Amateurs than was true of
those who had Democratic or Republican fathers. Because parties
have structured electoral opportunity in the past, as they do now,
it would have been surprising had any other finding emerged.
Hence the fact that the relationship, if not reversed, is substantially different for Republican challengers, suggests a more complex pattern.

Differences between the Republican sons of partisan or
Independent fathers disappear; contrary to the findings for Democratic challengers, GOP candidates whose fathers were Independent are *more* likely to have Careerist perspectives. Equal proportions, however, approximately one-half of each subgroup, are
Amateurs.

One explanation, quite tentative, would square with older
arguments about differences between Democrats and Republicans: a majority of the Democratic candidates, maturing during
the depression and residing in middle-class families where the
father was a member of the socially deviant party, were exposed
to a range of opinion which challenged some of the basic shib-
boleths of American middle-class life. Presumably, this might
lead to a different conception of the political career than is true
where politics is socially analogous to other forms of civic obliga-

tion, neither jarring conventional beliefs nor posing an occupational sequence distinctly alternative to a private career. Or so it seemed to Dean Acheson when he wrote twenty years ago that middle- and upper-status Democrats differed from Republicans precisely because of their attitudes toward the value of a career in public life.[25] Admittedly this explanation is highly speculative, but it does not seem outrageous, perhaps because the author is an occasional Democrat.

Theories of ambition and political advancement, however, must move beyond considering early socialization factors to empirically handling the variety of often conflicting childhood experiences which characterize both the ambitious and career-oriented as well as the less professionalized. Five enduring factors— what Eulau and Sprague call the career nexus[26]—appear in one form or another in almost all recruitment models: age, profession, social mobility, public office experience, and yeomanship in one of the two parties.

The first, age, is a major explanatory variable in Joseph Schlesinger's scheme and it is Schlesinger who has most forcefully and unpretentiously argued the central, predisposing role of age. "The younger a man is when he enters politics," the author asserts, "the greater the range of his ambitions and the likelihood of his developing a career commitment to politics."[27] Leo Snowiss provides some evidence[28] substantiating this argument, although he draws different implications from the findings. Snowiss shows that older Chicago Democratic congressional candidates tended to emerge in noncompetitive, inner-city districts but, in contrast to the younger, outer-city or suburban candidates, were the most thoroughly socialized as professionals; mainly because of long periods of party apprenticeship (presumably begun at a young age). The importance of age in this respect, as in Schlesinger's framework, is not indicated by age at time of candidacy, except when it is anchored in a long cycle of party activity. Thus, under one set of

25. Dean Acheson, A Citizen Looks at Congress (New York: McGraw-Hill, 1954).

26. Heinz Eulau and John Sprague, Lawyers in Politics (Indianapolis: Bobbs-Merrill, 1964, pp. 54–87.

27. Schlesinger, Ambition and Politics, p. 176.

28. In his "Congressional Recruitment and Representation," American Political Science Review (September 1966): 627–40.

conditions one would expect older candidates to be the most careerist; under another, the least.

Regrettably, the number in each cell is too small to permit the kind of multivariant analysis sufficient to disentangle the different effects of age and party work, but the data in table 3.5 are

### Table 3.5

### Generational Differences in Types of Political
### Commitment, Congressional Challengers
### (*In Percent*)

| Political Commitment | Democrats | | Republicans | |
|---|---|---|---|---|
| | 40 AND OVER | UNDER 40 | 40 AND OVER | UNDER 40 |
| Careerists | 41 | 52 | 28 | 25 |
| Transitionals | 25 | 33 | 18 | 30 |
| Amateurs | 28 | 14 | 52 | 43 |
| n.a. | 6 | 1 | 2 | 2 |
| *N* = | (89) | (53) | (105) | (52) |

not totally without interest. Those under age forty in the Democratic camp were slightly more likely to be Careerists, but their counterparts in the Republican party showed no such inclination. Larger proportions of older candidates from both parties were more likely to be Amateurs, providing some support for the idea that men in their forties, usually firmly entrenched in a nonpolitical career, will under normal conditions be prone to consider politics a secondary career or an avocation. But age gains in importance when levels of former party officeholding are considered by age groups: although 48 percent of the younger Democrats had never held any party office only 14 percent were Amateurs, indicating the independent effect of age and only age on Democratic challengers (34 percent of those forty and over had never held office; 28 percent were Amateurs).

The convergence of the second factor, a politician's profession, has repeatedly been used as a major variable in the equation of political ascent. Woodrow Wilson's dictum on the relation of law and politics has been cited so many times that many would dismiss yet another empirical test as further evidence that quanti-

### Table 3.6

### Occupations and Types of Political Commitment,
### Congressional Challengers
### (In Percent)

| Political Commitment | Democrats[a] | | | Republicans | | |
|---|---|---|---|---|---|---|
| | LAW | BUSINESS | PROFESSIONAL | LAW | BUSINESS | PROFESSIONAL |
| Careerists | 47 | 33 | 54 | 37 | 21 | 26 |
| Transitionals | 21 | 34 | 24 | 25 | 23 | 25 |
| Amateurs | 28 | 27 | 20 | 36 | 53 | 46 |
| n.a. | 4 | 6 | 2 | 2 | 3 | 3 |
| N = | (57) | (33) | (47) | (46) | (64) | (45) |

[a] The four Democratic candidates who were skilled workers are not included above.

tative political science "only documents the obvious." Unfortunately for common sense, and the obvious, the data in table 3.6 provide no such documentation: among Democratic challengers, lawyers are no more predisposed to Careerist or even Transitional attitudes than are other professionals, and are only slightly more career-oriented (or potentially career-oriented) than Democratic businessmen, notoriously the least professional in anecdotal accounts of campaigners. Common sense fares slightly better on predictions about Republicans since GOP attorneys do surface as Careerists more often than either the businessmen or other professionals—and more importantly—substantially less frequently as Amateurs. But the effects apparently depend on party and seem less related to a candidate's particular profession than the way he uses that profession to advance his particular set of political goals. Attorneys have no monopoly on political ambition, despite Schlesinger's assertion that "the lawyer in politics is to be equated with the careerist in politics."[29] Although Schlesinger's data are based on career patterns of governors, and hence are not comparable, these findings seriously undercut his and other arguments which see attorneys once they enter politics as decisively more oriented to the political vocation.[30]

29. Schlesinger, "Lawyers in Politics: A Clarified View," Midwest Journal of Political Science (May 1957): 29.
30. Eulau and Sprague seem to accept Schlesinger's conclusion, although their data on prelegislative public officeholding provide little evidence that it is true. See their analysis, Lawyers in Politics, pp. 65–66.

The third component almost always cited as operating to intensify political ambition among some, reducing it among others, is social mobility. The data presented in chapter 2, like other data on a variety of political leaders, document the statistically low level of intergenerational class movement for these challengers. A minority in each party are nevertheless mobile. If mobility does in fact generate a unique set of aspirations in politics, this should be reflected in substantially different career perspectives of mobiles and status stables.[31] As a glance at table 3.7 demonstrates,

Table 3.7

Intergenerational Social Mobility and
Types of Political Commitment,
Congressional Challengers[a]
(*In Percent*)

| Political Commitment | Democrats | | Republicans | |
|---|---|---|---|---|
| | STABLES | MOBILES | STABLES | MOBILES |
| Careerists | 44 | 58 | 27 | 32 |
| Transitionals | 25 | 29 | 26 | 14 |
| Amateurs | 25 | 19 | 46 | 52 |
| n.a. | 6 | 4 | — | 2 |
| N = | (80) | (36) | (93) | (45) |

[a] The mobility index is based on manual-to-nonmanual occupational movement. See table 4.5 for further elaboration.

this does seem to be occurring, particularly among Democratic challengers. Status mobiles (58 percent) more frequently than stables (44 percent) do anchor themselves to politics in a manner more career-oriented.

While most of the candidates who retained their class position through two generations could hardly be characterized as heroically assuming the WASP's Burden (since 44 percent were just as anxious for a career in politics as their mobile brethren), the differences do bear out other findings. Eulau and Koff found "that mobiles seem to be more prepared to take the risks of elec-

31. Surprisingly, the only published research focusing on this relationship for elective politicians is Heinz Eulau and David Koff, "Occupational Mobility and the Political Career," *Western Political Quarterly* (September 1962): 508–22.

tive office-holding than do status stables ... are more involved in
the political game and ... tend to be less occupationally business-
bound than status stables."[32]

On the other hand, the absence of any strong relationship for
Republicans suggests that the mobility function, like earlier
socializing factors, is not similar for candidates independent of
party.[33] The norm for all Republican challengers is closer to the
role of Amateur and the supposed differential impact of mobility
does not undermine that predisposition. Comparative examination of the occupations of Democratic and Republican mobiles—
on the assumption that the latter enjoy more prestigious, less
marginal, nonpolitical careers—[34]disconfirmed any expectation
that candidates differed because of variations in the formal character of their occupations. It may be that Republicans do in fact
enjoy higher status, more rewarding careers, but the data on this
point are silent.

Finally, the career perspectives of candidates in democratic
and plural societies, societies which are based in part on the
relevance of nonpolitical institutions for diffusing power and
opportunity, should be strongly shaped by differences in the pattern of public and party officeholding. In the case of the former,
no assertion has been more frequently repeated, no proposition
more persuasively reasoned, and no finding more ambivalent than
that contained in table 3.8. Consider the Democrats: 46 percent
of those with and 41 percent of those without public office experience are Careerists, while about equal proportions of the experienced and inexperienced are Transitional. True, 11 percent more
of those without former public office experience tend to the
Amateur's role, but the similarity of perspective seems compelling
given the almost universal expectation that men's ambitions are
shaped, modified, and tested in the arena of public office. I am
aware that the data don't discriminate between types or levels of
public office experience, but the surprising degree of ambition
among those without public service cannot be ignored.

Contrarily, Republican candidates seem to move in the predicted direction, just as they do ideologically; i.e., public office

32. Ibid., p. 521.
33. Eulau and Koff did not entertain this possibility since their data-base
was too small for analysis by party.
34. Bowman and Boynton, "Recruitment Patterns," p. 670.

Table 3.8

### Public Office Experience and Types of Political Commitment, Congressional Challengers
#### (*In Percent*)

| Political Commitment | Democrats | | Republicans | |
|---|---|---|---|---|
| | SOME PUBLIC OFFICE EXPERIENCE | NO PUBLIC OFFICE EXPERIENCE | SOME PUBLIC OFFICE EXPERIENCE | NO PUBLIC OFFICE EXPERIENCE |
| Careerists | 46 | 41 | 32 | 20 |
| Transitionals | 30 | 26 | 25 | 21 |
| Amateurs | 19 | 30 | 38 | 55 |
| n.a. | 5 | 3 | 5 | 4 |
| *N* = | (77) | (71) | (64) | (91) |

experience is more often associated with a "centrist" position for GOP challengers.[35] For one reason or another, the experience of actually holding office seems to play a much larger role in both the professional and ideological perspectives of Republican candidates. It is not clear whether Democrats perceive less dissonance between their ideological and professional roles and holding office, or whether they tend to hold different kinds of offices, or both. Party, not office, is again a powerful factor in the mosaic of political ambition and congressional candidacy.

The other "political" variable, party office experience, should also fundamentally influence the types of attitudes held by challengers when weighing the various advantages of building a career in politics. One commentator argues that the historical problem of third parties stems only partially from repeated electoral defeat. Rather the frustrated ambition of their leaders—successful in states but rarely elsewhere—leads them eventually to desert the ranks because the national opportunity system is monopolized by the two parties.[36] Similarly, one would expect candidates with higher levels of party office experience and more activity in party affairs, to anchor themselves more frequently to a political career. Table 3.9 contains evidence on this expectation.

For both parties, the effect of actually holding office—rather

35. See the next chapter where this is further developed.
36. Schlesinger, *Ambition and Politics*, pp. 201–2.

Table 3.9

## Party Office Experience and Types of Political Commitment, Congressional Challengers
### (*In Percent*)

|                        | Democrats |              |              | Republicans |              |              |
| ---------------------- | --------- | ------------ | ------------ | ----------- | ------------ | ------------ |
|                        |           | LOCAL        | NO OFFICE    |             | LOCAL        | NO OFFICE    |
| *Political*            | NATIONAL/ | EXPE-        | EXPE-        | NATIONAL/   | EXPE-        | EXPE-        |
| *Commitment*           | STATE     | RIENCE       | RIENCE       | STATE       | RIENCE       | RIENCE       |
| Careerists             | 55        | 51           | 31           | 33          | 29           | 17           |
| Transitionals          | 26        | 30           | 24           | 29          | 20           | 20           |
| Amateurs               | 15        | 14           | 42           | 35          | 46           | 61           |
| n.a.                   | 4         | 5            | 3            | 3           | 5            | 2            |
| *N* =                  | (41)      | (48)         | (56)         | (45)        | (63)         | (47)         |

than differences between national, state, and local experience—
seems to have most impact. Almost half the Democrats who had
not held party office were Amateurs, compared to 15 percent of
those with some experience in either local or national/state offices.
To some extent this is quite plausible given the character of the
index.[37] Likewise, Republicans without experience are much
more likely to fall in the Amateur's ranks. Again, there are no
significant differences between GOP candidates with only local
or national/state experience. Importantly the effect of party
yeomanship is not uniform for all political perspectives in the
Republican party. While having major consequences for these
attitudes, party work (or the absence thereof) is not related to
differences in ideological perspectives. Republicans may be professionalized by party office, but not at the expense of jettisoning
their basic ideological attachment to "conservatism."[38]

Models of recruitment, regardless of the analytical categories
applied or type of empirical data gathered, must still come to
terms with behavioral consequences. If one can distinguish between three different styles of commitment, which are in part a
function of the congressional challenger's early and contemporary network of social relations, the problem still remains:
what follows?

37. It is possible that some candidates who ranked "politics as a way of life"
very high were anchoring that evaluation in nonparty political activity, but this
seems remote for men who are, after all, candidates *of* parties.

38. The strategic implications of this are explored in subsequent chapters.

## Some Consequences: Ideological, Partisan, Strategic

Much of the payoff in studying political recruitment resides in connecting motivational profiles with other kinds of behavior. One would expect congressional challengers to differ in a variety of ways as a function of their orientation toward the political career.[39]

One model of recruitment, perhaps most often associated with the work of James Q. Wilson, provides a few more or less testable propositions about the ideological and political styles of "professionals" and "amateurs" in American politics.[40] For Wilson, they differ most consistently in their general approach to politics (not necessarily toward the political career), but by extension, his propositions should be applicable to the group under consideration here.

Leo Snowiss has utilized part of Wilson's argument in his study of the Chicago congressional delegation in the House of Representatives. He suggests that "machine and nonmachine recruitment systems can be shown to have general, systematic effects in the House [mainly] in the distinctions between ideological, issue-oriented liberal Democrats ['amateurs"] and non-ideological, machine liberals ['professionals"] . . ."[41] which lead to quite different styles of operation as congressmen. Likewise, the Goldwater phenomenon has been described as an ascendancy of "purists" over "pros."[42] Indeed, textbooks on American parties often treat this conflict as *the* source for the most enduring tensions within both organizations.

Three hypotheses seem consistent with these themes:

1. The greater (less) the tendency toward careerist orientations, the greater (less) the tendency of candidates in both parties to converge in the center on a general dimension of liberalism and conservatism; ·

---

39. Browning. "Hypotheses About Political Recruitment."
40. Wilson, *Amateur Democrat*, particularly chap. I.
41. Snowiss, "Congressional Recruitment," p. 638.
42. Aaron Wildavsky, "The Goldwater Pheomenon: Purists, Politicians and the Two-Party System," *Review of Politics* (July 1965). Some effects on the organization of Goldwater's campaign are developed in Karl Lamb and Paul Smith, *Campaign Decision-Making* (Belmont, Calif.: Wadsworth, 1968), particularly pp. 45–73.

2. Within the Democratic party, the greater (less) the tendency toward careerist orientations, the greater (less) the tendency to move toward the center on noneconomic (civil rights, foreign affairs, etc.) issues; and

3. Within the Republican party, the greater (less) the tendency toward careerist orientations, the greater (less) the tendency to move toward the center on *both* economic and noneconomic issues.

Evidence relating to each of these hypotheses is presented in tables 3.10 and 3.11.[43] The measures are a self-anchoring index

### Table 3.10

### Relationship of Career Commitment to Ideological Orientation, Congressional Challengers[a]

*(In Percent)*

| Self-Anchoring Position | Democrats | | | Republicans | | |
|---|---|---|---|---|---|---|
| | CAREER-ISTS | TRANSI-TIONALS | AMA-TEURS | CAREER-ISTS | TRANSI-TIONALS | AMA-TEURS |
| Liberal | 55 | 66 | 54 | 9 | 5 | 7 |
| Middle-road | 44 | 34 | 39 | 50 | 47 | 22 |
| Conservative | 1 | — | 3 | 38 | 48 | 70 |
| n.a. | — | — | 4 | 3 | — | 1 |
| N = | (64) | (40) | (36) | (42) | (36) | (75) |

[a] Candidates were classified on the basis of their response to the following question: "Next, we would like some idea about how you feel on certain policy issues being discussed around the country this year. On most issues, would you consider yourself liberal, middle of the road, conservative, or what?"

of liberalism-conservatism and responses to specific questions concerning federal intervention.

The relationship for Republicans, on the measure of generalized ideology, is remarkably strong and certainly consistent with the prediction. An overwhelming majority of GOP Amateurs, 70 percent, considered themselves conservative, while half as

43. Although Wilson specifically rejects the idea that professionals and amateurs in the Democratic party are distinguished by reference to liberalism, much of his treatment of intraparty conflict centers around those who do, and those who don't take their liberalism seriously, perhaps too seriously. Certainly the McCarthy-Humphrey struggle involved a great deal of this historic conflict.

## Table 3.11
## Types of Career Commitment and Differences on Six Components of Liberalism-Conservatism, Congressional Challengers[a]
### (*In Percent*)

| Issue | Democrats | | | Republicans | | |
|---|---|---|---|---|---|---|
| | CAREER-ISTS | TRANSI-TIONALS | AMA-TEURS | CAREER-ISTS | TRANSI-TIONALS | AMA-TEURS |
| On programs for minority and Negro rights, should the federal government: | | | | | | |
| do more | 31 | 45 | 56 | 42 | 8 | 18 |
| do same | 64 | 51 | 32 | 38 | 58 | 33 |
| do less | 4 | 3 | 10 | 20 | 32 | 44 |
| n.a. | 1 | 1 | 2 | — | 2 | 4 |
| On programs that work for disarmament . . . | | | | | | |
| do more | 45 | 71 | 66 | 31 | 13 | 26 |
| do same | 49 | 25 | 24 | 47 | 47 | 23 |
| do less | 6 | — | 6 | 20 | 39 | 45 |
| n.a. | — | 4 | 4 | 2 | 1 | 6 |
| On programs that encourage cooperation with Russia . . . | | | | | | |
| do more | 14 | 18 | 15 | 7 | 2 | 3 |
| do same | 81 | 72 | 73 | 41 | 27 | 28 |
| do less | 4 | 4 | 6 | 50 | 66 | 64 |
| n.a. | 1 | 6 | 6 | 2 | 3 | 5 |
| On programs to assist public education . . . | | | | | | |
| do more | 90 | 90 | 80 | 35 | 19 | 21 |
| do same | 10 | 9 | 15 | 43 | 48 | 23 |
| do less | — | — | 4 | 17 | 31 | 52 |
| n.a. | — | 1 | 1 | 5 | 2 | 4 |
| On programs that provide Medicare for the elderly . . . | | | | | | |
| do more | 90 | 78 | 83 | 43 | 11 | 18 |
| do same | 8 | 15 | 9 | 36 | 45 | 33 |
| do less | 1 | — | 2 | 17 | 42 | 41 |
| n.a. | — | 7 | 6 | 4 | 2 | 8 |
| On programs to help the poverty-stricken generally . . . | | | | | | |
| do more | 78 | 82 | 71 | 23 | 9 | 18 |
| do same | 21 | 17 | 27 | 51 | 51 | 41 |
| do less | 1 | 1 | 2 | 21 | 39 | 37 |
| n.a. | — | — | — | 5 | 1 | 4 |
| N = | (64) | (40) | (36) | (42) | (36) | (75) |

[a] The question used: "Much of what the federal government does can be judged in terms of whether it should do *more*, just about the *same*, or *less*. Please check the following to indicate what your judgment is about each of the following policies or program areas."

many of the Careerists, 38 percent, did so. This reinforces those arguments which have found conservatism an ideology profoundly hostile toward a set of skills and predispositions which make of politics, in Irving Howe's phrase, "steady work." Lest this be misunderstood, a similar criticism has often been directed at radicals and reform-oriented liberals.[44] In any event, the relationship for Republicans is linear and substantial.

Not so for Democratic challengers; in fact, the data for the three groups is curvilinear, with Transitionals more often identifying as liberals (although a majority of self-identified Democratic liberals were Careerists). On the other hand, no differences exist between Careerists and Amateurs in terms of their tendency to identify as liberal or middle of the road; small majorities of both subgroups thought of themselves as liberal.

Two interpretations seem plausible; either the validity of this subjective measure is suspect, or a professional orientation toward politics does not fundamentally modify a Democrat's generalized ideological commitment (and vice versa, or both). Although the validity of the self-anchoring device is treated intensively in subsequent chapters, further evidence, distinguishing on the basis of stands on particular issues, can be gleaned from table 3.11. The data are somewhat ambiguous.

Amateur Republicans, generally more conservative than Careerists, are not on all issues more opposed to federal intervention than Transitionals. GOP Careerists, however, do emerge as the most consistently "centrist" on the issues, economic and noneconomic. Yet they only approach Democratic candidates on the issue of civil rights where, peculiarly, they tend to resemble Transitional Democratic challengers (who most frequently identified as "liberal"). It should be remembered that this question was posed *after* the 1964 Civil Rights Act had been passed.

The responses of Democratic challengers on these items undercut my earlier findings by lending modest, and only modest, support to the Wilson position. Democrats tend to be

44. Among the recent, John Bunzel, *Anti-Politics in America: Reflections on the Anti-Political Temper and Its Distortions of the Democratic Process* (New York: Knopf, 1967). For a sometimes nasty, but somewhat justified critique of Bunzel (based on the absence of any empirical evidence to support or reject the by now monotonous assertions of liberals about the "radical" Right and Left in the United States), see Kenneth Sherrill's review in the *American Political Science Review*, (December 1968): 1342–44.

distributed about the same way on each of the economic issues
with major intraparty differences cropping up in two of the three
noneconomic areas. On civil rights and disarmament, both Transitionals and Amateurs more frequently supported the "liberal"
position than did their Careerist colleagues, but the relationship
does not hold for all noneconomic issues; e.g., there are no significant differences among Democratic challengers on the question of cooperation with the Soviet Union. Since further consideration of the ideological structure of both parties will be taken up in
the next chapter, the analysis here will be suspended.

Partly because of the imperfections of the data, partly because
of the apparent differential impact of party, the ideological consequences often associated with political "professionalism" appear
much more complex than is implied in the distinction between
amateurs and careerists. A second set of consequences, involving
psychological orientations to each of the parties, shares a position
equal to ideology in the configuration of presumed effects of
political careerism. Intensity of partisanship has been used to explain an enormous number of differences in the mass electorate
and party structure has played a dominant role in the explanatory
apparatus of most recruitment studies.[45] The institutionalization
of the House of Representatives rests on some stability in the roles,
values, and norms of party loyalty, just as the dominant mentality
of the professional politician is supposedly an abiding commitment
to the virtues of party solidarity. Some expectations therefore
follow for party candidates who are differentially motivated toward
a career in politics. Three measures of the partisan effect were
obtained—sense of party loyalty, perceptions of party sponsorship, and intensity of partisan identification—but only the first
two will be examined here.[46] Consider table 3.12.

For both parties, the differences run in expected directions:
Careerists substantially more often than Amateurs felt a "strong
sense of party loyalty" persuasive in their decision to enter the
campaign, a finding which is not exactly the most startling in the
history of serendipity. (The index was constructed partially on
indirect measures of party loyalty.) Yet there are some modestly
interesting surprises. Compare the Amateurs: Republicans are

45. Beginning with Seligman, "Recruitment in Politics."
46. Simply because an overwhelming majority thought of themselves as
strong partisans. The few exceptions will be dealt with below.

Table 3.12

Types of Political Commitment and Sense of Partisan
Loyalty, Congressional Challengers
(In Percent)

| Level of Party Loyalty[a] | Democrats | | | Republicans | | |
|---|---|---|---|---|---|---|
| | CAREER-ISTS | TRANSI-TIONALS | AMA-TEURS | CAREER-ISTS | TRANSI-TIONALS | AMA-TEURS |
| High | 57 | 37 | 24 | 57 | 47 | 36 |
| Medium | 36 | 53 | 26 | 22 | 39 | 31 |
| Low | 7 | 10 | 46 | 18 | 11 | 37 |
| n.a. | — | — | 4 | 3 | 3 | 6 |
| N = | (64) | (40) | (36) | (42) | (36) | (75) |

[a] The question asked candidates, to rank the importance of "a strong sense of party loyalty" as very, somewhat or not very important in explaining their decision to run for office. The categories above correspond to the three levels of intensity.

substantially less inclined to dismiss party loyalty as important than their Democratic Amateur counterparts, suggesting a reservoir of strong party loyalty combined with a sentiment of anti-politics among a minority of Republican activists. This inference is strengthened by fact that twice as many Democratic Amateurs (21 percent) also thought of themselves as weak party identifiers than did Republican Amateurs (9 percent). Also, weak identifiers within Democratic ranks were almost exclusively concentrated among the Amateurs, whereas there were no differences from group to group among Republicans. Although I have no evidence, this small proportion of Democratic challengers (four-fifths of whom were liberals) are probably psychologically closest to the mental set often noted for members of national, non-economic liberal interest groups such as the ADA; that is to say, highly active, highly informed but determinedly occasional and uncomfortable allies of the Democratic party and the political career.[47]

Contrarily, the greater proportion of weak partisans among Republican Careerists (18 percent compared to 7 percent for Democrats) is almost entirely a function of the entrance of larger numbers of southern GOP candidates in the 1964 campaign. Here one expects some degree of *partisan* mobility among the highly ambitious, depending on their perception of the opportunity

47. See Scoble, "Political Money."

structure in the South. The attitude was well expressed in the remarks of one "first time" Republican southerner (a Careerist and a winner):

> I represented a state railroad up here for a number of years, and, when I finished up business I would often spend the rest of the afternoon sittin' in the gallery, watchin' the action, sort of wishin' I was down there, but I wasn't active politically at home; didn't have the time. Well, one week, ————, the most prominent Republican in our state, came through, lookin' for a candidate, and some friends suggested he talk to me. I liked what he had to say—even though my daddy was a Democrat and I had always considered myself one, more or less. The statehouse crowd was corrupt, the local people seemed corrupt, and I didn't care to associate with any of them. The Republicans seemed like the only party that could restore any faith, it seemed like a great opportunity (although some of my Democratic friends scoffed), so I took it. . . .

If the two parties structure and monopolize political opportunity at the national level, one would anticipate that the highly ambitious would internalize this thoroughly (i.e., be more adept at "reality-testing") and hence more often consider the party significant in sponsoring their own candidacy. On the other hand, assumptions stemming from power motivation literature,[48] would probably lead to a prediction of greater internally initiated candidacies for the ambitious: the "Stevenson syndrome" (apart from its conscious use to maximize support and hence advance ambition) is stereotypically the quality most often associated with the Amateur Democrat.

But as the data in table 3.13 show, there are few differences between motivational groups. Careerists, Transitionals, and Amateurs tend to distribute in about the same way (within parties) over the factors relating to sources of instigation. In fact, the most striking difference here is not between motivational types, but between parties.

48. Browning and Jacob make clear, however, that the distinctive concern with power among successful politicians is neither excessive nor compulsive; see "Power Motivation and the Political Personality," pp. 75–90. This position accords with Lasswell's earlier argument on the constraints imposed on the power personality in his "The Selective Effects of Personality on Political Participation," in *Studies in the Scope and Method of "The Authoritarian Personality,"* ed. Richard Christie and Marie Jahoda (Glencoe, Ill.: Free Press, 1954).

## Table 3.13

### Types of Political Commitment and Sources of Instigation for Candidacy, Congressional Challengers

#### (*In Percent*)

| Sources of Instigation[a] | Democrats | | | Republicans | | |
|---|---|---|---|---|---|---|
| | CAREER-ISTS | TRANSI-TIONALS | AMA-TEURS | CAREER-ISTS | TRANSI-TIONALS | AMA-TEURS |
| Self-starting | 42 | 45 | 41 | 35 | 33 | 28 |
| Party-sponsored | 27 | 23 | 25 | 41 | 37 | 47 |
| Group-sponsored | 15 | 23 | 20 | 15 | 20 | 11 |
| Combination | 16 | 8 | 14 | 7 | 10 | 13 |
| n.a. | — | — | — | 2 | — | 1 |
| N = | (64) | (40) | (36) | (42) | (36) | (75) |

[a] The question: "Generally speaking, how did you first become interested in running for office?" Candidates then checked one of the following boxes: pretty much my own idea; suggested by party leaders; suggested by friends; combination (elaborate).

The Republicans are much more likely to perceive party as a major source of candidacy. Comparing Republican and Democratic challengers within types of political commitment, twice as many GOP Amateurs (47 percent compared to 25 percent Democratic); one and one-half as many Transitionals (37 percent compared to 23 percent); and similarly, one and one-half times as many Careerists (41 percent contrasted with 27 percent) considered party as the primary source for instigating candidacy. Just as Democrats are more often Careerists, so too they are more frequently self-starters, independent of differences in their orientation toward the political career. Because the n is too small to permit confident multivariate statistical treatment, I have not undertaken a separate analysis which simultaneously combined district competitiveness and motivation. But it should be emphasized that district competitiveness does not substantially affect the tendency of candidates to be Careerists, Transitionals or Amateurs.[49]

Considerable evidence on the relationship of party competi-

49. For example, in Democratic-dominant districts, 47 percent of the Democrats were Careerists; in competitive districts, 41 percent; in Republican-dominant, 46 percent. Among Republicans running in Democratic-dominant districts, 25 percent were Careerists; in competitive districts, 27 percent; in Republican-dominant, 39 percent (the latter were only 18 in number, however).

tion and career orientations has accrued for state legislative candidates, evidence that necessarily has often been extended to describe and explain the recruitment of congressional candidates.[50] Although these data are not sufficient to establish clear disconfirmation, they do lend support to David Leuthold's contention that ". . . even in districts where the party is sure to lose, congressional nominations in themselves are prestigious enough to attract a sizable proportion of candidates,"[51] making the recruitment function of parties quite different from what is apparently the case for state legislative contests. Moreover, they provide no evidence that differences in the perception of sponsoring agents (either internal or external) are a function of differences in the candidate's orientation toward a career in politics.

Ultimately, however, perhaps the most interesting set of consequences—and least amenable to test by the data collected for this study—involves electoral outcome. If success were simply a function of ambition (in private or public life), then much of the research on opportunity structures would be superfluous. A pluralist society rests on a group of mechanisms that, by definition, should encourage diversity and conflict; legislatures dominated by members like Wilbur Mills would be as dull as they would be deadlocked if overrun by ideologues.

The exchange seven years ago between Ralph Huitt and Donald Matthews on the contribution of "outsiders" to the Senate underscored this problem and anchored any empirical documentation of senatorial "effectiveness" in a broader context. To be sure, the operational criteria discriminating here between Careerists, Transitionals, and Amateurs does not suggest the polarization implied above; in fact, probably the opposite is shown. Neither the rejection or affirmation of careerism is so associated with one ideological or professional frame of reference that substantial diversity within motivational types is eliminated. Still, the possibility is of sufficient import that both popular and scholarly commentary has been concerned by the implications of the so-called decline of authentic pluralism in America.

Screening devices in the political and social structure of the

50. This problem, stemming from an absence of comparable data for congressional candidates, can be found in Malcolm E. Jewell and Samuel Patterson, *The Legislative Process in the United States* (New York: Random House, 1966), pp. 94–95.

51. Leuthold, *Electioneering in a Democracy*, p. 19.

United States are thought to both abound and promote heterogeneity.[52] Among them, the electoral arena has long been considered a major instrument in this regard. To what extent, then,
did the arena in 1964 factor out (or in) a disproportionately large
number of one or the other types?

Earlier, the analysis indicated that a small majority of
Democratic winners were Careerists and that a minority of GOP
winners (but of a larger proportion than the losers) were also
oriented to politics in career terms. But this finding, from the
viewpoint of evaluating the manner in which opportunity seems
therefore skewed toward challengers who are Careerists in congressional campaigns, is quite deceptive, as the data presented in tables 3.14 and 3.15 demonstrate.

### Table 3.14

### Types of Political Commitment and Electoral Margin in the 1964 Elections, Congressional Challengers

*(In percent)*

| Outcome and Margin | Democrats | | | Republicans | | |
| --- | --- | --- | --- | --- | --- | --- |
| | CAREER-ISTS | TRANSI-TIONALS | AMA-TEURS | CAREER-ISTS | TRANSI-TIONALS | AMA-TEURS |
| Winners | 51 | 26 | 48 | 13 | 13 | 5 |
| Losers | 49 | 74 | 52 | 87 | 87 | 95 |
| Won (61% plus) | 10 | 5 | 14 | 2 | 2 | 1 |
| Won (56–60%) | 4 | 3 | 10 | 4 | 11 | 1 |
| Won (55% or less) | 37 | 18 | 24 | 7 | — | 3 |
| Lost (45% plus) | 22 | 32 | 25 | 20 | 17 | 16 |
| Lost (40–44%) | 18 | 28 | 20 | 12 | 26 | 16 |
| Lost (39% or less) | 9 | 13 | 7 | 55 | 45 | 63 |
| N = | (64) | (40) | (36) | (42) | (36) | (75) |

Among Democrats, approximately equal proportions of
Careerists and Amateurs were successful (51 and 48 percent
respectively) or defeated (49 and 52 percent). It was the Transitionals who took a disproportionately larger responsibility in
defeat; only one-quarter were able to gain office.

Similarly, the magnitude of defeat tended to affect all groups
within the Republican ranks equally (although a slightly larger

---

52. That they abound is incontestable; that they encourage heterogeneity is a
question of continuing dispute.

## Table 3.15

## Types of Political Commitment and Electoral Fate
## of Freshmen in the 1966 Mid-term Elections[a]
### *(In Numbers)*

| Outcome and Margin | Democrats | | | Republicans | | |
|---|---|---|---|---|---|---|
| | CAREER-ISTS | TRANSI-TIONALS | AMA-TEURS | CAREER-ISTS | TRANSI-TIONALS | AMA-TEURS |
| Winners | 20 | 5 | 9 | 5 | 4 | 4 |
| Losers | 10 | 5 | 4 | 1 | — | — |
| Retired/other office | 1 | — | 1 | — | — | — |
| Won (61% plus) | 8 | 1 | 4 | 5 | 4 | 4 |
| Won (56–60%) | 3 | — | 1 | — | — | — |
| Won (55% or less) | 9 | 4 | 4 | — | — | — |
| Lost (45% plus) | 7 | 5 | 3 | — | — | — |
| Lost (40–44%) | 3 | — | 1 | 1 | — | — |
| Lost (39% or less) | — | — | — | — | — | — |
| Retired/other office | 1 | — | 1 | — | — | — |
| Totals | (31) | (10) | (14) | (6) | (4) | (4) |

[a] These figures are only for freshmen who were part of the original sample and who were subsequently interviewed. See chapter 1 for a complete enumeration of electoral outcomes.

number of Careerists were elected): 87 percent of the Careerists and 95 percent of the Amateurs were defeated in 1964. Likewise, the data for 1964 winners up for reelection in 1966 (shown in table 3.15) provide little evidence that the electoral system is disproportionately eliminating either Careerists or Amateurs. Neither the proportion nor the magnitude of victory or defeat was substantially different for either group. The more general consequences of the structure of defeat are considered later. These data are certainly consistent with the idea that Careerists, while more numerous in the Democratic party, nevertheless must face—apparently with no greater abundance of electorally convertible resources than their Amateur counterparts—the vagaries and risks of competitive, electoral politics.[53]

## Conclusion

Among these challengers, Democrats were more often career-oriented and ambitious, despite variation in backgrounds

53. An interesting question, one quite beyond the scope of this study, relates to the manner in which motivation is modified by continuing frustration, or is deflected into other, perhaps local, office-seeking behavior.

and structural conditions. Contrary to much theorizing, this does not seem a function of occupational marginality, nor do the data suggest Democratic challengers are using candidacy as an alternative channel of mobility. Lawyers in politics, specifically those who were Democratic candidates, were no more likely than other professionals to be particularly anxious for a career in politics, thus disconfirming some widely held beliefs about the ambition of politically engaged attorneys. Since Republican lawyers were more Careerist in their orientations, it seems clear that party, not profession, is the more important variable. Nor does former public office experience make much difference for Democratic candidates, although it does seem strongly related to the professionalization of Republicans.

On the other hand, party office experience has considerable impact on candidates of both parties. In part a reflection of the components of the index, it nevertheless also reinforces those arguments that have insisted on party activity as a central predisposing factor in forging careerist expectations in American politics.

Assumptions were then reversed, treating political commitment as an independent variable from which three consequences were predicted. Numerous observers have suggested that intraparty ideological conflict is essentially conflict between purists and professionals. Nevertheless, a self-anchoring measure of liberalism-conservatism produced no differences between Democratic Careerists, Transitionals, or Amateurs. But, among Republicans, the results were quite pronounced: a much larger majority of GOP Amateurs considered themselves conservative than was true of either Transitional or Careerist candidates.

On specific issues, tapping first economic, and then noneconomic dimensions, Republican Careerists were consistently more "centrist" on each item, although variation among the other two groups was not uniform. Democratic challengers tended to distribute in about the same way on each of the economic issues with major intraparty differences occurring in two of the three noneconomic areas; on civil rights and disarmament, Amateurs and Transitionals more frequently supported the liberal position. Still, these are differences of degree and the similarity on issue orientation, independent of career perspectives, should be remembered.

Two aspects of the congressional challenger's partisan orientation were then examined. Little evidence was generated supporting the belief that differences in the perception of sponsoring agents are related to the challenger's desire for a career in politics. Finally, although a majority of Democratic winners were Careerists, there were no differences in the proportion of Careerists and Amateurs who were able to win. While the data are hardly adequate, the electoral system does not appear to be differentially factoring out Amateurs; both motivational types in each party must contend with the stability of group-anchored (mainly party) voting behavior.

Motivationally diverse, congressional challengers must spend an enormous part of their effort simply acquiring the necessary resources to compete. The advantages that accrue to incumbents, who can devote their main attention to resource utilization, rather than acquisition, has been of long-standing concern to reformers. But, assuming that resources could and should be distributed more equitably, would the types of men and women who surface as candidates be fundamentally different?

Obviously the question contains substantial rhetoric. Unless one were able to manipulate experimentally the present distribution of resources and/or opportunity, little empirical evidence could be marshaled to test the assumption. The tiny shreds of comparative and cross-national data, stemming from environments where gaining resources is not so dependent on individual entrepreneurs, hardly suggests that candidates would be "better" qualitatively, at least in any way that political science might systematically examine. This problem is treated in detail in the final chapter of the book.

Demonstrably the existing electoral arena neither discourages the ambitious and future careerist, nor prevents participation by other than careerists. Both are important values in any properly functioning pluralist democracy. Linking citizens to popular control of the House requires something more than simply keeping parties open to candidates with diverse sets of career goals. The function most frequently attributed to political opposition is to provide alternatives about the the direction and content of public policy. Did these candidates do so?

# 4

# IDEOLOGY

Political conflict often moves in ironic cycles. At precisely the moment specialists on American parties have returned to documenting the extent of issue conflict between Democratic and Republican congressmen, new waves of discontent appear which find little that is different.

On occasion the more benign may concede here a point or there an exception, but these lapses are quickly remedied when those differences that do exist are dismissed as irrelevant, insignificant, or inadequate.

Again, as Lincoln Steffens and others found of New York in the late 1920s,[1] it is fashionable to insist on the distinction between "radical" and "conservative" or "liberal."[2]

Again, as the then young turk editors of the *New Republic* —Wilson, Soule, and Cowley—found themselves doing in 1931, conferences are held that question "the adequacy of America's dominant liberal ideology." And again the image of party candidates articulated by a Bryce or a Duverger takes hold: "fundamentally men expert in the winning of votes . . . not ideological

---

1. Similarities between the late 1920s and mid-1960s are traced by Christopher Lasch, *The New Radicalism in America* (New York: Vintage, 1965), especially pp. 251–308.
2. This is not to imply the distinctions aren't important; quite the contrary. Each has components that are very different, and these differences are surely as significant as the similarities suggested in the sometimes radical, sometimes conservative, attacks on the ubiquity of American liberalism.

groups nor class communities . . ." motivated by little other than personal gain.[3]

Yet, whether echo or choice,[4] growing empirical research suggests that ideology is an important and stable component of American party competition. The broad proposition entertained in this chapter, one suggested by Samuel Huntington 22 years ago[5] and recently modified by Herbert McClosky and others[6] who have returned to a concern with the role of ideology in American politics, is that congressional challengers tend to articulate and sustain a coherent partisan ideology in the face of an electorate for whom such matters are still inchoate or irrelevant, or both.[7]

3. Maurice Duverger, *Political Parties* (rev. ed.; New York: Wiley, 1963), p. 22.

4. The question of whether American parties offer a "significant" choice is one so obviously saturated by an individual's value preferences (in addition to empirically demonstrable evidence) that few answers will satisfy anyone. Since I believe that political scientists should make explicit their own value positions, I should add (if it is not already apparent) that mine usually dump me on the liberal-to-left wing of the Democratic party. Thus, while often finding party programs "inadequate" I rarely agree they are "insignificant" or "echos."

5. "A Revised Theory of American Political Parties," *American Political Science Review* (1950): 669–77. Unlike Huntington, this paper does not propose that the most ideologically conscious tend to emerge precisely in those districts where they would stand the best opportunity of winning, but rather that a coherent party ideology is not suspended by a majority of each party's candidates simply because the structure of party competition would permit possible electoral victory. This point is developed further above.

6. Besides McClosky's "Consensus and Ideology in American Politics," *American Political Science Review* (June 1964): 361–82; and McCloksy et al., "Issue Conflict and Consensus Among Party Leaders and Followers," *American Political Science Review* (June 1960): 406–27; a recent sample would include: John Soule and James Clarke, "Issue Conflict and Consensus: A Comparative Study of Democratic and Republican Delegates to the 1968 Conventions," *Journal of Politics* (February 1971): 72–92; Edmond Costantini and Kenneth Craik, "Competing Elites within a Political Party: California Delegates to the 1968 National Conventions," *Western Political Quarterly* (December 1969); Dwaine Marvick and Charles Nixon, "Recruitment Contrasts in Rival Campaign Groups," in *Political Decision-Makers*, ed. Dwaine Marvick (Glencoe, Ill.: Free Press, 1961); and Robert Hirschfield et al., "A Profile of Political Activists in Manhattan," *Western Political Quarterly* (1962): 489–97. Five recent books make this a central theme: Samuel J. Eldersveld, *Political Parties* (Chicago: Rand McNally, 1964); Robert Agger et al., *The Rulers and the Ruled* (New York: Wiley, 1964); Harry M. Scoble, *Ideology and Electoral Action* (San Francisco: Chandler, 1967); Gerald Pomper, *Elections in America* (New York: Dodd, Mead, 1968); Kenneth and Patricia Dolbeare, *American Ideologies* (Chicago: Markham, 1971).

7. The concept "ideology" has undergone such massive variation in use that discriminating observers will blanch at its instrusion here. Yet that old standby, the liberal-conservative continuum, has proved a useful organizing device for (some) political activists and (some) political scientists and is, Philip Converse suggests, "a serviceable yardstick for simplifying and organizing events in most Western poli-

Despite substantial countervailing electoral pressures, congressional challengers may in fact provide an indispensable communications network—cemented by a coherent if impure ideology —which sharpens rather than blunts party conflict, intensifying rather than modifying ideological differences.[8]

The intention here is to examine these tendencies empirically and under varying conditions. Six structural variables, including three social background and three political-environmental, will in turn be related to ideology, exploring the conditions under which candidates move toward or away from the "natural" liberal-conservative positions associated with each national party. The problem of party unity and electoral outcome is then considered, tracing the fate of liberals, moderates, and conservatives in the 1964 and 1966 elections. Finally, the chapter considers the significance of these findings for patterns of campaign behavior, recruitment, and party functions.

## The Measure of Ideology

The indicator employed throughout this chapter, a widely used and simple self-anchoring index of liberalism-conservatism, enjoys some distinct advantages but is also subject to certain limitations.

---

tics." It shares many attributes of formal ideologies, despite substantial change in particular issues and repeated efforts to refine by adding "corporate" or "radical" before either of these positions on the continuum. See his persuasive argument, "The Nature of Belief Systems in Mass Publics," in *Ideology and Discontent*, ed. David Apter (Glencoe, Ill.: Free Press, 1964), p. 214. The attitudes that have distinguished "liberals" and "conservatives" do, although imperfectly, meet most of the criteria of at least one variant of what commonly passes for ideology; a generally integrated set of beliefs about the political and social environment which embraces both empirical and normative (goal-directed and value-justifying) components. While this will hardly satisfy some, it seems to be at the core of other more elegant and comprehensive usages. See David Minar, "Ideology and Political Behavior," *Midwest Journal of Political Science* (November 1961): 317–31; William Connolly, *Political Science and Ideology* (New York: Atherton, 1967), pp. 2–3; or Robert Lane, *Political Ideology* (Glencoe, Ill.: Free Press, 1962), pp. 13–16.

8. Using the definition above, there is no logical or empirical contradiction between a politics which is simultaneously "ideological" *and* "brokerage" although many elements of the "new" and "old" Left would deny this, as would most students (e.g., Daniel Bell) who take as their model the classic struggles of the European Left and Right. A highly useful empirical examination of this theme is Robert Putnam, "Studying Political Elites: The Case of 'Ideology,' " *American Political Science Review* (September 1971): 651–81.

The alternative most frequently suggested involves scaling individuals on the basis of responses to specific issues. By deriving cumulative or summated scale scores on a sample of issues, one is able to rank-order persons in a rough but reliable fashion and, with Guttman techniques or factor analysis, explore the internal consistency of various opinion clusters.[9] Since data on the candidate's orientation toward specific issue areas was obtained in this study, and as later analysis shows, the relationship between self-classification and these items was strong but far from perfect, a Guttman scale was also attempted. Using the Cornell technique, five items were combined,[10] but neither the coefficient of reproducibility (.82) nor of minimal marginal reproducibility (.52) met minimum standards of reliability. One of the five issue areas (civil rights) was then dropped, some item "shuffling" undertaken, and the other four recombined. Each related to domestic economic orientation. Although the coefficient of reproducibility improved (.85), it still did not reach a satisfactory minimum. Hence cumulative scales are not used in the analysis.

Quite apart from questions of technical reliability, earlier examination on the Guttman scale and on a scale of Likert-type summated liberalism suggested some rather severe problems of validity with both these "objective" ideological measures. Each distinguished reasonably well between Republican conservatives and *all* Democratic challengers, but, particularly among Democrats, neither sufficiently tapped what appear to be genuine *intra*party differences. Large majorities of the latter, whether considering themselves "liberal" or "middle of the road," clustered in the upper three positions of each scale.[11] Yet intuitively these two different psychological reference points suggest important distinc-

9. The use of factor analysis with attitude data is rejected by many statisticians because social science has not yet created attitude scales which meet interval assumptions of measurement. Lewis Guttman and James Lingoes have developed a new set of programs for multivariant analysis on ordinal level data—smallest space analysis—which may enjoy increasing use in attitude research. For an example, see Glendon Schubert, "Ideological Distance: A Smallest Space Analysis Across Three Cultures, *Comparative Political Studies* (October 1968): 319–47.

10. Each related to the conventional question of federal domestic intervention and were directed at the following areas: regulating business; providing medical care for the aged; providing aid to assist public education; providing help for the poor generally; engaging in programs to assist Negroes and other minorities.

11. On an eleven-point Guttman rank-ordering, 86 percent of the Democratic challengers scored one, two, or three.

tions among the candidates, distinctions that command empirical examination. [12] Because I am concerned with ideological conflict *within* as well as *between* the two parties, it was necessary to opt for a measure that did discriminate between candidates.

Previous research has demonstrated that the highly educated and politically sophisticated are much more capable than the typical citizen of organizing a variety "of idea-elements into more tightly constrained wholes." [13] Thus one can anticipate that abstractions such as "liberal" and "conservative" are operationally more reliable as devices for classifying and predicting the behavior (including opinions) of the highly active in American politics. The fact that substantial variation does exist—whether one uses objective or subjective tests—underscores the complexity, the lack of complete unidimensionality, and the tentativeness of these and other simplified ideological dimensions. Certainly self-classified liberals or conservatives are going to possess opinions that will be interpreted differently by different observers in different environments. But a similar problem applies equally to other measures of ideology. The qualification is no more, or no less, applicable to alternative operational criteria. When used in conjunction with other measures, the self-anchoring index provides a standardized and serviceable tool for large-scale research on the attitude structure of political activists.

## Profiles

The assumption of a Left-Right spatial model of party conflict, postulated by Anthony Downs and others, is predictably

12. Democratic nonincumbents were almost exclusively nonsouthern Democrats and one would expect maximum homogeneity among this group on general questions relating to economic intervention, particularly in 1964. The Vietnam war had not really surfaced as a divisive issue, although one year later my interviews with freshmen showed that some were becoming increasingly restless as American involvement grew more massive. However one might feel about events surrounding the 1968 campaign, and the impact of "New Politics" or the stability of the New Deal coalition, it seems clear that many of the issues political scientists have been using for the past twenty years are undergoing substantial modification. The situational character of all our operational measures reinforces the need for developmental studies, perhaps using a modified panel technique, on the way politicians adjust "old" labels to "new" issues or vice-versa. Chapter 6 examines change and continuity among winners between 1965 and 1970.

13. Converse, "Nature of Belief Systems," p. 229. McClosky has also provided some evidence along these lines, noting the strong association between scale scores and self-classification for leaders, but not followers, in his "Consensus and Ideology in American Politics," p. 375.

## Table 4.1

### Subjective Ideological Position of Congressional Challengers, 1964[a]

#### (In Percent)

| Self-Anchoring Position | Democrats | Republicans |
|---|---|---|
| Liberal | 59 | 8 |
| Middle of the road | 37 | 34 |
| Conservative | 1 | 53 |
| Mixed[b] | 2 | 4 |
| Meaningless terms | 1 | 1 |
| N = | (145) | (158) |

[a] Candidates were classified on the basis of their response to the following question: "Next, we would like some idea about how you feel on certain policy issues being discussed around the country this year. On most issues, would you consider yourself liberal, middle of the road, conservative, or what?"

[b] A category used to classify those who indicated a position between the choices above.

more applicable to a socially atypical group of highly active citizens than it is to the electorate.[14] As the data in table 4.1 show, candidates do in fact form "ideological communities," particularly between but also within parties. The association between party and issue position (not unexpectedly) is far from one to one. However, majorities (although not over-whelming) bunch at that position conventionally associated with each of the national parties.

Obviously identification as "liberal," "middle of the road," or "conservative" does not mean, as stressed earlier, that there are rigidly prescribed patterns of behavior that are liberal or conservative. But the distinction does have important consequences, both on specific opinions as well as behavior. Between that 59 percent among the Democrats who thought of themselves as liberal and the 53 percent among Republicans who identified as conservative, there are large and consistent differences in responses to the six

14. Anthony Downs, *An Economic Theory of Democracy* (New York: Harper, 1957), particularly pp. 96–142. This is a phenomenon stressed in the work of McClosky, Eldersveld, and James Q. Wilson and entertained more formally in the reformulation of Downs by Donald Stokes, "Spatial Models of Party Competition," reprinted in Angus Campbell et al., *Elections and the Political Order* (New York: Wiley, 1966), pp. 175–76. Some counterevidence is beginning to appear. See the various contributions of Gerald Pomper, Richard Boyd, Richard A. Brody, Benjamin I. Page, and John H. Kessel to the *American Political Science Review* (June 1972): 415–70.

# Table 4.2

## Six Tests of Attitude Consistency: Subjective and Objective Components of Liberalism-Conservatism[a]

### (In Percent)

| Issue | Democrats[b] LIBERALS | MODERATES | Party Distance[c] | Republicans LIBERALS | MODERATES | CONSERVATIVES | Party Distance |
|---|---|---|---|---|---|---|---|
| **On programs for minority and Negro rights, should the federal government:** | | | | | | | |
| do more | 57 | 27 | *30* | 38 | 26 | 19 | |
| do same | 40 | 62 | | 54 | 53 | 30 | |
| do less | 1 | 8 | | 8 | 16 | 47 | *31* |
| n.a. | 2 | 3 | — | — | 5 | 4 | |
| **On programs to assist public education ...** | | | | | | | |
| do more | 79 | 73 | *6* | 69 | 19 | 8 | |
| do same | 6 | 13 | | 8 | 46 | 14 | |
| do less | — | 2 | | 8 | 16 | 56 | *45* |
| n.a. | 15 | 8 | | 15 | 19 | 20 | |
| **On programs to provide medical care for the elderly ...** | | | | | | | |
| do more | 96 | 73 | *26* | 85 | 28 | 8 | |
| do same | 4 | 13 | | 15 | 47 | 33 | |
| do less | — | 2 | | — | 16 | 43 | *37* |
| n.a. | — | 10 | | — | 9 | 16 | |
| **On programs to help the poverty-stricken generally ...** | | | | | | | |
| do more | 87 | 60 | *27* | 54 | 19 | 12 | |
| do same | 13 | 37 | | 33 | 63 | 31 | |
| do less | — | — | | 12 | 12 | 50 | *38* |
| n.a. | — | 3 | | — | 6 | 7 | |
| **On programs to regulate labor unions ...** | | | | | | | |
| do more | 9 | 12 | | 31 | 56 | 60 | *4* |
| do same | 66 | 67 | | 54 | 35 | 22 | |
| do less | 22 | 17 | *5* | 15 | 9 | 6 | |
| n.a. | 3 | 4 | | — | — | 12 | |
| **On programs that encourage cooperation with Russia ...** | | | | | | | |
| do more | 21 | 6 | *15* | 31 | 2 | 3 | |
| do same | 74 | 81 | | 54 | 42 | 19 | |
| do less | 3 | 6 | | 15 | 49 | 74 | *25* |
| n.a. | 2 | 7 | | — | 7 | 4 | |
| *N =* | (83) | (57) | | (12) | (56) | (83) | |

[a] The question used: "Much of what the federal government does can be judged in terms of whether it should do *more*, just about the *same*, or *less*. Please check the following to indicate what your judgment is about each of the following policies or program areas."

specific issue areas presented in table 4.2. Moreover, the manner in which moderates (middle of the road) of each party differ is testimony to the psychological framework the parties provide in mediating the ideological attitude of "moderation."

Conventionally, differences between parties in two-party systems have been conceived as embracing three zones, two on the polar ends and one in the center, composed of groups from both parties who are closer to each other than to their respective poles. On the three social welfare issues presented here, the spread suggests a different arrangement, with both the liberal and moderate Democrats joined by the few (8 percent) liberal Republicans constituting one bloc, moderate Republicans a second, and conservative Republicans a third. The tilt on these dimensions is surely "left." The relative absence of disagreement between liberal and moderate Democrats on each of these issues shows how the argument over federal intervention—among nonincumbents—had become a party issue and not simply a division between different wings within each party.

Although similar evidence has been provided for the parties in Congress,[15] it should be remembered that Democratic challengers are contesting disproportionately in districts outside the South. On two of the noneconomic issues, one dealing with civil rights and the other with foreign policy, the distribution described above undergoes some rearrangement. The civil rights question, raised *after* the 1964 Civil Rights Bill had been passed, provides the closest approximation of an issue on which candidates are distributed by ideology and not by party affiliation; i.e., liberal Democrats and Republicans on the Left, moderates of both parties in the Center, conservative Republicans on the Right.

---

[b] Only two Democratic candidates claimed to be conservatives; they have not been included in this analysis.

[c] A simple measure based on the percentage difference (for Democrats) between liberals and "middles" favoring *more* activity on each issue, and (for Republicans) between conservatives and middles favoring *less* activity.

---

15. Among which, see Julius Turner, *Party and Constituency* (Baltimore: Johns Hopkins University Press, 1951); Duncan MacRae, Jr., *Dimensions of Congressional Voting* (Berkeley: University of California Press, 1959); David B. Truman, *The Congressional Party* (New York: Wiley,1959); Lewis A. Froman, Jr., *Congressmen and Their Constituencies* (Chicago: Rand McNally, 1963); David R. Mayhew, *Party Loyalty Among Congressmen* (Cambridge, Mass.: Harvard University Press, 1967).

Interestingly, however, one out of five of the conservative Republicans felt the federal government should do more in this area although 47 percent also believed government should do less. This question, excluding the labor union item which sought to invert expected responses, also saw a dropoff in the unanimity of support given by liberal Democrats for domestic intervention. While a majority (57 percent) favored increased federal activity, the much larger than normal proportion who were willing to see the federal government continue present levels of activity (40 percent) lends some support to the notion that liberals, like conservatives, are most consistent on economic issues.

The other noneconomic item, a question on relations with the Soviet Union, uncovered two significant patterns. First, although one-fifth of the liberal Democrats felt the United States should do more on programs encouraging cooperation with Russia, huge majorities in both liberal and moderate Democratic camps were agreed on continuing present policy. Among Republicans, the issue evoked not only the most consistent nay-saying response for the conservatives (74 percent advocated "less"), but it also moved about half (49 percent) of the moderates into this category. The recent forays of Richard Nixon in the area of Soviet and Chinese relations seem all the more remarkable in light of data like this. Moderate and conservative Republicans were moved toward the most unanimity on this question and on the need for increased regulation of labor. Again, the few liberal Republicans were closer to Democrats than they were to either wing of their own party.[16]

These data are of course derived exclusively from nonincumbents and any ideological differences (or similarities) between Democratic and Republican challengers could be quite deceptive from the viewpoint of alternatives presented the electorate in specific districts. It is possible that nonincumbents are more like their incumbent opponents in most districts while pairs of congressional candidates differ from district to district. Thus my data would show substantial party differences, since only nonincum-

16. Leroy Rieselbach has demonstrated, however, that few presidents can rely on a generalized ideology of "internationalism" when attempting to build support for specific programs, if the president's strategy is based on expectations of party differences that were more obvious in the immediate postwar period. See his *The Roots of Isolationism* (Indianapolis: Bobbs-Merrill, 1966), pp. 141–64.

bents are considered, when in fact district rather than party was the critical variable. I cannot directly test this hypothesis, but other evidence suggests that it is more often the exception than the rule.

First, a direct test of this problem has been undertaken by John L. Sullivan and Robert E. O'Connor, comparing policy stands and voting behavior of matched pairs of challengers and incumbents in the 1966 election. Their findings strongly support the above argument:

> ... the electorate was offered a substantively significant choice in the Congressional election of 1966 ... winning candidates in that election generally voted as their pre-election issue-stands predicted ... Democratic candidates were almost invariably more liberal than their ... Republican opponents [when both were competing in the same district].[17]

Second, substantial research has demonstrated that the parties tend to differ on roll-call votes in the House in a manner quite consistent with the findings presented here for nonincumbents. The independent effects of constituency, while significant, do not substantially alter this basic partisan division. Third, previous studies that have compared the voting behavior of successive incumbents from different parties have consistently shown that substantial differences in behavior do occur, that the "particular incumbent does make a difference"; i.e., he votes differently from his predecessor on similar issues.[18] Intensive comparative analysis of the few (83) challengers who were successful in 1964 with their predecessors on four Great Society issues corroborated this finding. I'm not suggesting that individual challengers don't alter some positions in specific districts, but my findings as well as others sug-

17. Sullivan and O'Connor, "Electoral Choice and Popular Control of Public Policy: The Case of the 1966 House Elections," *American Political Science Review* (December 1972): 1256–68.

18. See the citations in note 15. These studies, based on roll-call voting behavior, are subject to the same logical problem since they deal only with incumbents. But the probability of interparty differences disappearing under the impact of constituency (outside the South) is remote, particularly in light of the extensive constituency controls examined in each of the above. Further, Lewis Froman has shown that there is even significant variation among congressmen from the same party, although his analysis is restricted to votes on reciprocal trade. Froman, *Congressmen*, chap. 8.

gest that congressional challengers and their incumbent opponents differ significantly on public policy.

Table 4.2 also presents a rather simple index of ideological distance *within* the parties on each issue. The bitter division within the presidential wing of the Republican party during 1964, while not to be anticipated as universally occurring in each congressional district, is still partially reflected in the degree of intraparty conflict suggested by differences on four of the six issues.

Considering differences between moderates and liberal-conservatives for each party as an indication of significant intraparty conflict (liberals are clearly out of the Republican party's ideological ballpark, statistically and attitudinally), the GOP is certainly the more divisive. On federal aid to education, 56 percent of the conservatives, but only 9 percent of the moderates, felt the federal government should do less, a difference of 45 percent. On three other issues, poverty, Medicare, and civil rights, the moderates and conservatives were separated by a spread greater than 30 percent. For Democrats the civil rights issue was the only one which approached this magnitude in showing substantial intraparty conflict; 57 percent of the liberals, but only 27 percent of the moderates, believed the government should do more.

Congressional challengers, whether potential winners or doomed losers, are not simply an aggregate of individuals contesting in isolated constituencies on issues relevant only to their districts. Like Eldersveld has shown for the organizations in Detroit,[19] or Scoble has argued of the NCEC,[20] these party candidates constitute groups in ideological terms. The foregoing analysis indicates these "communities of co-believers" are neither monolithic entities nor ideological oligarchies but there is substantial unity. If, as this study suggests, they provide some degree of ideological coherence for each national party, then an important question centers on those factors which tend to magnify, mediate, or reduce this cohesion: how tough is the cement?

## Social Sources of Ideological Pluralism

The belief in a widespread and sharp generational conflict between the old and the young is part of the persistent proverbial wisdom of American politics. Like all proverbial knowledge, how-

19. Eldersveld, *Political Parties*, pp. 528–35.
20. Scoble, *Ideology and Electoral Action*, pp. 26–61.

ever, this belief tends to ignore the considerable social and political research which has established the profound continuity, the extensive sources of stability, which characterize the transmission of values from one age to another.[21] Yet student unrest, the McCarthy or McGovern campaigns, and the generous publicity heaped on the behavior of young political leaders are often treated as typical (rather than atypical) of substantial cleavages in the belief systems of two generations.

Usually, the old guard (itself a term reflecting this wisdom) is pictured as representing the forces of moderation, if not reaction, against a newer, more liberalizing younger generation. Among others, Harvey Lehman[22] and David Walker[23] have argued that age in recruitment is a factor which affects the ideological outlook of candidates and that youthful politicos are more often the selection of forces of protest and unrest.

Consider thus the data in table 4.3. The so-called generational split does exist, but in precisely the opposite direction from that expected. For both parties, those *under* forty were more often in the conservative ranks than those forty and over. Among Democrats, 62 percent of the candidates over forty considered themselves liberal while slightly less than one-half, 48 percent, of their counterparts who were under forty thought of themselves as liberal. Of Republicans, 64 percent under forty identified as conservative while this was true for only 46 percent of their older colleagues.

Two interpretations of this rather striking and unexpected finding are possible. First, an argument can be made that the reversal is not really unexpected if one assumes that it is the youth

21. The work on political socialization is large and growing. On this point, see Richard Dawson and Kenneth Prewitt, *Political Socialization* (Boston: Little, Brown, 1968); Fred I. Greenstein, *Children and Politics* (New Haven: Yale University Press, 1965); Robert Lane, *Political Ideology* (New York: Free Press, 1963), particularly pp. 268–83. Cf. Edward Greenberg, ed., *Political Socialization* (Chicago: Atherton, 1970). Even among those who were the center of popular "generation gap" literature, college radicals, some evidence exists which suggests that it was less a "gap" and more an extension of the traditionally liberal, highly involved political activity of their parents. For some not very reliable, but highly suggestive data, see S. M. Lipset and Philip Altbach, "Student Politics and Higher Education in the United States," in *Student Politics*, ed. S. M. Lipset (New York: Basic Book, 1967), pp. 199–253.

22. Harvey Lehman, *Age and Achievement* (Princeton, N. J.: Princeton University Press, 1959).

23. David Walker, "The Age Factor in the 1958 Congressional Elections," *Midwest Journal of Political Science* (February 1960): 1–26.

Table 4.3

Comparative Ideological Position of Congressional
Challengers, by Age and Party
(*In Percent*)

| Ideology | All Candidates | | Democrats | | Republicans | |
|---|---|---|---|---|---|---|
| | 40 AND OVER | UNDER 40 | 40 AND OVER | UNDER 40 | 40 AND OVER | UNDER 40 |
| Liberal | 34 | 26 | 62 | 48 | 10 | 4 |
| Middle of the road | 36 | 41 | 33 | 52 | 38 | 30 |
| Conservative | 26 | 32 | 2 | — | 46 | 64 |
| n.a. | 4 | 1 | 3 | — | 6 | 2 |
| N = | (195) | (105) | (89) | (53) | (105) | (52) |

organizations in the Republican party, such as the Young Americans for Freedom (YAF), which most closely approximate "pure" conservatism and who are most insistent on sustaining doctrinal purity against the pragmatic, electorally oriented drive of their elders. However, a similar argument must then apply equally to younger members of the Democratic party, but this clearly is not the case. Nor is it true that Democratic candidates under forty no longer felt the term "liberal" adequately descriptive of contemporary choices since they in fact consciously identified as "middle of the road."

Nevertheless, on the assumption that younger candidates, regardless of subjective orientation, do in fact differ on post-New Deal, noneconomic issues, and that these differences are not adequately handled within the conventional space of liberalism-conservatism, analysis was undertaken by age on the civil rights issue. Although the differences are reduced, the distribution is still in the same direction: 43 percent of the older but 40 percent of the younger Democratic candidates believed the federal government should do more in this area; 27 percent of the GOP candidates forty and above felt the federal government should do less on civil rights while 38 percent of the younger Republican challengers considered less activity appropriate. To the extent federal intervention in civil rights is an issue that goes beyond the older economic conflict, younger men are no more likely than older candidates to favor such extension.

A second interpretation, one consistent with some of Joseph

Schlesinger's work on ambition theory,[24] would hold that younger candidates, more ambitious and career-oriented than their elders, are more flexible ideologically because that ideology is tempered by realistic appraisals of the opportunity structure. But this argument fails to explain the findings for Republicans.

The relationship between age and ideology is complex and it is doubtful the operational measures used here are powerful enough to embrace some rather important components in a generational conflict, such as style, which surface in situations where age differences are a factor. An excellent example, partially involving just such a conflict, was the Halleck-Ford leadership struggle during 1965.[25] Also, the cutting point employed, forty years, is obviously not appropriate for youth-adult political conflict although it does fit the requirements for generational battles among political leaders, who are rarely under thirty. The fact is that the common proposition about generational conflict receives little confirmation from these data, and possibly might be quite contrary to expectations. This should serve as considerable warning to those who see younger leaders as an unqualified source for liberalizing tendencies in the two national parties.

Another social-background factor, occupation, is also thought to be intimately related to ideology. Lawyers, in particular, have consistently been the target of reformers for their presumed conservative bias, even though two studies that tested this assertion found little evidence that attorneys differed from nonattorneys in this respect. David Derge, for example, concluded that lawyers in legislatures will neither be concentrated among those supporting, nor opposing, progressive legislation[26] and another study found that legislator-attorneys actually scored slightly higher on a liberalism scale than was true of nonlawyers.[27] The evidence on this score shown in table 4.4 assumes some significance then, since

24. Joseph Schlesinger, *Ambition and Politics* (Chicago: Rand McNally, 1966), p. 176.

25. Robert L. Peabody, *The Ford-Halleck Minority Leadership Contest, 1965* (New York: McGraw-Hill, 1966). I also introduced two control variables—constituency and district competitiveness—in an earlier report. Neither reduced substantially the paradox of this finding on age and ideology. See my "Party, Ideology, and the Congressional Challenger," *American Political Science Review* (December 1969): 1226.

26. David Derge, "The Lawyer as a Decision-Maker in the American State Legislature," *Journal of Politics* 21 (August 1959): 431.

27. Heinz Eulau and John Sprague, *Lawyers in Politics* (Indianapolis: Bobbs-Merrill, 1964), pp. 126–27.

## Table 4.4

### Occupations and Political Ideology, Congressional Challengers, by Profession and Party

### (In Percent)

| Ideology | All Candidates | | | Democrats | | | Republicans | | |
|---|---|---|---|---|---|---|---|---|---|
| | LAW | BUSI-NESS | PROFES-SIONAL[a] | LAW | BUSI-NESS | PROFES-SIONAL | LAW | BUSI-NESS | PROFES-SIONAL |
| Liberal | 32 | 18 | 42 | 51 | 45 | 75 | 9 | 6 | 9 |
| Middle 'of the road | 48 | 38 | 26 | 44 | 48 | 25 | 52 | 32 | 22 |
| Conserva-tive | 18 | 37 | 30 | 4 | — | — | 37 | 55 | 64 |
| n.a. | 2 | 7 | 2 | 1 | 7 | — | 2 | 7 | 5 |
| N = | (103) | (97) | (101) | (57) | (33) | (47) | (46) | (64) | (45) |

[a] The professional category included the four skilled workers and one candidate who listed her profession as "housewife."

there are differences between lawyers and nonlawyers, but these differences are more complicated than lawyer/nonlawyer distinctions suggest.

First, among Republicans, attorneys are a distinctly moderate group. Compared to both GOP businessmen and other professionals, lawyers less frequently think of themselves as conservative: 37 percent of the attorneys, but 55 percent of the businessmen and 64 percent of the other professionals are self-designated conservatives. On the other hand, about equal proportions of Democratic lawyers and businessmen fall into the moderate and liberal categories while three-fourths of the other professionals, heavily dominated by educators and journalists, consider themselves liberal and only 24 percent identified as middle of the road. The nonlawyer professionals in both parties emerge on the polar positions substantially more frequently than either the business or legal types among the candidates.

One explanation, strictly speculative, is that professionals in both parties are less dependent on the brokerage skills associated with business and with law, and hence occupationally less inclined to adopt a position reflecting such style. It should be noted, however, that sizable proportions of lawyers and businessmen within each party are equally inclined to the modal position of their parties so that differences *among* lawyers or businessmen are perhaps as important as differences between lawyers *and* other (nonbusiness) professionals.

The third social-background factor, intergenerational social mobility, has frequently been cited as a major determinant of political belief systems. Lipset and others[28] have argued that upwardly mobile voters in the United States tend to be even more conservative in their party choice than those middle-class individuals whose fathers held occupations similar to their own.

Alternatively, some have asserted that it is precisely those coming from working-class backgrounds and moving into middle-class roles who retain a commitment to the original group's ideology.[29] Some evidence regarding these two contrary positions is given in table 4.5. The operational criteria is a manual-to-nonmanual index. Taken as a group, upwardly mobile candidates tend to be slightly more liberal than status stables, but only small

## Table 4.5

### Intergenerational Social Mobility[a] and Political Ideology, Congressional Challengers, by Party

#### (*In Percent*)

| Ideology | STATUS STABLES | STATUS MOBILES | Democrats | | Republicans | |
|---|---|---|---|---|---|---|
| | | | STABLES | MOBILES | STABLES | MOBILES |
| Liberal | 28 | 41 | 54 | 78 | 6 | 11 |
| Middle of the road | 38 | 31 | 40 | 22 | 37 | 38 |
| Conservative | 29 | 26 | 2 | — | 53 | 47 |
| n.a. | 5 | 2 | 4 | — | 4 | 4 |
| N = | (173) | (81) | (80) | (36) | (93) | (45) |

[a] The mobility index is a manual-to-nonmanual intergenerational classification based on occupations. Although somewhat more refined instruments have been used in other studies (cf. Heinz Eulau and David Koff, "Occupational Mobility and the Political Career," *Western Political Quarterly* [September 1962]: 511), this is widely found in the sociology literature and has the advantage of emphasizing the implied effects of class movement. On the other hand, it probably understates the degree of mobility once both father and son have moved into nonmanual categories. Still, the percent mobile noted here (about one-third) is approximately the same as found by Eulau and Koff for stage legislators, even though they applied a more precise test. Of the 303 nonincumbents, 49 could not be classified because their fathers were farmers or because they did not respond to the question. All the mobiles above were upward in their movement.

28. Seymour M. Lipset, *Political Man* (New York: Doubleday, 1960), pp. 253–58.

29. Heinz Eulau and David Koff, "Occupational Mobility and the Political Career," *Western Political Quarterly* 15 (September 1962): 507–22.

differences exist between these two groups in terms of the frequency with which they identify as conservatives.

An important difference emerges when one examines the differential effect of mobility within each party, however. Social mobility is apparently unrelated to the ideological preference of Republican candidates; there is neither evidence of an unusual infusion of moderate or liberal noblesse oblige among those who are stable, nor signs that the mobile compensate by disproportionately adopting a conservative stance. But, among Democrats, the upwardly mobile are much more inclined to identify as liberals (78 percent) than are the stables (54 percent).

Heinz Eulau and David Koff have noted that "When they first come to politics, mobile politicians tend to be more oriented toward their occupational success than do status stable politicians," looking at political life as a mechanism for advancing their occupational careers.[30] Although this aspect of recruitment is quite beyond the scope of this book, it is clear that ideological perspectives, often thought to be in direct conflict with career advancement, are also dominant in the world view of mobile politicians. This is particularly true of Democratic candidates.

Ironically, the data can be interpreted as lending modest support to both the Lipset and the contrary proposition: among candidates who were mobile, a slight majority (58 percent) were nominees of the more conservative party, although they were a distinct minority within that party and were no more likely to identify as conservative, moderate or liberal than their status-stable counterparts. On the other hand, fewer mobiles were Democratic candidates, but the tendency of this group to identify as liberal was much more pronounced than was true for those Democrats who were stable in status.

## Political Sources of Ideological Pluralism

"Congressional recruitment is essentially a process for organizing power."[31] The political party has generally been the primary agency through which power is organized.

Building on the pioneering efforts of Turner and MacRae,[32]

30. Ibid., p. 522.
31. Snowiss, "Congressional Recruitment," p. 628.
32. Turner, *Party and Constituency*; and MacRae, *Dimensions of Congressional Voting*.

numerous studies have sought to ascertain the effects of party competition and constituency characteristics on the roll-call voting behavior of legislators, although only a handful have dealt in a comprehensive way with the interrelationship of party, constituency, recruitment processes, and the professional and ideological styles of those selected in these environments.[33]

Two strands of inquiry have dominated the roll-call studies of the past fifteen years; one dealing with legislative party cohesion, the other with ideology. Considerable evidence has piled up since MacRae's early research showing that departures from party regularity in voting occur most frequently—when they do occur at all—among legislators from districts that are most competitive and "least typical" socially and economically of their own parties.

Further, the results on specific measures of liberalism-conservatism, although inconsistent and characterized by exceptions, tend to confirm MacRae: ideological departures occur most frequently—and it should be stressed again, when they do occur—among legislators from districts that are electorally marginal and environmentally atypical of their own parties.[34] The majority of these studies have focused on state legislatures. Lewis Froman, however, has shown the first proposition (party regularity) to be false for Democrats and only partially true for Republicans in the House when interparty competition is the independent variable, and the second proposition (ideological deviance) generally accurate (with some major exceptions) using both competitiveness and constituency as independent variables.[35]

The reasoning behind both these hypotheses is quite plausible—candidates seek to maximize their electoral appeal by (1) moving toward the rival party in districts where the opposition party is dominant, (2) pursuing a middle-of-the-road course in districts where the parties are evenly matched, and (3) assuming polar positions where their own party is dominant and the problem of reelection not critical. These propositions have never been systematically explored with challengers in legislative

33. Among which, see Sorauf, *Party and Representation*; Wahlke, Eulau, et al., *The Legislative System*; and Snowiss, "Congressional Recruitment."

34. Most of these studies are extensively summarized and critically examined in Eulau and Hinckley, "Legislative Institutions," pp. 122–50.

35. Froman, *Congressmen*, pp. 85–122. Wayne Shannon has disputed Froman's findings, arguing he exaggerates the amount of ideological deviance. See Shannon's "Electoral Margins and Voting Behavior in the House of Representatives," *Journal of Politics* (November 1968): 528–45.

campaigns, a group to whom they would presumably be quite relevant.

Although the indices of competition and constituency presented in tables 4.6 and 4.7 are not very elegant, the hypothesis linking ideology to party structure receives little confirmation by the data presented here. Among Democrats, for example, approximately equal proportions tend to identify as liberal or middle of the road, despite variation in the degree of interparty competition. And this holds even for those districts which are overwhelmingly dominated by the opposition (the GOP's share of the total vote never dipped below 60 percent).

For Republicans, there is in fact a tendency for a greater proportion of candidates contesting marginal districts to identify on the polar position (conservative) than those candidates secure in Republican dominant districts (who are more often moderates), but the small number of challengers contesting in districts domi-

### Table 4.6

### Party Structure and Recruitment: Relationship of Electoral Competition to Political Ideology, Congressional Challengers, by Party[a]

#### (In Percent)

| | Democrats | | | Republicans | | |
|---|---|---|---|---|---|---|
| *Ideology* | DEMOCRAT DOMINANT | COMPET-ITIVE | REPUBLICAN DOMINANT | DEMOCRAT DOMINANT | COMPET-ITIVE | REPUBLICAN DOMINANT |
| Liberal | 53 | 57 | 57 | 9 | 4 | 5 |
| Middle of the road | 30 | 39 | 40 | 35 | 29 | 55 |
| Conservative | 7 | 1 | — | 51 | 61 | 38 |
| n.a. | 10 | 3 | 3 | 4 | 5 | 2 |
| *N* = | (13) | (61) | (71) | (98) | (42) | (18) |

[a] The index of party competition is a modified version of the one used in Lewis Froman, *Congressmen and Their Constituencies* (New York: Rand McNally, 1964), p. 29. Categories were collapsed because of the relatively small number of candidates in each cell. The following conventions were used above: Competitive districts were those in which the opposition had won at least 45 percent of the vote in the five elections preceding 1964 at least once or had actually won the district. Party-dominant districts are those in which the opposition had not won once in the five preceding elections nor been able to gain more than 44 percent of the vote. About one-fourth of the districts were redrawn in the 1961–63 period, 42 of which are included in the totals above. Electoral totals for these are based solely on the 1962 and 1964 elections. However, those districts in which the 1964 winner was a Democrat, but the preceding elections had been won by a Republican with more than 55 percent of the vote were placed in the Republican-dominant category. Data source: *Congressional Quarterly Almanac* 19 (1963): 1173–84.

## Table 4.7

### Urbanism and Recruitment: Relationship of Constituency to Political Ideology, Congressional Challengers, by Party[a]

#### (In Percent)

| Ideology | Democrats | | | | Republicans | | | |
|---|---|---|---|---|---|---|---|---|
| | URBAN | SUBURBAN | RURAL | MIXED | URBAN | SUBURBAN | RURAL | MIXED |
| Liberal | 61 | 63 | 51 | 65 | 13 | 7 | 5 | 6 |
| Middle of the road | 35 | 36 | 44 | 35 | 43 | 39 | 28 | 39 |
| Conserva- tive | 4 | — | 2 | — | 38 | 46 | 66 | 50 |
| n.a. | — | 1 | 3 | — | 6 | 8 | 1 | 5 |
| N = | (23) | (39) | (63) | (20) | (47) | (28) | (65) | (18) |

[a] The classification of districts is taken from *Congressional Quarterly Almanac* 19 (1963): 1173–84. "Mixed" districts were those for which *CQ* could not determine a predominant character. The urban, suburban, rural include those few (38) which *CQ* classified as "mixed, but predominantly . . ." A discussion of criteria, cutting points, etc., is contained in the almanac.

nated by their own party makes any analysis here risky. The differences between Republicans running in competitive and Democratic-dominant districts are, however, in a direction consistent with MacRae's prediction, but the proportion is just barely large enough to qualify as significant; 51 percent in Democratic-dominant compared to 61 percent in competitive districts were conservative, showing a mild dropoff effect among Republicans confronted with an intractable Democratic district.

The effects of constituency, measured by an urban-suburban-rural typology, are more consistent with expectations, particularly for Republicans. Excluding those districts which could not be classified (included in the table as "mixed"), table 4.7 shows a sharp and monotomic increase in the proportion of Republican conservatives and a decrease in moderates as one moves from urban to suburban to rural constituencies. This is almost the same result found by Froman for congressional incumbents and helps to explain why there are more conservative Republicans in competitive districts: the most competitive Republican districts tend also to have the most rural constituencies.[36]

36. See the discussion on this point by Froman, *Congressmen*, pp. 118–19. Among the competitive districts included above, 49 percent were rural.

Similarly, while there are no significant differences between the proportions of suburban and urban Democratic candidates who are liberal, the percentage does drop among rural Democrats. Though it is probably true, as Robert Friedman has argued,[37] that if present economic and social trends continue, the urban-rural dichotomy will cease to have a distinctive, measurable difference independent of party, it does not follow that some cleavages, particularly *intra*party conflict, will not continue to be rooted in the character of these different constituencies. Still, these data, as well as Froman's and others, raise substantial questions of interpretation.

A large majority of rural Republicans and a small majority (51 percent) of rural Democrats do think of themselves as conservative and liberal respectively. The differences between Republicans and Democrats are obviously much greater than differences within each party, regardless of whether candidates are contesting in urban, suburban, or rural districts. Party is still the most powerful variable for explaining interparty differences, while the party system (based on competition) is unrelated and constituency factors are only mildly operative on the rare deviance that does exist.

This interpretation is similar then to most of those studies which have examined both *intra* and *inter*party differences—but often in their concern with deviancy, homogeneity in outlook has been underplayed. Perhaps Snowiss is correct when he suggests that the more important differences are really between "machine" and "amateur" liberals, or between the "old" Republican conservatives and the "newer" pragmatic variety, and these differences can be explained by reference to party environments which are quite distinctive in terms of organizational resources, structure, and professional ethos.[38] This is a task clearly beyond the capability of these data.

Another independent variable, former officeholding, was selected because it taps two dimensions of the process many have

37. Robert Friedman, "The Urban-Rural Conflict Revisited," *Western Political Quarterly* (June 1961): 959.

38. This finding applies only to the Chicago delegation, a group conspicuous for the extensive number of "machine" liberals. Large-scale comparative research, as Snowiss suggests, will be necessary before the generality of such an argument can be tested.

argued leads candidates for public office to converge rather than differ on issues of public policy, expanding rather than restricting their electoral appeal.

Edmond Costantini has shown[39] that California's Democratic officeholders as a group, while more ideological than the rank-and-file party members in the electorate, are still more "centrist" than active, committed party workers. Moreover, the simple effect of actually holding office, where one is forced to deal with the wide variety of conflicting desires, aspirations, and needs of a polyglot constituency, often results in a political "education" for even the most ideological officeholder in a democratic polity— the less wordy but more popular description for which is copping out.

Since Costantini used a scale reflecting position on specific issues, these data are not quite comparable, but one would still expect differences between those who have held public and party —but particularly *public*—office and those who have not. This expectation is totally disconfirmed for Democrats, but remarkably borne out for Republicans, as a glance at the data in table 4.8 will indicate.

Virtually no difference exists between Democratic candidates with or without prior office experience, but for Republicans

### Table 4.8

#### Public Office Experience and Political Ideology, Congressional Challengers, by Party

#### (*In Percent*)

| Ideology | Democrats | | Republicans | |
|---|---|---|---|---|
| | SOME PUBLIC OFFICE EXPERIENCE | NO PUBLIC OFFICE EXPERIENCE | SOME PUBLIC OFFICE EXPERIENCE | NO PUBLIC OFFICE EXPERIENCE |
| Liberal | 55 | 56 | 11 | 7 |
| Middle of the road | 40 | 38 | 48 | 20 |
| Conservative | 4 | 3 | 36 | 63 |
| n.a. | 1 | 1 | 5 | 10 |
| N = | (74) | (71) | (64) | (91) |

39. Costantini, "Intraparty Attitude Conflict: Democratic Party Leadership in California," pp. 956–72.

Table 4.9

Party Office Experience and Political Ideology,
Congressional Challengers, by Party

(*In Percent*)

| Ideology | Democrats | | | Republicans | | |
|---|---|---|---|---|---|---|
| | NATIONAL STATE | LOCAL | NO OFFICE | NATIONAL STATE | LOCAL | NO OFFICE |
| Liberal | 60 | 59 | 56 | 7 | 11 | 4 |
| Middle of the road | 34 | 41 | 41 | 44 | 30 | 39 |
| Conservative | 2 | — | 1 | 46 | 56 | 53 |
| n.a. | 4 | — | 2 | 3 | 3 | 4 |
| N = | (41) | (48) | (56) | (45) | (63) | (47) |

the difference is quite large: 63 percent of the GOP candidates who had no public office experience considered themselves conservatives, but only 36 percent of those who had held public offices did so, a difference of 27 percent.

On the other hand, party office experience apparently has little effect (see table 4.9) on tendencies to anchor oneself in either a centrist or polar position, even when different levels (national, state or local) are considered. This is consistent with the belief that, at least for Republicans, there is a distinct difference in the way party and public officeholding socializes candidates; the former maximizing partisan ("purist") attitudes, the latter undercutting such perspectives.

The finding for Democratic candidates suggests that either these men perceive less dissonance between their ideology and officeholding or they hold different kinds of offices than do Republicans, or both. Among Republicans it is clear that intraparty conflict and ideological purity is emphasized by the entry of candidates with little public officeholding experience. Alternatively, countervailing forces may begin to operate when Republicans have managed to endure the tribulations of public office. But the experience apparently had differential effects, depending on party and ideological position. The explanation offered above is quite tentative.

The organizational decentralization of American political parties is legendary, a phenomenon which has led most of the "responsible party" theorists to assume that clear-cut alterna-

## Table 4.10

### Cleavage and Consensus in the Ideological
### Orientation of Candidates to Party Organizations[a]
#### (In Percent)

| Candidate Considers Self in Relation to: | Democrats | | Republicans | | |
|---|---|---|---|---|---|
| | LIBERAL | MIDDLE-ROAD | LIBERAL | MIDDLE-ROAD | CONSERVATIVE |
| Local party | | | | | |
| more liberal | 47 | 21 | 69 | 30 | 1 |
| about same | 48 | 69 | 31 | 67 | 76 |
| more conservative | 4 | 8 | — | 2 | 1 |
| n.a. | 1 | 2 | — | 1 | — |
| State party | | | | | |
| more liberal | 36 | 13 | 77 | 26 | 5 |
| about same | 61 | 73 | 15 | 65 | 63 |
| more conservative | 1 | 12 | 8 | 9 | 31 |
| n.a. | 2 | 2 | — | — | 1 |
| National party | | | | | |
| more liberal | 16 | 2 | 92 | 58 | 14 |
| about same | 81 | 42 | 8 | 39 | 52 |
| more conservative | 3 | 54 | — | 3 | 30 |
| n.a. | — | 2 | — | — | 4 |
| N = | (83) | (57) | (12) | (56) | (83) |

[a] The question: "On most issues today, would you consider yourself more liberal, about the same, or more conservative than each of the following:"

tives can only be provided by the nationalization of each party. The data presented in table 4.10 suggest a different problem.

For liberal Democrats, the national party is clearly the most congruent reference point ideologically and the local party least so: 81 percent considered themselves in harmony with the national party, whereas 48 percent felt ideologically similar to the local organization and 47 percent considered themselves "more liberal." But for conservative Republicans, the reverse is true: 76 percent considered themselves congruent with the local party, while 52 percent felt comfortable with the national organization. This occurred in a campaign when the national Republican apparatus was led by a symbol of forthright conservatism.

On the other hand, moderates within the Democratic camp felt distinctly more harmonious with the local and state parties and less so with the national (54 percent felt "more conservative"). The tendency in all three wings of the GOP was to consider the local and state parties most congruent, but larger proportions of conservative candidates felt closer to either the national or local apparatus than either the moderates, or, obviously, the few liberals. These images were certainly affected by the character of the national campaign of 1964, and although no evidence exists, one can surmise that conservative Republicans would not have meshed with the national party even as well as they did if a more typical GOP presidential candidate had surfaced.

Contrary to one assumption of the responsible-party school, conservative Republican candidates seem to maintain doctrinal purity when their orientation is localized, and usually in the face of a more or less determined move by the party's presidential wing to broaden the appeal nationally. Thus ideological coherence is maximized in the Republican party by psychologically decentralizing tendencies and in the Democratic party by nationalizing forces.

These findings also suggest another line of speculative inquiry. A huge majority of these candidates face demonstrably hostile electoral conditions and it stretches the imagination to believe that any amount of institutional tinkering with the national party organization (regardless of what else might be accomplished) would in fact generate even more candidates who identified clearly as liberal or conservative; among Republicans the very opposite would in all probability occur. Giving the national organizations power to impose policy control on candidates would generate more liberal Republican challengers. While this might make liberals happier, it would also reduce the range of ideological choice between parties.

Despite the electoral environment, and the powerful countervailing social and organizational features of American political life, it seems remarkable that a majority of congressional challengers do in fact continue to offer what this observer takes to be a clear choice—at least in districts outside the South.

## Ideology and Electoral Outcome

Two observations can be made about the character of congressional campaigns in the United States. First, as argued earlier, the behavior of the challenger, including his ideological stance, is probably the least influential factor bearing on electoral outcome.[40] Second, given the necessary conditions, even a small increase in the number of incumbents defeated by challengers can have significant consequences for the output of the House of Representatives.

The data presented in tables 4.11 and 4.12 can be interpreted as providing some evidence consistent with the first argument: liberals and moderates are distributed among winners and losers in about the same proportion as they are among Democratic non-incumbents as a whole. Nor does table 4.12 show any evidence that indicates moderate Democrats tended to gain victory—when they did so—by a larger margin than liberals, an assumption implicit in some campaign theories. There are no appreciable differences in either the margin of victory, or defeat, between Democratic moderate and liberal candidates.

I am aware that no evidence regarding different campaign resources, strategies, activities, etc. of liberals or moderates is provided here. Rather, it is assumed that these factors, more or less under the control of individual candidates, are evenly distributed among both groups. The question involves the common argument that a liberal (and by extension, a conservative)[41] ideology can only be sustained in districts that are leaning to the other party at the expense of electoral victory. These data suggest that a candidate's general position (within the usual ideological bounds) is unimportant.

Among Republicans, the magnitude of defeat affected all wings almost equally, except that the few (16) winners considered here were disproportionately conservative, but 87 percent of the GOP conservatives running in 1964 were defeated, just as were 94 percent of the Republican moderates and 92 percent of the liberals. As V. O. Key once observed in another context, when the rain falls, it falls equally on the willing and unwilling. Although the data are far from satisfactory, they do lend some support to the notion that the more important determinants of electoral out-

40. Lewis A. Froman, "A Realistic Approach to Campaign Strategies and Tactics," in *The Electoral Process*, ed. M. Kent Jennings and Harmon Zeigler (Englewood Cliffs, N.J.: Prentice-Hall, 1966), p. 4.

41. Robert Erikson provides some data on *incumbents* which suggest that Republican conservatives suffer disproportionately in elections. See his "The Electoral Impact of Congressional Roll Call Voting," *American Political Science Review* (December 1971): 1018–33.

Table 4.11

Electoral Outcome and Ideology in the 1964
Congressional Elections, by Party
(*In Percent*)

|  | Democrats | | Republicans | |
|---|---|---|---|---|
| *Ideology* | WINNERS | LOSERS | WINNERS | LOSERS |
| Liberal | 54 | 59 | 4 | 9 |
| Middle of the road | 39 | 39 | 27 | 35 |
| Conservative | 2 | — | 70 | 51 |
| Mixed | 2 | 2 | — | 4 |
| n.a. | 2 | — | — | 1 |
| *N* = | (63) | (82) | (16) | (142) |

Table 4.12

Ideology and Electoral Margin in the 1964
Congressional Elections, by Party
(*In Percent*)

|  |  |  | Democrats[a] | | Republicans | | |
|---|---|---|---|---|---|---|---|
| *Outcome* | DEMO-CRATS | REPUB-LICANS | LIBER-ALS | MODER-RATES | LIBER-ERALS | MODER-RATES | CONSERVA-TIVES |
| Winners | 33 | 9 | 40 | 44 | 8 | 6 | 13 |
| Losers | 67 | 91 | 60 | 56 | 92 | 94 | 87 |
| Won (61% plus) | 6 | 1 | 6 | 8 | 8 | 2 | — |
| Won (56–60%) | 6 | 3 | 7 | 11 | — | — | 6 |
| Won (55% or less) | 21 | 5 | 27 | 25 | — | 4 | 7 |
| Lost (45% plus) | 29 | 18 | 26 | 29 | 15 | 16 | 17 |
| Lost (40–44%) | 27 | 22 | 21 | 21 | 23 | 26 | 10 |
| Lost (39% or less) | 11 | 50 | 13 | 6 | 54 | 53 | 60 |
| *N* = | (145) | (158) | (83) | (57) | (12) | (56) | (83) |

[a] The two self-identified conservative Democrats scored a 100 percent victory.

come are structural, involving the constituency and the pattern of party competition in each district.

One other fact about electoral success—rare as it may be for challengers—is suggested by these figures. Those Democrats who did win in environments that were either competitive or in constituencies generally not oriented to the Democratic party, were also invariably the most vulnerable in the next elections. Although I'll deal later with the behavior and fate of the Republican and Democratic freshmen of 1964, some indication of what happened in 1966 is presented in table 4.13.

This election, of course, reversed the Democratic victories

## Table 4.13

### Electoral Fate in the 1966 Mid-term Elections of Freshmen in the 89th Congress, by Party and Ideology[a]

#### (In Numbers)

|  | Freshmen | | Democrats | | |
|---|---|---|---|---|---|
| Outcome | DEMO-CRATS | REPUB-LICANS | LIBER-ALS | MODER-ATES | CONSERVA-TIVES |
| Won (61% plus) | 18 | 14 | 6 | 5 | 4 |
| Won (56–60%) | 4 | — | 3 | 1 | — |
| Won (55% or less) | 17 | — | 9 | 7 | — |
| Lost (45% plus) | 19 | — | 12 | 7 | — |
| Lost (40–44%) | 4 | 1 | 2 | 2 | — |
| Lost (39% or less) | — | — | — | — | — |
| Retired/other office | 4 | 3 | 2 | 2 | — |
| Total losers | 23 | 1 | 14 | 9 | — |
| Total winners | 39 | 14 | 18 | 13 | 4 |
| Other[b] | 4 | 3 | 2 | 2 | — |
| Totals | (66) | (18) | (35) | (23) | (4) |

[a] The three freshmen who entered in the second session and three former congressmen who ran in 1964 were omitted from these figures. The ideology classification includes three Democrats and two Republicans who either didn't respond to the original questionnaire or were not subsequently interviewed. They were classified on the basis of federal role scores. Since only one Republican freshman was defeated, Glenn Andrews (Alabama), breakdowns for the GOP would be pointless.

[b] Among those who voluntarily left the House, Demorats Charles Farnsley (Ky.) retired; Paul Krebs lost his seat through reapportionment in New Jersey; Robert Sweeney ran for the attorney general's office in Ohio; Teno Roncalio contested for United States senator from Wyoming. Both Sweeney and Roncalio were defeated. Among Republicans, all three were southerners and all ran for governor: Howard "Bo" Calloway in Georgia; James Martin in Alabama; Prentiss Walker in Mississippi. All were defeated.

of 1964, giving the Republicans a net gain of 48 seats, 10 more than the Democrats had managed two years before, and an unusually high off-year gain in congressional elections (the average off-year switch since 1950 has been 25). The lone Republican loser, Glenn Andrews of Alabama, was widely believed to be "too moderate" on civil rights.

Parenthetically, if Andrews was in fact defeated on the civil rights issue, and there is every reason to believe he was, this case should serve as a reminder of the inapplicability of the generalizations explored above to individual campaigns. Like the finding of Miller and Stokes on constituency opinion,[42] single issues can become powerful determinants of electoral outcome. But the data again underscore the argument here entertained, since there are no significant differences in the electoral margin of defeat, or victory, among those Democratic moderate and liberal freshmen up for reelection in 1966.

## Conclusion

It seems pointless to reiterate that American political parties are aggregations of extraordinarily diverse, often conflicting, social and political units and then professionally gun down those who long for the classic, presumably well-organized and clear ideological choices associated with continental political systems. Just as there are tendencies in the party system fostering homogeneity, so too there are countervailing forces creating significant choice.

Popular control over policy implies that voters will be given alternatives by competing candidates. The data examined here suggest that congressional challengers in the United States are by and large performing that function. Whether liberalism and conservatism are meaningful alternatives shall be left to the individual judgment of the reader. They apparently seem so to these candidates, most of whom empirically resist being poured into those old standbys—the twin bottles—of intellectual contempt.

Differences between the two parties are not a function of

42. The Hays-Alford contest in the fifth district of Arkansas, the example cited by these authors, was extraordinary: 100 percent of the voters knew who Hays and Alford were and apparently also thought Brooks Hays, a twenty-year veteran, too soft on civil rights. He was defeated in a write-in campaign for Alford.

differences in the social backgrounds of their respective candidates (with one minor exception),[43] but rather a result of the way similar backgrounds are apparently differentially internalized. The small social cleavages that do exist between the candidates are reinforced by the fact that the majority of social "deviants" nominated by Republicans were almost without exception defeated.

Among Democrats, the most influential sources promoting ideological consistency around liberalism were (1) the entry of candidates whose careers are not rooted in either business or law, (2) the availability of candidacy to men and women who are socially mobile and, to a lesser extent, (3) the environment of suburban and urban constituencies. Intraparty differences for Democrats do not seem to be related to either the structure of party competition or to differences in public or party officeholding experience.

On the other hand, those factors responsible for increasing the probability that greater numbers of Republicans will be conservative were (1) an absence of public office experience (but not party office),[44] (2) contesting in a rural constituency, and like Democratic liberals, (3) coming from a professional career other than law or business. Contrary to some expectations, Republican businessmen are less likely than professionals (excluding law) to consider themselves conservative. Although competitive districts tended to more consistently produce conservatives (contradicting the belief that competitiveness makes for moderating tendencies), this is more an expression of the large number of competitive districts which are also rural.

Unlike the Democrats, social mobility had no demonstrable effect on the ideology of GOP candidates, neither making them

43. Professionals among the Democrats were more often educators, journalists and ministers than were Republicans, but the differences are not substantial.

44. A similar lack of experience was noted by Aaron Wildavsky for Goldwater supporters at the 1964 convention in his "The Goldwater Phenomenon: Purists, Politicians and the Two-Party System," *Review of Politics* 27 (July 1965): 393–94. Polsby points out that Goldwater appealed, in addition, to a considerable number of party professionals, regardless of misgivings about the electoral consequences, simply because they agreed with his specific programs. But he adds that 74 percent of the delegates—an unusually high figure—had not been to either of the two previous conventions. See Polsby, "Strategic Considerations," in Milton C. Cummings, Jr., *The National Election of 1964* (Washington, D.C.: The Brookings Institute, 1966), pp. 100–101.

more conservative nor liberal. Centrist tendencies among Republicans were most often pronounced in both suburban and urban constituencies with slightly fewer conservatives (and slightly more moderates and liberals) competing in urban areas.

All of these relationships, however, should be considered in the light of substantial similarity of commitment. There is a large core of Democratic liberalism and Republican conservatism which withstands almost any environmental factor introduced. But this appears to be more true of Democrats than Republicans.

Some evidence is presented which very tentatively supports the argument that for most districts the electoral outcome is little dependent on whether a challenger is conservative or liberal, a finding which undercuts the belief that it is electorally profitable for parties to enter campaigns on the assumption that moving to the middle will produce short-run gains (whatever else might be the reason for adopting such strategy). And it is precisely because large numbers of ideologically oriented nonincumbent candidates do not act "rationally" in this sense that when the rain falls, and a few are elected, large enough majorities (or minorities) are created to move (or prevent from moving) major public innovations in social policy. As one Democratic freshman sarcastically remarked, "We were the cannon fodder of the Great Society." But if these data and other material to be examined later are accurate, it was not because he supported the domestic policy of the Johnson Administration. Liberal Democrats, like many others, have always underestimated the powerful pull of straightforward party voting. And many of these freshmen had to attempt reelection in traditionally strong Republican districts.

# 5

# CAMPAIGNS

In the litany and practice of American politics, congressional elections are accorded a supporting, if enduring, role.

The presidential struggle, for obvious reasons, overshadows all other contenders. Indeed, national elections staged without presidential aspirants have acquired that peculiarly American designation, off-year. The nearest analogue to congressional campaigns is underground theater—this despite the increasing deluge of personal accounts, hard and soft sale "how to" campaign manuals, the Movement for a New Congress, and the steady outpouring of sophisticated case studies by political scientists.[1] Data on the number, type, and quality of underground film devotees would be difficult to obtain. But I doubt that such information

1. The most comprehensive study of congressional electoral behavior, using aggregate data in the tradition of V. O. Key, is Milton C. Cummings, Jr., *Congressmen and the Electorate; 1920–1964* (New York: Free Press, 1966). Three recent books—Robert Huckshorn and Robert Spencer, *The Politics of Defeat* (Amherst: University of Massachusetts Press, 1971), David Leuthold, *Electioneering in a Democracy* (New York: Wiley, 1968), and John Kingdon, *Candidates for Office* (New York: Random House, 1968)—provide a variety of empirical materials on congressional campaigns. Among the better case studies, see David Paletz, "The Neglected Context of Congressional Campaigns," *Polity* (Winter 1971):195–218; John Bibby and Roger Davidson, *On Capitol Hill* (New York: Holt, 1966), pp. 30–71; Conrad F. Joyner, "Running a Congressional Campaign," in *Practical Politics in the United States*, ed. C. Cotter (Boston: Allyn & Bacon, 1969); William J. Gore and Robert Peabody, "The Functions of the Political Campaign: A

would compare unfavorably with what we know about their electoral counterparts in House campaigns:[2]

—less than 5 percent of American adults have ever participated in any campaign activities (other than voting) relating specifically to a House race;

—59 percent of those adults living in a district contested by both an incumbent and challenger in 1958 indicated they had neither read nor heard anything about either candidate for Congress;

—only one in five adults felt they knew "something" about both candidates;

—among those who could comment on one or both candidates, less than 3 in 100 referred to anything having to do with legislative issues;

---

Case Study," *Western Political Quarterly* (March 1958): 55–70; and John C. Donovan, *Congressional Campaign: Maine Elects a Democrat* (New York: Holt, 1958). Lewis Froman has attempted to formulate a series of prescriptive statements, based on modern empirical research, in his "A Realistic Approach to Campaign Strategy and Tactics," in *The Electoral Process*, ed. L. Harmon Zeigler and M. Kent Jennings (Englewood Cliffs, N.J.: Prentice-Hall, 1966). On the policy consequences, and lack thereof, of close campaigns, see Charles O. Jones, "The Role of the Campaign in Congressional Politics," in Zeigler and Jennings, *Electoral Process*, pp. 21–42. A forthcoming volume by David M. Olson, *The Congressman and His Party* (Boston: Little, Brown) focuses intensively on aspects of incumbent-district campaign relationships. Two lively and compelling personal accounts are Stimson Bullitt, *To Be a Politician* (New York: Doubleday, 1959), and Rodney G. Minott, *The Sinking of the Lollipop* (San Francisco: Diablo Press, 1968). Political campaign handbooks, written by professional campaign managers, political scientists, journalists, and others, are always in abundance on local newsstands. For recent, more sophisticated efforts by political scientists, see Edward Schneier, William T. Murphy, and others (for the Movement for a New Congress), *Vote Power: The Official Activist Campaigner's Handbook* (Englewood Cliffs, N.J.: Prentice-Hall, 1970), or Donald Herzberg and Jack Peltason, *The Student's Guide To Campaign Politics* (New York: McGraw-Hill, 1970). Professionals, expansive types that they sometimes are, occasionally enjoy telling it to the public; among the many, see Herbert M. Baus and William C. Ross, *Politics Battle Plan* (New York: Macmillan, 1968). Much of the folklore and science of campaign management, strategy, and payoffs is extensively analyzed in Dan Nimmo, *The Political Persuaders* (Englewood Cliffs, N.J.: Prentice-Hall, 1970).

2. Most of these findings come from the Representation and Congress study of Warren Miller and Donald Stokes. See their two articles, "Party Government and the Salience of Congress," *Public Opinion Quarterly* (Winter 1962): 531–46; and "Constituency Influence in Congress," *American Political Science Review* (March 1963): 45–56.

—a majority were unable to identify which party held control of Congress during the two years preceding the survey;

—almost 9 out of 10 voters cast their ballot for the candidate who shared their partisan affiliation;

—most importantly, 71 percent had neither read nor heard anything about the challenger.

Of course these figures are subject to considerable constraint and variation, over historical time and by each campaign, district, and region.[3] Just as the larger electoral process oscillates between periods of "strong" and "weak" ideological focus, so too individual congressional districts are responsive to the push and pull of greater issue concern.[4] The stunning upset victories of electoral underdogs—a Paul Sarbanes, Ron Dellums, or Dale Alford—seem to occur under conditions of increasing issue focus in specific districts. Such periods probably produce dramatic shifts in levels of information, emotional involvement, and issue sophistication. Congressional voters thus possess *both* actual and potential influence over incumbent congressmen since they have proved capable, from time to time, of wielding sanctions for non-compliant behavior.[5]

3. Thirteen years have elapsed since Miller and Stokes collected their data. It is difficult to believe the events of the past decade have not been reflected in substantial changes in the congressional electorate. Yet secondary analysis on SRC's 1964 and 1968 data reveals that on basic information items—knowledge of candidates' names, for example—the national electorate continues to have distressingly little recall ability. That short-run forces, associated with specific campaigns, can increase the salience of issues in presidential campaigns has been convincingly illustrated by John Osgood Field and Ronald A. Anderson, "Ideology in the Public's Conception of the 1964 Election," *Public Opinion Quarterly* (Fall 1969): 380–98. Regrettably, nothing of this sort has been applied to a sample of congressional districts. The impact of single issues, discussed earlier, does have significant consequences for constituency behavior, however. But we still need follow-up studies to assess change over time.
4. These two concepts are developed in Donald Stokes, "Spatial Models of Party Competition," reprinted in Angus Campbell et al., *Elections and the Political Order* (New York: Wiley, 1966). Application of this classification to the 1968 presidential campaign, with suggestive data, has been undertaken by Herbert F. Weisberg and Jerrold G. Rusk, "Dimensions of Candidate Evaluation," *American Political Science Review* (December 1970): 1167–86.
5. A point emphasized by Miller and Stokes but often neglected by those who interpret their findings to mean that constituents have little or no influence over congressional behavior. See their comments in "Constituency Influence in Congress," p. 55.

More typically, however, challengers enter the race with all the liabilities implied by the above data. Add to these problems the substantial advantage in resources (money, manpower, information) held by incumbents, and one has a convincing explanation of membership stability in the House of Representatives.

Two observations seem to follow. First, as I suggested in chapter 1, the behavior of the challenger, including his ability to mobilize generous financial support, is the least influential factor bearing on the decision making of an overwhelming majority of voters. Losers are almost always convinced that another $5,000, or $25,000, would have reversed the outcome. And so it might in some districts. But twenty years of careful empirical research, plus the (only twice interrupted) thirty-eight-year minority status endured by the GOP, despite a consistent 3–1 financial advantage, belies this fantasy.[6] Money may be the mother's milk of politics, but other types of nourishment are needed if the candidate is to avoid being orphaned by the voters.

Since the more important determinants involve characteristics of the constituency, their attitudes toward issues, party identification, educational-income levels, and so forth, changing the current shape of party dominance will be subject to transformation in these deeper, more long-run considerations.

Congressional campaigns, as argued earlier, are paradoxical contests. Individual candidates cannot usually produce through their campaign efforts the necessary wherewithal for widespread party upsets in any single election. But meaningful opposition will erode (parties will not be able to capitalize on long-run shifts) unless candidates are provided enough incentives to make campaigning worthwhile during the interim.

The analysis of the past three chapters has focused on how the dominant parties provide three types of incentives: alternative channels of social representation, careerist and noncareerist modes of political participation, and opportunities to present programmatic-ideological alternatives on public policy. Measured against the standards of the classic socialist-capitalist parties of Western Europe, the Republican and Democratic organizations are clearly deficient. But they are not, I believe, utterly without redeeming social value.

6. Although this advantage might be revealed to be considerably less if adequate data were available on district-level fund raising and expenditures.

This chapter directs attention toward campaign-related resources provided by various levels of party organization to candidates—as perceived by the candidates. A detailed analysis of the size and scope of party resources is quite beyond the more limited perspective entertained here. Rather I will concentrate on candidate perceptions because these perceptions are central in examining the incentive system needed for sustaining opposition at the district level. Data are presented showing how candidates evaluate the assistance given by national and local party organizations. As in previous chapters, some theoretically useful independent variables are introduced, examining particularly the differential impact of party competition and constituency characteristics. Resource acquisition, however, is only one side of the coin. As John Kingdon wryly comments, ". . . right or wrong, most candidates believe campaigns affect outcomes."[7] Brief attention then turns to candidate evaluation of the electoral impact of utilizing resources in different ways.

## Party Resources

American parties are not universally esteemed for their ability to bestow handsome favors on potential candidates. Following the decline of the classic machines of the late ninteenth century, party reformers of various ideological stripe have sought (with only a modicum of success) to increase the potential resource base of both national organizations. But most candidates would still agree with one challenger (a winner from the Midwest) who lamented, "Blessed are those who do not expect very much, for they will not be disappointed."

Nor is this attitude peculiar to congressional challengers. David Olson notes that most incumbents "view both the national *and* local level party as relatively ineffectual in their campaign (italics mine)."[8] Complaints by younger congressmen are more commonly directed at the two primary national campaign organizations involved in House elections, the Democratic Congressional Campaign Committee (DCCC) and the National Republican Congressional Committee (NRCC). To be sure, both have in-

7. Kingdon, *Candidates for Office*, p. 109.
8. Olson, *Congressman and His Party*.

creased the type and amount of services available over the past ten years, but, for reasons discussed below, their contributions, financial and otherwise, constitute a small proportion of the total needed or utilized. National-level committees are not alone in this respect. Frequent rumblings were also aimed at the paucity of assistance generated by local (mainly county) organizations, whether reflected in money, campaign workers, research and data needs, or other campaign-related assistance.

Even in those counties where candidate recruitment is tightly controlled by organizations which approximate the stereotype "machine," candidates are normally expected to develop much of their own resource base. Said one, another midwesterner, ". . . they looked at three things: my record in the party, how I got along with labor, and whether I could raise enough money; and not necessarily in that order. While we didn't have to spend as much as some of my colleagues here [due to one-party dominance in his district], if I hadn't been able to guarantee that I could gain financial backing, I would have been passed over."

These "organizational insufficiencies," to use Frank Sorauf's apt phrase,[9] are certainly responsible for the rise of professional campaign management firms[10] as well as the potential clout of a variety of nonparty but highly active electoral operations (COPE, NCEC, AMPAC, MNC, etc.). Most challengers, however, were wary of campaign management firms—because of the high fee plus commission arrangements—and few in 1964 deeply involved professional firms in their campaigns.[11]

Realistically or not, challengers initially looked to the national party committees for substantial financial assistance. What did they get?

Reliable estimates about campaign contributions and ex-

9. In his *Party Politics in America* (Boston: Little, Brown, 1968), chap. 3.

10. See Nimmo, *Political Persuaders*, pp. 34–42, for a discussion of other reasons.

11. *Congressional Quarterly* is probably the best continuing source on the mushrooming professional campaign management industry. There is great variety in how far individual candidates permit such firms significant influence over actual campaign decision making. I do not have adequate data on this question for challengers; about one-third of the winners, reinterviewed in 1965 and 1966, indicated they had used the services of a campaign management firm rather extensively. Most of the others contracted for specific jobs (e.g., advertising, polls), but did not actually retain the services of a full-fledged management firm.

penditures are impossible to obtain; responsible (e.g., Citizen's Research Foundation) sources suggest that five major national party committees contributed $2.47 million to all House candidates, $1.9 million going to Republicans and $553,000 to Democrats.[12] Mean disbursements by the DCCC to Democratic challengers were $1,511 (incumbents received $1,224). The NRCC distributed an average of $1,914 to 234 nonincumbent candidates, while providing $2,851 to 153 incumbents. This includes expenditures by the Republican Congressional Boosters Committee, which I will include in NRCC figures. Both parties concentrated higher disbursements on marginal districts, whether an incumbent was contesting in such a campaign or not.

The NRCC provided an average contribution of $3,317 for its marginal incumbents, $2,505 for marginal challengers. DCCC's behavior was slightly less incumbent-oriented; marginal challengers received an average of $1,498, incumbents facing a stiff battle, $1,742.

1964 was also an exceptional year for Democratic "downtown" money, funds raised by other national committees and redirected to congressional races. By contrast, in 1970 neither the DNC, nor any of its characteristic fronts, raised or distributed money to congressional candidates. But in 1964, independent of the Democratic Study Group's activity, a variety of presidential committees operating under the DNC parceled out generally small amounts to a significant minority of challengers and incumbents.

Three committees, the President's Club for Johnson Committee (PCJC), the Johnson-Humphrey Committee (JHC), and the Humphrey for Vice-President Committee (HVP), distributed $156,300 to congressional candidates. The largest proportion, 72 percent, went to challengers. Of 204 Democratic challengers,[13]

12. Two intensive studies have provided the bulk of information surveyed here: Kevin L. McKeough, *Financing Campaigns for Congress: Contribution Patterns of National-Level Party and Non-Party Committees, 1964* (Princeton, N.J.: Citizen's Research Foundation, 1970); and Stephen Wasby, "National Party Contributions to Non-Incumbent Candidates: The Democrats in 1964," *Social Science Quarterly* (March 1968): 573–85.

13. Actually, seven of the 204 Democratic nonincumbents were not challengers in the strict sense since they had defeated Democratic incumbents in the primary. With one exception (a primary involving Carl Elliot), all were heavily favored to win in the general election. They did. Twelve other Democratic "chal-

84 received assistance from PCJC, 8 from the JHC, 5 from the HVP (4 of whom were contesting in Minnesota). A fortunate challenger, one competing in a marginal district, *may* have been able to obtain an additional $2,300 from these sources.[14]

One other party source, the DSG (operating under the pseudonym Democrats for Sound Government) raised and distributed $36,750 to candidates, the bulk of which was provided by a subvention from the National Committee for an Effective Congress.[15] The DSG allocated a mean contribution of $564 to 56 challengers.

Consider, however, the average out-of-pocket *cash* costs borne by most candidates. Estimates vary widely, but one official on the DCCC estimated that an urban district with "reasonable" opposition probably required an investment of $40,000. Expenses in suburban and rural districts, according to the same person, fell between $25,000 to $35,000. Other sources put the 1964 cost for a tough urban-suburban campaign at somewhere between $65,000 and $85,000.[16]

Two years *earlier*, David Leuthold found that San Francisco Bay Area campaigns with stiff opposition cost between $50,000 and $60,000; sure winners spent between $20,000 and $30,000.[17]

---

lengers" were also strongly favored since they were competing in districts formerly held by Democratic incumbents who had retired. Eleven were successful. These 19 candidates received an average disbursement from the DCCC of $2,100.

14. One fortunate candidate received $15,000 from the Humphrey group; one other, $12,500. Both were Minnesotans. See McKeough, *Financing Campaigns*, pp. 44–45. This money was apparently raised in Minnesota and earmarked for congressional races. Interestingly, both lost.

15. The NCEC has experimented with a variety of fund-raising and disbursing techniques as it has sought to assist primarily liberal Democratic and Republican senatorial candidates. The 1964 election was the first major effort of this group to redirect its efforts to House races, using block grants-in-aid to the Democratic Study Group and the Committee to Support Moderate Republicans. Much of this money was earmarked for specific candidates, supported by the DSG or CSMR, but actual disbursements were apparently carried out by the latter two organizations. CSMR went out of business after the 1964 election, resurfacing as "Republicans for Progress" in 1966 and 1968. Their total reported disbursements have never exceeded $10,000. The DSG, on the other hand, has been able to increase its funding ability, spending $170,030 in 1968. On the NCEC, see Harry M. Scoble, *Ideology and Electoral Action* (San Francisco: Chandler, 1967), particularly pp. 94–100.

16. Interviews with winners. Although they may have overestimated costs, other reports tend to square with their estimates. It seems just as likely that they were underestimating actual expenditures.

17. Leuthold, *Electioneering*, p. 75.

More recently, Lee Potter, now executive director of the NRCC, estimated that a close House race in 1970 cost between $60,000 and $100,000, with that figure dropping to $40,000 in rural areas.[18]

Moreover, as Will Rogers was fond of saying, "It costs a lot of money to get beat with these days." National-level financial support decreased as the possibilities of electoral victory faded. The cheapest congressional campaign, one reported by a Republican who received 27 percent of the vote, was estimated at $12,000. The same candidate reportedly received $1,400 from national-level sources, including nonparty committees.

Huckshorn and Spencer estimate that in 1962 challengers in lopsided districts were even less fortunate, since 54 percent apparently received no financial support from any national party committees. Using only money as a measure of national party contributions can be misleading, however, since it underestimates challenger perceptions of the *relative* role of national party activities vis-à-vis other levels of party organization. The analysis later suggests that it is precisely in hopeless districts where candidates—primarily Democrats—tend to see the national apparatus as the most helpful.

Still, since there is normally an *inverse* relationship between time spent in office and out-of-pocket campaign costs, combined with the increasing ease most incumbents have in raising money, the impact of this inequality falls heavily on potential challengers.[19]

Perhaps the point is belabored. Neither party is capable of adequately sharing costs with candidates or other party units for a normal congressional campaign. The luckiest Democratic candidate, competing in a tight, marginal district, might have received $5,000 from all national-level party committees. Add to this figure $3,500–$5,000 from nonparty sources (mainly COPE); the result is that only one-sixth to one-tenth of total campaign-related expenses come from national finance sources. Nor are Republicans much better off in this respect. Despite their consistent ability to raise and spend more money, the luckiest GOP

18. *Congressional Quarterly Weekly Report*, 5 December 1969, p. 2439.

19. Exceptions to this rule occur when (1) incumbents face tough primary opponents (although generally fund raising is still easier); (2) after reapportionment struggles when the normal distribution of party strength and/or district boundaries are threatened.

challengers were fortunate in receiving (adding NRCC/RCBC and AMPAC/BIPAC) more than $10,000, again one-sixth to one-tenth the total cost.[20]

Monetarily, American party organizations stand little danger of rapidly nationalizing congressional campaign finance. What other resources were provided by the national party apparatus?

Although most challengers would simply have preferred more cash, all four national committees produced and distributed large volumes of strategic and issue-oriented information—weekly newsletters, position papers, tailor-made evaluations of the incumbent's roll-call and bill-initiating activity. Both national committees have research divisions which provide ongoing publications designed for candidates and party officials. The Republicans' *Fact Book for Republican Campaigners* is updated biannually and is generally considered to be an excellent, if highly partisan, document. Larry O'Brien's famous campaign manual, first used in the 1960 Kennedy campaign, was revised in 1962 and 1964. This manual, the *Democratic Congressional Campaign Manual*, was distributed to each candidate early in the campaign.

The utility of such party-generated material, from the perspective of candidates, is difficult to ascertain. Leuthold notes that most of the nonincumbents he studied did little more than glance at national publications.[21] On the other hand, Huckshorn and Spencer found that their sample of challengers were more inclined to rate national party research activities favorably—particularly those involving detailed records of the incumbent's voting behavior.[22]

The information-seeking behavior of challengers is beyond this chapter's scope, but occasional comments by winners indi-

20. AMPAC is the American Medical Association's Political Action Committee; BIPAC, the Business-Industry Political Action Committee. BIPAC's traceable allocations amounted to $155,100, the overwhelming majority of which went to Republican candidates. AMPAC's activities are impossible to trace for 1964 since they followed the practice of subventing national money to state committees, who in turn disbursed it to candidates. See McKeough, *Financing Campaigns*, pp. 8–15. Republican party committees, during strategic campaigns, have also been capable of upping this amount considerably. In 1966, the average disbursement of the NRCC/RCBC to 46 challengers who contested against Democratic freshmen was slightly over $10,000. This, combined with other national money, was a substantial increase over 1964. More on this in the next chapter.

21. Leuthold, *Electioneering*, pp. 56–59.

22. Huckshorn and Spencer, *Politics of Defeat*, pp. 156–57.

cate that at least some found such information useful, although wishing that each committee would focus its reporting with greater depth. Moreover, the national campaign committees must compete with a burgeoning variety of public and private research organizations, as well as dozens of "one-shot" horseback operations. These range from the hucksterlike Campaign Associates (Wichita, Kansas) whose pitch to prospective candidates is that ". . . the ability to capitalize on available know-how and apply known techniques is the *only* thing that separates winners from losers" (only $27.95 for "48 action-packed pages in 12 monthly installments") to the careful candidate and issue background materials prepared by either the Center for Political Research, located in Washington, D.C., and associated with the *National Journal*, or the staff of the National Committee for an Effective Congress. Consumer protection is a policy in which congressional candidates increasingly have a personal stake.

The standard Washington-based campaign conference, conducted by the parties for potential candidates, is apparently on the increase. During the 1970 elections, for example, the Democratic Study Group sponsored two four-day sessions for candidates, one in March and one in May, drawing approximately one hundred persons. Whether they have any meaningful impact is another question. In addition, each national committee on occasion "lends" professional campaign specialists to selected contestants. But this practice is not widespread, in part because many candidates and their managers resent "external" intrusion in the conduct and direction of the campaign.

Other services, often coordinated by either the parties' downtown national committees or the House campaign committees, tend to be more incumbent-oriented. For example, the Democrats' Congressional Support Program, organized after the 1964 election and directed primarily at the needs of freshmen, was designed to provide a variety of services—constituency, research, computer mailings, and so forth—but collapsed in the wake of the Republicans' 1966 victories. More detailed consideration of this program will be deferred until later in the book, but each party has struggled for ten years to provide stable, continuing candidate-oriented services in this regard. Despite the heroic efforts of various congressmen, presidential assistants, and party committee staffers, at last glance, neither party seemed on the verge of a stunning resolution of the problems associated with such activity.

The more important question here is how challengers perceived such efforts, miniscule as they might appear, judged from the multitude of local needs, expectations, and problems that characterized each candidate's campaign.

Consider the data presented in table 5.1. Estimates by candidates are provided for both "national" and "local" party organizations. Surprisingly, there are few differences between parties on estimates given for national and local assistance. Among Republicans, 59 percent believed the national apparatus had provided "considerable" or "some" assistance, 48 percent thought the local organization had been of that much utility. Similarly for

Table 5.1

## Levels of Campaign Assistance Provided Congressional Challengers from National and Local Party Organizations[a]

(*In Percent*)

|  | Democrats | Republicans | Democrats WON | Democrats LOST | Republicans WON | Republicans LOST |
|---|---|---|---|---|---|---|
| National party |  |  |  |  |  |  |
| considerable | 26 | 22 | 20 | 29 | 25 | 21 |
| some | 30 | 37 | 38 | 24 | 31 | 36 |
| not much | 27 | 26 | 28 | 25 | 37 | 24 |
| none | 16 | 15 | 14 | 22 | 7 | 19 |
| n.a. | 1 | — | — | 1 | — | — |
| Local party |  |  |  |  |  |  |
| considerable | 18 | 25 | 23 | 12 | 56 | 21 |
| some | 34 | 23 | 44 | 25 | 31 | 22 |
| not much | 36 | 37 | 20 | 50 | 13 | 39 |
| none | 12 | 14 | 13 | 13 | — | 17 |
| n.a. | — | 1 | — | — | — | 1 |
| *N* = | (145) | (158) | (63) | (82) | (16) | (142) |

[a] Estimates are derived from candidate response to the following question: "We would like to know something about your estimation of the local, state, and national party organizations as each related to your campaign. In the *general* election, how much help (campaign literature, financial assistance, staff help, etc.) did you receive from the (local/state/national) party organizations?" I've dropped the data on state party organization because most candidates were agreed that it provided little assistance.

Democratic candidates: 56 percent considered the national and 52 percent the local party of some or considerable help.[23]

Not surprisingly there tends to be a reasonably high degree of overlap in perception (with one major exception, discussed below) with approximately six of ten candidates judging the contributions of both levels similarly. While I can't cite more specific supporting evidence, this finding suggests that organizational contributions are in general cumulative—the greater the involvement of one level of party organization, the greater the involvement of another.

Anecdotally, Republicans are usually thought to be better organized, richer in resources, more adept at their deployment. But this is not upheld by the data from these candidates; differences between Democrats and Republicans are quite small. The only exception, a difficult one to interpret given the tiny number, is the large (56 percent) proportion of Republican winners who felt their *local* party had been extremely generous. Since these fortunate few were not disproportionately enthusiastic about national-level contributions, perhaps this does reflect potent GOP organizational capabilities in a limited number of districtricts.[24] As the data clearly show, the simple fact of winning tends to increase, just as losing decreases, favorable evaluations of organizational contributions. This cognitive difference supports Kingdon's "congratulation-rationalization" hypothesis because it is a perceptual change quite consistent with the tasks of explaining and/or rationalizing electoral outcome.[25]

23. I am aware that problems of intersubjective comparability are legion with these data: one man's "considerable" may be another's "not much." My concern, however, is with candidates' perceptions in the aggregate, or as later in the analysis, by important structural subgroups. Perception, not some arbitrarily created "objective reality" is the important factor in incentive theory. Similar problems obtain with candidate definitions of "local" party organization. That construct most often refers, among candidates and others, to a combination of district county units, and I suspect, but cannot demonstrate, that most of these challengers were thinking of county organizations as the "local" party. Supporting evidence for this can be found in Olson's forthcoming volume, *Congressman and His Party*, chap. 2; and in Paul T. David, Ralph M. Goldman, and David C. Bain, *The Politics of the National Party Conventions* (Washington: Brookings Institution, 1960).

24. Of the nine Republican candidates who believed local parties contributed substantially to their campaigns, five were southerners, a fact that southern Democrats might consider worth pondering.

25. Kingdon does not consider perceptions of party organizational differences, but the above inference seems appropriate: *Candidates for Office*, pp. 34–39.

Moving from those candidates who felt generally advantaged to those less sanguine, some rather interesting comparisons emerge. Among losers, in both parties, it is clearly the *local parties that are perceived as the least* useful: 63 percent of the Democratic losers indicated the local organizations had provided little ("not much" and "none" in the table) support contrasted with 47 percent who made a similar judgment about the national organizations. Differences are less pronounced for Republican losers, but in the same direction (56 and 43 percent respectively). To the extent either level seeks to compensate for the resource discrepancy between challenger and incumbent in these districts, it is clearly the national parties that are perceived as the most credible. On the other hand, among winners the reverse seems to be occurring: local rather than national party assistance is most frequently counted favorably.

For both parties, however, it is the national committees that seem to be performing in the most consistent manner. Winners and losers are closest in their perceptions of how much (or little) bounty was distributed by this level while disagreement tends to be substantial about local contributions. Nor should one expect otherwise. The enormous variability of the American party system is usually attributed to factors that sharply differentiate party organizations at the state and local (county) level: differences in structure, urbanization, electoral competition, social-economic groupings, issue salience, historical peculiarities. Estimating precisely which of these variables has the most impact on candidate perception is an impossible task with the data at hand. Still, two factors—constituency and party competition—can be operationalized and a rough measure of their impact undertaken.

## Constituency, Competition, Resources

Typologies of electoral competition are widely used because of the presumed effects of competitiveness on a variety of dimensions relating to the behavior of public officials. As noted in earlier chapters, the correlates of competition are not uniform. Some researchers have found a high degree of association between single-party dominance and the existence of disciplined, well-organized local structures.[26] Others have noted that

26. See Leo Snowiss, "Congressional Recruitment and Representation," *American Political Science Review* (September 1966): 627–39; and Frank Sorauf,

single-party dominance in congressional districts, even outside
the South, does not lead to particularly strong party organizations.
Olson, for example, argues that ". . . majority status might be a
necessary, but is certainly not a sufficient, condition for [well-
organized] party types."[27]

Spirited competition, or semipermanent minority status, on
the other hand, almost always serve as powerful deterrents to
hierarchical politics. Candidate-centered party organizations
occur in all three types of electoral environments, but they tend
to be most frequent in competitive and minority areas.[28]

Theoretically and intuitively, one would expect candidates
to differ in their perceptions of national and local party assistance
as one moved from majority through competitive to minority
districts. Such expectations can be formalized thus:

—For the *national* party organizations, the greater (less) the
degree of electoral control possessed by the incumbent's party,
the greater (less) the relative impact of national contributions on
the challenger's campaign; and,

—For the *local* party organizations, the greater (less) the degree of electoral control possessed by the challenger's own party,
the greater (less), the relative impact of local organizational contributions on the candidate's campaign.

Evidence regarding both these hypotheses is presented in
table 5.2. Looking first at national-level contributions, the data
seem modestly, and only modestly, consistent with proposition
one. Democratic challengers were somewhat more likely to rate
national assistance of greater significance if they were competing
in strong Republican or competitive districts. Differences between
Republicans are much less distinguished in this respect (22 percent competing in Republican districts thought the national apparatus made considerable contributions compared to 21 percent
of those competing in Democratic areas). However, GOP candidates standing in Republican districts were much more likely
(62 percent) to discount national contributions than were either

*Party and Representation* (New York: Atherton, 1963). As both authors argue, the
important variables seem to be urbanization and single-party dominance, rather
than simple majority status.

27. Olson, *Congressman and His Party*, chap. 2.
28. Ibid.

## Table 5.2

### Levels of Campaign Assistance Provided Congressional Challengers, by District Competitiveness[a]

*(In Percent)*

| | Democrats | | | Republicans | | |
|---|---|---|---|---|---|---|
| | TEND DEMO-CRATIC | COMPET-ITIVE | TEND REPUB-LICAN | TEND DEMO-CRATIC | COMPET-ITIVE | TEND REPUB-LICAN |
| National party | | | | | | |
| considerable | 7 | 22 | 30 | 21 | 23 | 22 |
| some | 30 | 36 | 25 | 36 | 42 | 16 |
| not much | 38 | 29 | 22 | 22 | 26 | 44 |
| none | 25 | 13 | 23 | 21 | 18 | 18 |
| n.a. | — | — | — | — | 1 | — |
| Local party | | | | | | |
| considerable | 23 | 24 | 29 | 18 | 45 | 16 |
| some | 38 | 37 | 29 | 21 | 26 | 27 |
| not much | 7 | 27 | 50 | 43 | 23 | 27 |
| none | 32 | 12 | 12 | 16 | 6 | 30 |
| n.a. | — | — | — | 2 | — | — |
| N = | (13) | (61) | (71) | (98) | (42) | (18) |

[a] The Index of Party Competition is discussed in chapter 4.

those running in competitive districts (44 percent) or Democratic strongholds (43 percent).

More important, I believe, is the very weak association between competition and perception. If national distribution strategies, and candidate perceptions, were "rational" in the economic sense (winning as a prime value), then there should have been large and consistent differences between candidates running in competitive areas and all other districts. Obviously this is not the case.

Does it hold for local organizations? Somewhat better, but the association is still rather small. A larger proportion of Republican challengers competing in Democratic districts, 59 percent, were inclined to dismiss local organizational contributions than was true of national efforts, but the similarity between candidates, independent of electoral differences, seems more compelling. Note, for example, the closeness in perception among GOP candidates for whom the hypothesis would predict the greatest differences, i.e., those competing in Democratic-dominant and Republican-dominant districts. One major party difference does occur at the local level: Republican challengers in competitive races were much more likely than their Democratic counter-parts to evaluate local-level party contributions favorably. This accords with anecdotal notions that outside such places as Chicago, the GOP is more capable of sustaining effective local organizational networks than Democrats—at least when the smell of victory is strong.

A plausible explanation, however, for the general lack of strong support for either hypothesis resides in the psychology of defeat. Presumably those candidates who lost, particularly in close races, would be much more likely to depreciate *all* organizational contributions to their campaigns. Rationalization in this respect provides a non-personal scapegoat for defeat. While the *N*s are too small to permit a confident test, data controlling for outcome are presented in table 5.3. If candidate evaluations were solely a function of winning or losing, then losers should share the same evaluation of party contributions, independent of differences in competitiveness. Clearly the data do not support this assumption.

For example, 26 percent of the Democrats who *lost* in competitive races still thought local parties gave them "considerable" assistance, while this was true of only 2 percent who lost in Republican districts. Comparable proportions are also found for Republicans competing in these two types of districts. To be sure, the data do show that some amount of congratulation-rationalization is occurring since there are suggestive differences between winners and losers within the same type of district. Outcome, independent of the district's habitual voting behavior, does have a powerful impact on perception of local party assistance. But it does not completely eliminate the local organizational realities within which challengers must compete.

Moving to national-level data, it is again evident that challengers, despite differences in outcome and in competitiveness, order the contributions of the national parties in a more even manner. Losers in all three types of districts, of course, tend to see national inputs as less contributive, just as winners are more generous in their perceptions. Still, as noted previously, the na-

## Table 5.3

## Levels of Campaign Assistance Provided Congressional Challengers, by District Competitiveness and Electoral Outcome

### (In Percent)

| | Democrats | | | | | | Republicans | | | | | |
|---|---|---|---|---|---|---|---|---|---|---|---|---|
| | TEND DEMOCRATIC | | COMPETITIVE | | TEND REPUBLICAN | | TEND DEMOCRATIC | | COMPETITIVE | | TEND REPUBLICAN | |
| | WON | LOST[a] | WON | LOST | WON | LOST | WON[b] | LOST | WON | LOST | WON | LOST |
| **National party** | | | | | | | | | | | | |
| considerable | 8 | * | 20 | 26 | 33 | 30 | — | 22 | 18 | 26 | 40 | 15 |
| some | 31 | — | 37 | 36 | 43 | 16 | — | 35 | 36 | 42 | 20 | 15 |
| not much | 38 | — | 30 | 26 | 19 | 24 | — | 24 | 26 | 23 | 20 | 46 |
| none | 23 | — | 13 | 12 | 5 | 28 | — | 18 | 9 | 7 | — | 24 |
| n.a. | — | — | — | — | — | 2 | — | 1 | 9 | 2 | 20 | — |
| **Local party** | | | | | | | | | | | | |
| considerable | 23 | — | 20 | 26 | 29 | 2 | — | 18 | 55 | 39 | 40 | 7 |
| some | 38 | — | 50 | 23 | 39 | 24 | — | 20 | 27 | 26 | 20 | 23 |
| not much | 8 | — | 20 | 39 | 32 | 58 | — | 44 | 9 | 26 | 20 | 31 |
| none | 31 | — | 10 | 12 | — | 14 | — | 15 | — | 7 | — | 39 |
| n.a. | — | — | — | — | — | 2 | — | 3 | 9 | 2 | 20 | — |
| N = | (13) | (—) | (31) | (30) | (21) | (50) | (3) | (95) | (8) | (34) | (5) | (13) |

[a] No Democratic challengers in districts which tended Democratic lost.
[b] Only 3 Republican challengers contested in districts usually voting Democratic; all were in the South.

tional organizations are less subject to the sharp variation evident
in the local data. This is particularly true when one compares the
evaluation of winners and losers in competitive districts; first for
the local, then for the national, parties. The House campaign
committees do seem to be providing some compensation for the
uneven contributions of local party organizations in the United
States.

The second structural variable, a rough typology of urban-
suburban-rural constituency characteristics, is introduced to test
the impact of ecological setting.

Reformers have for years singled out the various ways in
which legislative and other institutions have given disproportionate representation and power to rural, essentially parochial,
interests over the emergent needs of an urban-suburban majority. Occasionally bitter disputes have arisen, particularly in
the national campaign committees of the Republican party, over
the stepchild status of its urban candidates and party organizations. Outside the South, less frequent but trenchant criticism
among Democrats has been directed to the party's disproportionate assistance going to labor-dominated urban constituencies
at the expense of suburban "islands" of issue-oriented liberals.

A glance at the data presented in table 5.4 may assist in
putting this struggle over relative deprivation in context. Urban
Republican candidates do more frequently feel national and local
party organizations contribute little to their campaigns (26 percent said they received *no* assistance from the national committees, compared to 11 percent of their suburban and rural
counterparts). But 53 percent also reported receiving some or
considerable help. Rural and suburban Republican challengers
do appear to be somewhat more advantaged: 60 percent of the
rural and 68 percent of the suburban candidates reported this
much campaign assistance. Which comparison one decides to
emphasize depends on one's vantage point.

National party assistance goes where parties think they stand
a chance of winning. Republicans tend to lose disproportionately
in urban areas; one-half their urban candidates, therefore, dismissed the national party as not being very helpful. But then so
did one-third of the GOP's suburban and rural candidates. Nor
were the latter doing so because they believed their local organi-

Table 5.4

Constituency Characteristics and Levels of Campaign
Assistance Provided Congressional Challengers[a]

(*In Percent*)

|  | Democrats | | | Republicans | | |
|---|---|---|---|---|---|---|
|  | URBAN | SUBURBAN | RURAL | URBAN | SUBURBAN | RURAL |
| National party |  |  |  |  |  |  |
| considerable | 22 | 26 | 27 | 17 | 25 | 26 |
| some | 26 | 38 | 25 | 36 | 43 | 34 |
| not much | 35 | 15 | 29 | 21 | 21 | 28 |
| none | 17 | 18 | 19 | 26 | 11 | 11 |
| n.a. | — | 3 | — | — | — | 1 |
| Local party |  |  |  |  |  |  |
| considerable | 26 | 21 | 13 | 17 | 32 | 29 |
| some | 22 | 36 | 37 | 23 | 21 | 25 |
| not much | 39 | 36 | 38 | 49 | 32 | 34 |
| none | 13 | 7 | 12 | 11 | 11 | 11 |
| n.a. | — | — | — | — | 4 | 1 |
| N = | (23) | (39) | (63) | (47) | (28) | (65) |

[a] See chapter 4 for a discussion of the index of constituency characteristics. I've omitted 20
Democrats and 18 Republicans who competed in districts *Congressional Quarterly* classified as
"mixed."

zations were making up the difference. Approximately four of
ten rural and suburban challengers also saw the local networks as
not very contributive (six of ten urbanites felt this way).

Contrarily, if emphasis focuses on the compensatory function
supposedly performed by the national party, then the GOP is
certainly deficient. Not sustaining urban candidates more forcefully further denies them the possibility of capitalizing on long-
run constituency changes that may be occurring in these districts.
The ecology of a district obviously has some impact on resource
distribution within the Republican party, but these data also
point to other factors of equal importance.[29]

29. Among which may have been the idiosyncracies of the 1964 election.
Goldwater's southern strategy, and the national committee figures who helped im-
plement it, were not distinguished by an abundance of sympathy for northeastern
or other urban areas. The NRCC seemed less biased in this respect, as Mc-
Keough's data on financial support for non-Goldwaterites show, although the House

The small but predictable differences among Republicans are not duplicated for Democrats. Urban challengers are just as likely to see the national and local organizations as helpful *or* useless as their suburban counterparts. It is the rural challengers, competing, if you will recall, almost exclusively outside the South, who differ in their evaluations most frequently. But, as the data show, these differences are scarcely substantial: 13 percent of the rural Democratic challengers accorded their local organizations a considerable role, compared to 26 and 21 percent of their urban and suburban colleagues respectively. Even this tiny variation disappears when one compares the three groups on their evaluation of national party activities.[30]

These findings, generally in accord with those of Olson for incumbents,[31] are at variance with others who have focused on a single metropolitan area or a single state, and who've found evidence of considerable organizational clout.[32] Generalizations about organizational inputs to congressional campaigns will be enhanced when political science generates large-scale comparative studies which can handle national, regional, and metropolitan factors. Obviously my data are quite limited in this regard.

Overwhelmingly, the impression left by the above analysis is that neither level of party organization is performing in a manner acceptable to a large majority of challengers: i.e., in a fashion that approaches giving them resource equality with incumbents. Whether national and/or local party organizations should, or could, increase that acceptability is a question I shall defer until later.

Scanty as resources for most of these candidates are, each is still faced with the task of utilizing what little they've accumulated. Candidates, like guerrillas, must ultimately deploy for the struggle.

---

committee did give disproportionately to rural Republicans. See McKeough's analysis, *Financing Campaigns*, pp. 19–28. Although I cannot document it, I suspect my data do not simply mirror the whims of Messrs. Goldwater, Burch, White, et al., but reflect deeper limitations in the Republican electoral base.

30. Nor is regional variation important, except that northeastern candidates were more likely to consider the *national* party bountiful. Cf. Olson, *Congressman and His Party*, chap. 2.

31. Ibid.

32. Snowiss, "Congressional Recruitment."

## Techniques

"The entire question of what kinds of campaign techniques are most effective," observes Frank Sorauf, "remains largely a matter of conjecture and abundant popular wisdom."[33] The persuasive verbal artillery of modern campaign technology, and the "New Politics" of the technologists, tends to obscure the truth of Sorauf's observation.

Despite the increasing appeal of Comprehensive Systems Planning, Master Battle Plans, Multi-Media Expertise, "481" Bogeymen, most congressional candidates still appear to operate on a principle of disjointed disgorge:[34] since it is impossible to ascertain with precision what the relative costs and benefits of opting for one set of techniques over another might be, one simply does as much as one can afford of everything.

Television is bought, radio and newspaper advertising slots obtained, volunteer organizations mobilized (or created), doorbells rung, cocktail parties and coffees given, business and community groups addressed, mailings undertaken, baptisms and bar mitzvahs attended, billboards utilized, offices and factories visited, sniping (usually) encouraged, even, one suspects, babies still kissed. To what end?

Twenty-five years of mass communications research has spawned a variety of theories, and substantial empirical research, on the question "Who says what to whom, when, and with what effect?"[35] Moreover, a small but growing number of sophisticated studies on the personal factor—direct contact by activists with voters—suggests that such activity does indeed predispose

33. Sorauf, *Party and Representation*, p. 250.
34. A derivative principle of that cosmic philosophy, Disjointed Incrementalism. Specifically, it is a synonym for what Gore and Peabody refer to as "the spray of stimuli," and a variation on Jones' dictum for all candidates: "Keep moving, keep firing, and don't look back." See Gore and Peabody, "Functions of Political Campaign," p. 65; and Jones, "Role of Campaign," p. 29.
35. Summaries are provided in Joseph Klapper, *The Effects of Mass Communication* (Glencoe, Ill.: Free Press, 1961); Bernard Berelson and Morris Janowitz, eds., *Reader in Public Opinion and Mass Communication* (2nd ed.; New York: Free Press, 1966); Arthur Cohen, *Attitude Change and Social Influence* (New York: Basic Books, 1966); Daryl J. Bem, *Beliefs, Attitudes, and Human Affairs* (Belmont, Calif.: Wadsworth, 1970); Bernard Hennessy, *Public Opinion* (2nd ed.; Belmont, Calif.: Wadsworth, 1970); and Howard Mendelson and Irving Crespi, *Polls, Television, and the New Politics* (San Francisco: Chandler, 1970).

the elector toward the activists' cause.[36] But, from the viewpoint of candidates, the important question is still one of relative pay-offs from different investment strategies, and the costs—financial, personal, organizational.

Lewis Froman's attempt to synthesize modern social science findings into a set of maxims for campaign strategy[37] is impressive, although the difficulties in implementing Froman's approach have recently been put to empirical test.[38] One other strand of inquiry, more germane here, stems from efforts to explain why candidates emphasize certain clusters of techniques rather than others. Eulau, Zisk, and Prewitt argue that the partisan milieu encourages candidates either to move toward *personal* (e.g., door-to-door canvassing) or *impersonal* (mass media) campaign techniques.[39]

Congressional campaigns, unlike statewide operations, are often dependent on the ability of candidates to penetrate sub-areas within a larger metropolitan or regional locale; hence massive doses of local television or newspaper advertising are usually considered too costly for the amount of potential returns. V. O. Key's data, for example, show that House candidates averaged about 30 minutes of television time during the 1960 campaigns (in sustaining *and* nonsustaining hours), compared to a mean of 10 hours for senatorial candidates. Comparable figures of AM radio were 1 hour and 25 minutes for the average House candidate, to 11.5 hours for the average U.S. Senate aspirant.[40] Unfortunately, these data are somewhat outdated and reflect only slots of 5 minutes or more. Most candidates rely on shorter spots and have

36. Daniel Katz and Samuel J. Eldersveld, "The Impact of Local Party Activity upon the Electorate," *Public Opinion Quarterly* 25 (1961): 1–24; Peter H. Rossi and Phillips Cutright, "The Impact of Party Organization in an Industrial Setting," in *Community Political Systems*, ed. Morris Janowitz (Glencoe, Ill.: Free Press, 1961); Raymond Wolfinger, "The Influence of Precinct Work on Voting Behavior," *Public Opinion Quarterly* 27 (1963): 372–86; William T. Murphy, "Student Power in the 1970 Elections: A Preliminary Assessment," *P.S.* 4 (Winter 1971): 27–32.

37. Froman, "Realistic Approach to Campaign."

38. Paletz, "Neglected Context of Congressional Campaigns."

39. Heinz Eulau, Betty Zisk, and Kenneth Prewitt, "Latent Partisanship in Non-Partisan Elections," in Jennings and Zeigler, *Electoral Process*, pp. 226–28.

40. Recomputed from data cited by Herbert Alexander, "Broadcasting and Politics," in Jennings and Zeigler, *Electoral Process*, p. 89.

probably increased the amount of time spent and money devoted to television utilization. The presumed potency of television
exposure is clearly evidenced by the widespread anxiety among
incumbent congressmen over attempts to abolish the "fair time"
rule. But the relatively large margin between House and Senate
candidates during 1960 is still indicative of the very different environments in which these candidates must compete.

Three factors impinge on challengers' estimates of which
campaign techniques hold high payoffs: partisan structure,
whether the district is predominantly Republican, Democratic, or
competitive; social demography, whether the district is primarily
urban, suburban, or rural; and whether the candidate wins or
loses. The latter is important if Kingdon's thesis can be generalized across the board; i.e., losers should disproportionately exag-
gerate the impact of relatively remote sources of influence, while
winners should more frequently see factors under their own
control as decisive.

Data are first presented by party and electoral outcome.
Following earlier studies,[41] I have divided the techniques into
two classes: personal and impersonal. Table 5.5 gives initial results.

Generally, differences between parties are not substantial,
although GOP candidates do see impersonal techniques, particularly newspaper support, as more potent than do Democrats. More important, as the data show strikingly, the impact of
electoral outcome moves candidates to quite different evaluations
about techniques. Losers, in both parties, are substantially more
likely to see newspaper support and, among Democrats only,
television, as quite significant in determining outcome. Three-
fourths of the Republican challengers, winners and losers, placed
a high value on television (as did 78 percent of the Democratic losers). Only Democratic winners departed from this judgment, with 47 percent perceiving it as somewhat or not very important.

The findings on newspaper support, which one imagines reflects the disproportionately pro-Republican character of the
American press (Spiro Agnew's opinions notwithstanding), also
accords with expectations: 75 percent of the Democratic winners

41. Eulau et al., "Latent Partisanship."

### Table 5.5

### Evaluation of Campaign Techniques Among
### Congressional Challengers, by Party and
### Electoral Outcome[a]
### (*In Percent*)

| | Demo-crats | Repub-licans | Democrats | | Republicans | |
|---|---|---|---|---|---|---|
| | | | WON | LOST | WON | LOST |
| **PERSONAL AND DIRECT:** | | | | | | |
| (A) *Door-to-door Canvass* | | | | | | |
| very important | 63 | 68 | 65 | 60 | 100 | 64 |
| somewhat or not very important | 37 | 32 | 35 | 40 | — | 26 |
| (B) *Small-group Appearance* | | | | | | |
| very important | 63 | 53 | 79 | 51 | 87 | 48 |
| somewhat or not very important | 37 | 47 | 21 | 49 | 13 | 52 |
| **IMPERSONAL AND INDIRECT:** | | | | | | |
| (C) *Television Use* | | | | | | |
| very important | 68 | 75 | 53 | 78 | 75 | 75 |
| somewhat or not very important | 32 | 25 | 47 | 22 | 25 | 25 |
| (D) *Newspaper Support* | | | | | | |
| very important | 46 | 59 | 25 | 62 | 43 | 60 |
| somewhat or not important | 54 | 41 | 75 | 38 | 57 | 40 |
| N = | (145) | (158) | (63) | (82) | (16) | (142) |

[a] The question asked candidates to evaluate the impact of various techniques on the outcomes of their elections.

discounted its importance, while 62 percent of the losers saw newspapers as very important.[42]

On measures of more personalized campaign techniques, majorities in both camps, winners and losers, tended to see door-

42. While evidence on the effect of newspaper support is contradictory, I'm inclined to agree with the thrust of John Mueller's argument that it is consistently overestimated by communications researchers, particularly when such support

to-door canvassing as a major factor, diverging only on their estimates of the value of small-group appearances. Here, overwhelming majorities of Democratic and Republican winners (79 and 87 percent respectively) felt such appearances vital while their less fortunate colleagues were very much divided: only 51 percent of the Democratic losers and 48 percent of the GOP losers were willing to concede that much impact to small-group appearances.

Turning to the effects of party milieu and social demography (tables 5.6 and 5.7), the impact of electoral outcome is somewhat modified, at least within each party. Consider, for example, Democratic perspectives in competitive districts. Whereas the findings examined above showed no differences between winners and losers on the question of door-to-door canvassing, Democratic winners in vulnerable districts are much more likely than losers to consider this important. On the other hand, winners were still likely to sustain their favorable predisposition to small-group appearances, independent of differences in party competitiveness. Similarly for the two types of impersonal techniques. The early and substantial differences between Democratic winners and losers on the impact of television are reduced when one compares these two groups in competitive districts.

Differences among Republican winners and losers, except on the measure of newspaper support, remain about as they were in table 5.5. When GOP challengers compete in Democratic districts, they are much more likely to perceive newspaper support as influential: 66 percent (all losers) of those who stood in Democratic districts considered newspaper support highly powerful. However, only 45 percent of those running in competitive, and 46 percent in GOP-dominated districts, both groups also losers, placed this much importance on newspaper support. It seems likely that this divergence is a simple function of running in districts where the press departs from its usual behavior and moves toward endorsement of Democratic candidates; i.e., the urban Northeast and the South.[43]

---

revolves around low salience campaigns. See Mueller, "Ballot Patterns and Historical Trends in California," *American Political Science Review* 63 (December 1969): 1204–6. Cf. James E. Gregg, "Newspaper Editorial Endorsements and California Elections, 1948–62," *Journalism Quarterly* (Autumn 1965): 532–38.

43. This is strictly an impression. One of the potentially most fruitful contributions of the Nader Project on Congress is the data being collected on the type, scope, and duration of media coverage of congressional candidates.

Table 5.6 Party Competition, Electoral Outcome, and Evaluation of Campaign Techniques Among Congressional Challengers (*In Percent*)

| | Democrats | | | | | | Republicans | | | | | |
|---|---|---|---|---|---|---|---|---|---|---|---|---|
| | *Tend Democratic* | | *Marginal* | | *Tend Republican* | | *Tend Democratic* | | *Marginal* | | *Tend Republican* | |
| | WON | LOST | WON | LOST | WON | LOST | WON | LOST | WON | LOST | WON | LOST |
| **PERSONAL AND DIRECT:** | | | | | | | | | | | | |
| (A) *Door-to-door Canvass* | | | | | | | | | | | | |
| very important | 46 | —[a] | 70 | 45 | 71 | 72 | —[b] | 68 | 55 | 61 | 80 | 31 |
| somewhat or not very important | 54 | — | 30 | 55 | 29 | 28 | — | 32 | 45 | 39 | 20 | 69 |
| (B) *Small-group Appearances* | | | | | | | | | | | | |
| very important | 85 | — | 76 | 55 | 76 | 50 | — | 54 | 81 | 41 | 60 | 31 |
| somewhat or not very important | 15 | — | 24 | 45 | 24 | 50 | — | 46 | 19 | 59 | 40 | 69 |
| **IMPERSONAL AND INDIRECT:** | | | | | | | | | | | | |
| (C) *Television Use* | | | | | | | | | | | | |
| very important | 39 | — | 60 | 70 | 57 | 78 | — | 74 | 81 | 84 | 40 | 70 |
| somewhat or not very important | 61 | — | 40 | 30 | 43 | 22 | — | 26 | 19 | 16 | 60 | 30 |
| (D) *Newspaper Support* | | | | | | | | | | | | |
| very important | 23 | — | 20 | 51 | 33 | 70 | — | 66 | 36 | 45 | 40 | 46 |
| somewhat or not very important | 76 | — | 80 | 49 | 67 | 30 | — | 24 | 74 | 55 | 60 | 54 |
| N = | (13) | (—) | (31) | (30) | (21) | (50) | (3) | (95) | (8) | (34) | (5) | (13) |

[a] No Democrats who competed in Democratic-dominant districts lost.

[b] Only three Republicans competing in Democratic-dominant districts won.

Table 5.7

Constituency Characteristics and Evaluation of
Campaign Techniques Among
Congressional Challengers*

(*In Percent*)

| | Democrats | | | Republicans | | |
|---|---|---|---|---|---|---|
| | URBAN | SUBURBAN | RURAL | URBAN | SUBURBAN | RURAL |
| **PERSONAL AND DIRECT:** | | | | | | |
| (A) *Door-to-door Canvass* | | | | | | |
| very important | 52 | 62 | 62 | 74 | 61 | 63 |
| somewhat or not very important | 48 | 38 | 38 | 26 | 39 | 37 |
| (B) *Small-group Appearances* | | | | | | |
| very important | 65 | 62 | 65 | 53 | 50 | 55 |
| somewhat or not very important | 35 | 38 | 35 | 47 | 50 | 45 |
| **IMPERSONAL AND INDIRECT:** | | | | | | |
| (C) *Television Use* | | | | | | |
| very important | 65 | 62 | 71 | 66 | 75 | 78 |
| somewhat or not very important | 35 | 38 | 29 | 34 | 25 | 22 |
| (D) *Newspaper Support* | | | | | | |
| very important | 48 | 49 | 41 | 66 | 68 | 46 |
| somewhat or not very important | 52 | 51 | 59 | 34 | 32 | 54 |
| N = | (23) | (39) | (63) | (47) | (28) | (65) |

aThese data exclude 20 Democrats and 18 Republicans who were competing in districts *Congressional Quarterly* classified as "mixed."

Constituency characteristics, measured by the urban-sub-urban-rural trichotomy, has little impact on the candidates' evaluations, as a review of table 5.7 documents. Nor are the original differences between winners and losers modified by controlling for constituency (table not shown). One suggestive finding, however, centers on the perspectives of rural candidates. Rural America as the celebrated center of "friends and neighbors" *Gemeinschaft* politics takes a slight bruising from these findings. Congressional challengers in both parties are slightly *more* likely to evaluate television positively when they are competing in *rural* districts than are their cousin candidates in suburban or urban districts. But the differences are minute, itself an important qualification of the presumed effects of rural vs. suburban or urban life. As the data show, there are *no* differences in evaluation of personal, direct, and small-group contact measures as one moves from those urban-suburban centers of galluping alienation and social disorganization to the agrarian fiber of American politics.[44]

Whatever the impact of the new technology and media-centered campaigns, majorities of these candidates, win or lose, are still convinced that traditional, direct-contact activities are important determinants of electoral outcome. Obviously, they also agree that "swingin' through midsummer barbecues in shad-belly vests" isn't enough. The media, particularly television, are clearly considered major instruments. And such perception has presumably led candidates to utilize these media more heavily.

Regrettably, whether using any of these techniques more frequently than others actually influenced the ultimate outcome is a question about which the data examined here are coldly silent.

Political scientists and others have only recently begun to construct experimental, and quasi-experimental, designs to test the persuasiveness of different campaign appeals,[45] but I suspect we are still a long way from seriously being able to "offer immense opportunities to politicians in aiding them to make appropriate choices" among campaign strategies and tactics.[46] Nor am I much persuaded by the arguments of Lewis Froman and others that the state of the discipline enables us to do so, even if

44. David Olson notes that while *Congressional Quarterly* usually classifies in excess of 75 districts as "predominantly rural" (I've used CQ classifications above), the American Farm Bureau, as of 1969, argued there were only 31 congressional districts that were "authentically rural," i.e., with no city over 25,000 population in the district. Thus the above could be very deceptive. See Olson's discussion on this point. *Congressman and His Party*, chap. 2.

45. See the studies cited above, note 36.

46. Froman, "Realistic Approach to Campaign," p. 19.

one's values move one in this direction. I still believe that campaigns can (and increasingly, should) be educational in the old-fashioned sense. Restructuring the existing relationship between candidates and the public is one of the most important long-run effects serious congressional opposition might have on the American political system.

Every two years a sizable number of challengers go through the sometimes tedious, often strenuous process of gaining nomination, chasing campaign resources, experimenting with different techniques, knowing, as V. O. Key once observed, ". . . the voice of the people consists mainly of the words 'yes' and 'no' and at times one cannot be certain which word is being uttered."

While a majority of these candidates were ultimately defeated, a strategic minority were able to win—by dint of luck, superior campaign organization, and skills, or by riding the crest of long- or short-run changes in the character of their constituencies. Some were confident of that exquisite moment; all, whether reinforced or surprised by the verdict, had to begin preparing for other battles in other places. Their equation had changed. Moving from the external environment of competitive electoral politics to the struggle for recognition in the House, no matter how much the question of reelection haunts each freshman legislator, constitutes a substantial shift to a new set of problems.

# 6

# LEGISLATING

Anecdotes about the trials and tribulations of freshmen in the House of Representatives are legion. While it may be true that a congressman's life is the "shortest distance between two years,"[1] much of the new member's interest and time must still focus on developing a frame of reference for dealing with the internal processes of institutional life in the House.

Two interrelated political factors sharply impinged on the way these successful challengers confronted their sudden transformation from electoral underdogs to representatives. First, the massive defeat of Barry Goldwater by Lyndon Johnson had given the Democratic party its greatest presidential victory since 1936. Second, the GOP House delegation, shrunken since 1958, stood at its lowest point (140) since the 1930s, when the first session of the 89th Congress convened in January 1965. Armed with a huge majority (295) in Congress, the liberal-labor wing of the Democratic party went to work and during the first ten months pumped out a series of long-simmering and significant social reform measures. Analogies with the New Deal are exaggerated but most commentators agree that the 89th was the most productive and innovative Congress of the post-World War II period.

1. Pirated from David Paletz who borrowed it from Charles Clapp who recorded it in one of the Brookings sessions.

In the course of such intense legislative activity, freshmen on both sides of the aisle were rapidly introduced to three axioms of congressional reality: as an institution, the House is first an oligarchy, frequently a hierarchy, sometimes a community.[2] Moreover, a "minority mentality" was being strongly reinforced among the few Republican newcomers. As Irwin Gertzog has convincingly demonstrated,[3] and my data later corroborate, the feeling of being demolished by a liberal blitzkreig was added to the normal frustrations of adaptation in the House. While many Democrats also chafed under standard operating procedures, few were faced with that feeling of cumulative helplessness, procedural *and* policy, that marked the experience of their GOP cohorts. Indeed, for most Democrats, problems of accommodation revolved exclusively around organizational questions, particularly seniority and its prerogatives.

Three years later, as disputes over Vietnam, race, and poverty deepened, a new generation of Democratic freshmen (and more senior members) would develop indictments of policy output and House procedures which certainly exceeded earlier Republican discontent. But in 1965, the enthusiasm—one is tempted to say illusions—associated with major legislative achievement temporarily sidetracked many liberals from their usual objections to problems in the House.

2. This hardly needs documentation, but some good places to begin are Clem Miller, *Member of the House* (New York: Scribners, 1962); Morris Udall and Donald Tacheron, *The Job of the Congressman* (rev. ed.; Indianapolis: Bobbs-Merrill, 1970); Leroy Rieselbach's introduction to his collection of readings, *The Congressional System* (Belmont, Calif.: Wadsworth, 1970), pp. 1–27; and Richard Fenno's two articles, "The Internal Distribution of Influence: The House," in *Congress and America's Future,* ed. David Truman (Englewood Cliffs, N.J.: Prentice-Hall, 1965), and "The Freshman Congressman: His View of the House," in *American Governmental Institutions,* ed. Aaron Wildavsky and Nelson W. Polsby (Chicago: Rand McNally, 1969).

3. Gertzog is working on a large-scale study of freshman adaptation in the House. For preliminary reports, see his "Frustration and Adaptation: The Adjustment of Minority Freshmen to the Congressional Experience" (Paper delivered at the 1966 annual meeting of the American Political Science Association), and "The Socialization of Freshman Congressmen: Some Agents of Organizational Continuity" (Paper delivered at the 1970 annual meeting of the American Political Science Association). A collection of essays on the freshman experience has been organized by the LRS: Walter J. Oleszek, ed., "The Freshman Legislator: Selected Articles," mimeographed (Washington, D.C.: Legislative Reference Service, 1968). For a model of decision making which explores the cue-taking behavior of freshmen on votes, see William Mishler et al., "Determinants of Institutional Continuity: Freshman Cue-Taking in the U.S. House of Representatives," in *Legislatures in Comparative Perspective,* ed. Allan Kornberg (New York: David McKay, 1973).

Conservatives, not liberals, were generally the harshest critics of the 89th Congress. Predictably, this criticism was rarely directed toward institutional characteristics (except seniority). GOP conservatives focused on policy output and majority leadership, two features that are in principle highly situational and divorced from a serious structural critique. The latter, as always, was more frequently articulated by a minority of Democrats, despite the congruence between their ideology and the 89th's policy orientation.

This chapter focuses on the way these freshmen evaluated and adapted to the strengths and weaknesses of life in the House—as an institution generally, as reflected in committee work, and in the interaction of party leaders and members. Since the worklife of the House is concentrated in committees, I will also examine the assignment process and the propensity to change original assignments over three sessions (89th, 90th, 91st).

One theme of the book has been the programmatic orientation of candidates as it affects the responsiveness of American political parties. An important question revolves around how *pre*-congressional policy stands are related to their subsequent behavior as representatives. Data are examined to test some basic notions in linking candidate promise to leadership fulfillment.

## Socialization and Freshman Congressmen

Legislatures, like all social systems, are sustained and/or transformed by their ability to incorporate the values and expectations of new generations while socializing them to the values of existing tribal customs and practices. Insofar as representative institutions share universal tribal functions, the House is subject to certain "laws" of organized group behavior. Numerous students of legislative behavior have sought to isolate and explore those factors that facilitate responsiveness and creativity while guaranteeing organizational continuity.[4] "Rules of the Game,"

4. Among which Donald R. Matthews, *U.S. Senators and Their World* (Chapel Hill: University of North Carolina Press, 1960); John Wahlke, Heinz Eulau, William Buchanan, LeRoy Ferguson, *The Legislative System* (New York: Wiley, 1963); Allan Kornberg, *Canadian Legislative Behavior* (New York: Holt, 1967); Nelson Polsby, "The Institutionalization of the House of Representatives," *American Political Science Review* (March 1968): 144–49; and, most recently, Charles Bell and Charles Price, "The Rules of the Game" (Paper delivered at the 1969 American Political Science Association Meetings). Directly relevant to this chapter is Gertzog, "Socialization of Freshman Congressmen," pp. 2–5.

"Normativeness," "Operational Codes," are all expressions for dealing with critical aspects of the socialization and decision-making process in legislatures. Gertzog proposes that the ". . . ability of an organization to adequately indoctrinate new members to its rules, procedures, and goals is affected by [its] capacity to provide clear and unambiguous rules." Ultimately, the effectiveness of these rules depends on the judicious use of a sanction system (positive and negative) to deal with aberrant behavior.[5]

On a continuum of organizational normative "tightness," democratically elected legislatures are rarely armies, goosestepping to the same drummer. There appears to be substantial variation from country to country, and within the United States from state to state, in the extent to which legislative bodies develop, communicate, and enforce elaborate formal and informal codes.

Various factors tend to encourage substantial latitude without leading to anarchy or decisional stalemate. Some are characteristic of the institution, some characteristic of the members recruited.[6] Since the House does not control recruitment of members, except in the most limited legal sense of overseeing the Constitutional requirements regarding citizenship, state residence, and age, it cannot impose strict screening measures for membership. Nor does (or has) the House successfully ousted many members who have consistently violated internal norms.[7] To be sure, there are hundreds of subtle (and not so subtle) ways in which the "outsider" is made to feel uncomfortable in that

5. Ibid.
6. Ibid.
7. The most sensational recent case, overturned by the Supreme Court, was Adam Clayton Powell. The Court ruled that, while the House had the authority to expel members for "due cause," they must first seat any duly elected representative who meets the Constitutional requirements of age, state residence, and citizenship. While Powell had apparently engaged in some questionable practices, the harshness of the move against him (he was first stripped of his chairmanship and seniority by the Democratic Caucus, then denied a seat in the House) seemed clearly a case of moralizing overkill. The coalition that voted not to seat him, in my judgment, was moved by diverse motives, including some only slightly disguised racism, considerable resentment over his personal life style, Democratic and Republican electoral opportunism, down-home Puritanism. The rhetoric, however, was always that he had "tarnished" the public "image" of the House. This carried substantial irony since (according to Gallup) public evaluation of Congress was at its highest postwar peak during the prior session, a period when Powell had chaired the most productive legislative committee in the 89th Congress. Observed one congressman: ". . . a little less Protestant Bible-beating hokey, and a little more productive social legislation, would go a lot further in redeeming the image of this place."

role. "Going along to get along," that monotonously cited Rayburnism, is a powerful but usually nonpolicy oriented incentive for the individual member.[8] If the individual can bear short-run deprivations of *internal* influence, perhaps status, maybe some esteem, then he can usually be sure that electoral longevity will eventually bring him some amount of institutional power.[9] Finally, although House and party subgroups have increasingly been attempting to provide formal sessions of "introduction and orientation" for new members, this is not considered a major function and is usually given limited attention.[10] In short, the institutional capacity to compel appropriate behavior among members appears extremely constrained.

Consider, however, the characteristics of most entering freshman representatives. Sociologically they are hardly proletarians or Brahmins, nor (yet) middle-class dropouts. Most have endured the

8. Powell's policy views were not instrumental in the decision to deny him a seat. However, the House of Representatives did once (excluding the Civil War cases and a polygamist) deny membership to a duly elected candidate because he was ideologically out of the "mainstream." The case, of course, involved socialist Victor Berger, a pacifist and opponent of World War I, twice elected to Congress from the fifth district of Wisconsin (Milwaukee) and twice denied a seat. The precise legal grounds used to exclude Berger involved a section of the 14th Amendment, developed to prevent Confederate politicians from taking seats after the Civil War, which adds to the normal qualifications a clause about "engaging in insurrection or rebellion . . . or giving aid and comfort to enemies. . . ." Berger had been convicted in a lower court under the Espionage Act, a conviction that was later overturned by the U.S. Court of Appeals. Under current legal doctrine, it is extremely doubtful that the "aid and comfort" phrase could be given enough precision to justify exclusion of American communists, let alone socialists. But, as Chafee points out, the House was less interested in legal precision than it was in condemning opposition to the war as un-American. The Supreme Court never ruled on the Constitutionality of the House decision, but in 1923, after the Department of Justice had dropped charges against Berger, he was finally seated—without one dissenting vote. The most authoritative account of this episode is still Zechariah Chafee, Jr., *Free Speech in the United States* (Cambridge, Mass.: Harvard University Press, 1942), pp. 241–85.

9. It is difficult to know what sort of precedent has been established for the role of party caucuses in light of the Democrat's decision to strip John Bell Williams and Albert Watson of seniority after they supported Goldwater. Williams resigned, was elected governor of Mississippi, while Watson bolted, became a Republican, and was reelected to the House from South Carolina. Short of ousting a member, this is probably the most powerful deprivation the House (in this case, party) can visit upon a maverick.

10. Jointly sponsored by the American Political Science Association and party leaders in the House, these bipartisan three-day sessions were first started in 1960 and have now become a fixture of each biennial session. Party subgroups have initiated further sessions, restricted to representatives from their respective sides of the aisle, which are also becoming institutionalized.

tribulations of public or party office prior to contesting for the House, and an overwhelming majority consider themselves strong party types. Although many waged tough campaigns as opposition candidates, that role was performed consistent with notions characteristic of a *loyal* opposition.

No matter how sharp policy disagreement had been, or would become, the dialogue never approached nor even slouched toward radically different political visions. No matter how critical the candidate's stance vis-à-vis ongoing practices in the House, that attitude fell far short of calling for the conversion of the institution into a Committee of Public Safety or a "People's Assembly." No matter how despairing, or confident, over the distributive and representative capabilities of the existing congressional system, all seemed firmly committed to sustaining or improving the operational credo of the House—tolerance and respect for policy differences, mutual adjustment, some apprenticeship and specialization, some compromise, ultimate authority through majority decision making. Even those with strongly critical postures were still convinced that reform was preferable to massive institutional rearrangement: reform in representativeness (more blacks, Chicanos, women, and other spokesmen for the exploited should be seated); in structure (more internal democracy, efficiency, and less arbitrary decision making by party leaders should be encouraged); in responsiveness (national priorities should be changed through the transformation of public policy).

Quite literally, the recruitment process has churned up men and women who are predisposed to consider the House of Representatives a venerable and workable institution, despite any perceptions of flaws or unresponsiveness. Successful challengers thus enter the House "presocialized" and, in my opinion, this fact is a far more powerful guarantor of organizational continuity than any of the sanctions or rewards that the institution possesses independently.

This said, members still pursue a bewildering variety of personal adaptive strategies, reflect a broad range of negative and positive orientations toward the House and its output, engage in intense and contentious conflict over public policy, and in general behave in ways that prevent institutional ossification. It should be clear that I disagree, empirically and normatively, with those who would dismiss such differences as superficial because "all

those people play the game" and are hence "in the system."
While insider-outsider distinctions are occasionally useful, pre-
occupation with them will retard our ability to understand how
(and why) some political institutions remain static while others
are transformed. As one representative observed:

> If there was ever a lost generation, we are it. The kids don't
> trust anyone over 30, and the old bull elephants of the
> House don't trust anyone under 60. Those of us in between
> are the limbo generation.[11]

Factors in the adaptation of freshman representatives which
produce both cleavage *and* consensus may provide clues about
the capacity of the House to inculcate and promote meaningful
political change (including internally) while preserving its organizational integrity.[12]

## Power and Participation in Committees

Compared to the first few months of a typical session in the
1890s, the 89th Congress was a model of efficient and predictable
behavior patterns. No matter how new and confusing House
procedures were to freshmen, the overwhelming expectation
among veterans was one of orderly and stable change. New
faces would constitute less than 25 percent of the membership;
two or three chairmanships would shift to men with more than
twenty years' service; the Republicans would select a new minority leader in a spirited but hardly bitter fight, a representative
with "only" sixteen years of service.

The contrast with H. Douglas Price's description of the
House circa 1896 is striking. Membership turnover typically
ranged between 40 and 60 percent. Translating a normal session
into modern terms, House freshmen would have witnessed
McCormack giving up the Speakership to become a freshman
senator and being succeeded by Carl Albert. "After the next
election, Albert would be challenged for the leadership by Wilbur
Mills, who would then be dumped from Ways & Means and
made chairman of Banking and Currency. Clarence Cannon,
the latter-day watchdog of the Treasury, would be switched to

11.  Thomas M. Rees (D.-Calif), "Newsletter," 12 February 1970, p. 2.
12.  Gertzog, "Socialization of Freshman Congressmen."

chairman of Interior. If this sounds unlikely, consider further that Albert would then leave the House to become a freshman Senator, and that Mills, Cannon, and the new chairman of Ways and Means would be defeated at the next election. Cannon's successor, George Mahon, would serve a couple of terms and then run for Governor of Texas."[13]

Sixty years later the Democrats' decision to strip Williams and Watson of seniority was considered a tidal wave in an otherwise unflappable sea of growing professionalism and slow (painfully so, for most newcomers) advancement through the ranks of seniority to positions of potential power.

None of these successful challengers was naive about the consequences of this historical transformation, particularly as it affected three major areas of congressional practice: obtaining a desirable committee position, participating in committee and House policy deliberations, and their general relationship to the House and its leadership.

The criteria used by Democrats on Ways and Means and the Republican Committee-on-Committees for making freshman assignments have been explored extensively by others.[14] Uppermost for both the freshman and his decision-making colleagues, however, is that it be useful for the neophyte's particular constituency and that it comport with his interests and/or subject-matter expertise. However, the vote-getting/constituency-servicing convertibility of a particular assignment is difficult to ascertain, and strong subject-area expertise is precisely what freshmen most lack. Conflict and disappointment are inevitable.

To the extent the 89th was representative, data presented in table 6.1 reinforce the widely held belief that the inability to secure a desirable assignment is the first, but certainly not the

13. H. Douglas Price, "The Congressional Career: Risks and Rewards" (manuscript, Harvard University, 1963).

14. Nicholas A. Masters, "Committee Assignments in the House of Representatives," reprinted in Rieselbach, *Congressional System*, pp. 46–48, originally from the *American Political Science Review* (1961). More recently, see George Goodwin, Jr., *The Little Legislatures: Committees of Congress* (Amherst: University of Massachusetts Press, 1970). An imaginative attempt to apply a linear programming model to the assignment process, generating different kinds of assignments for freshmen than they receive in reality, has been undertaken by Eric Uslaner, "Congressional Committee Assignments: A Linear Programming Technique" (Paper delivered at the 1971 annual meeting of the American Political Science Association).

Table 6.1

Evaluations by Freshmen of Their Original Committee
Assignment in the House of Representatives,
89th Congress

| Rankings | Democrats % | N | Republicans % | N |
|---|---|---|---|---|
| First choice within realistic limits | 43 | (24) | 16 | (2) |
| First choice within context of delegation caucus | 12 | (7) | — | — |
| Second choice | 33 | (17) | 42 | (6) |
| Lower than second choice | 12 | (7) | 42 | (6) |
| | 100 | (55) | 100 | (14) |

strongest, source of frustration and discouragement among new
members. These data also show that minority freshmen more frequently felt substantially deprived in this regard, primarily because Republican seat ratios had been reduced. Almost half
(six of the fourteen interviewed) indicated their assignment—
even given realistic expectations—was still lower than their
*second* choice. Said one unusually embittered Republican:

> I know we lost slots on the better committees because of the
> election and all that, and I think, no I know, my delegation
> dean fought hard for me ... but damn it, I had already
> scaled down my original desire, developed two realistic
> choices (where there were vacancies), talked to everyone
> involved, and still didn't get either one. They put me on
> ——— and, this is galling, told me to have patience and
> something would be done later. Like patting a schoolboy
> on the head. ...

Other Republican freshmen, although disappointed, were
more inclined to accept a bad assignment as a short-run evil,
likely to be changed if they were reelected:

> The leadership was strapped [on numbers and openings]
> so I just said, "Put me where you think I can do most good
> and I'll be back in later with my real choices."

Almost all freshmen, Republican or Democratic, understood
the powerful claim of seniority on openings and simply

acquiesced. One southwestern Democrat described the process by saying:

> Our delegation always caucuses before coming back and the senior men get first choice. Then the new members make a selection based on what is left, what sort of advice the old-timers give them, and so forth. Luckily the Agriculture Committee was enlarged and I got my choice even though our state has two men on the committee.

Ideological considerations in the appointment of freshmen seem to have been nonexistent although they are among the more powerful factors as the years pass and members begin lobbying for the exclusive committees.[15] Only one freshman, an early antiwar eastern liberal, mentioned such considerations:

> It was second choice. I wanted Foreign Affairs, but I couldn't get it. I think my stand on Vietnam hurt me . . . it got around, although nobody said anything . . . and I ended up on ————.[16]

Three factors seem to explain the generally low-key reaction to committee assignments: (1) despite misgivings about other aspects of seniority, most freshmen accept it as fair in the distribution of new assignments; (2) a considerable minority (43 percent) of the Democrats were in fact able to obtain their first preference; and (3) among those disappointed, all believed they would be able to initiate a successful move and/or that committee assign-

15. On the ideological underpinnings of what constitutes "responsible committee members," see John Manley, *The Politics of Finance* (Boston: Little, Brown, 1970), and Richard F. Fenno, *The Power of the Purse* (Boston: Little, Brown, 1966). Very different expectations seem to structure recruitment to Education and Labor, as Fenno shows in another study, "The House of Representatives and Federal Aid to Education," in *New Perspectives on the House of Representatives*, ed. Robert Peabody and Nelson Polsby (Chicago: Rand McNally, 1963), pp. 195–237. It is an interesting but idle piece of speculation to envision the behavior of the Committees on Committees if either were ever confronted by a sizable number of serious radicals in their freshman delegations.

16. I nosed around during 1966–67, asking various inside friends about the accuracy of this member's assertion, but, like all such enlightened gossip, one never knows how to treat the results. For whatever it's worth (nor much, I concede) the score was 4–2 against his belief. As I suspect most readers know, the House Foreign Affairs Committee, whatever else it did, was not conspicuous for its sustained questioning of American involvement in Vietnam. There were, however, some prominent early antiwar critics on the committee, including Representatives Diggs, Fraser, and Rosenthal.

ments were simply not that critical during the first two years of a representative's career.

The last point, particularly, was instrumental in providing a cushion for the frustrated. None, even those who believed they were treated callously, felt moved enough to challenge party decisions in the way Shirley Chisholm (D.-N.Y.) successfully did at the beginning of the 91st Congress. For the more timid of the 89th who survived the next two elections, the data in tables 6.2 and 6.3 strongly support expectations of movement. Among Democrats, 50 percent (17) had switched their original major assignment; while among Republicans, 73 percent (8) undertook similar movement. The majority of this activity, of course, was lateral across "semiexclusive" committees. Only one Democrat and two Republicans were left with "nonexclusive" committee status in the 90th Congress and each of these shifted upward in the 91st. Interestingly, one of the Republicans, Jack Edwards (R-Ala.), who held two nonexclusive assignments through his first four years, jumped to the Appropriations Committee in the 91st Congress. Other than Barber Conable (R.-N.Y.), who moved from Science and Astronautics to Ways and Means, Edwards was the only GOP freshman from the 89th to gain an exclusive assignment during this six-year period.

Among Democrats, the most difficulty in changing the formal status of a major assignment was experienced by one member who was originally assigned to Government Operations, then shifted to Merchant Marine during the 90th, and finally to Science and Astronautics, a semiexclusive committee, at the beginning of the 91st.

The fact that exclusive committees are almost always beyond the reach of freshmen was contradicted by only one case in the 89th Congress. The reasons for this exception underscore a unique combination of fortuitous events and individual assets. Because this combination reflects such a powerful aggregation of perfect factors—a royal flush in the appointment process of freshmen— I'll quote the individual's account at some length:

> Besides my expertise and party experience [auditor general of a large state, deputy Democratic state chairman], the factors that really counted were the agreement of my delegation to back me unanimously and the hard work of our senior person. None of the senior people on our delega-

## Table 6.2

### Changing Committee Assignments of Congressmen First Elected to the 89th Congress, 1965–70 (Major Assignment Only)[a]

|  | 89th Dem (1965–66) | 89th Repub (1965–66) | 90th Dem (1967–68) | 90th Repub (1967–68) | 91st[b] Dem (1969–70) | 91st[b] Repub (1969–70) |
|---|---|---|---|---|---|---|
| **Exclusive Committes** | | | | | | |
| Appropriations | 1 | — | — | — | 1 | 1 |
| Rules | — | — | — | — | — | — |
| Ways & Means | — | — | — | 1 | — | 1 |
| **Semiexclusive** | | | | | | |
| Agriculture | 11 | 1 | 6 | 1 | 5 | — |
| Armed Services | 6 | — | 5 | 1 | 3 | 1 |
| Banking & Currency | 3 | 2 | 3 | 2 | 3 | 2 |
| Education & Labor | 3 | 1 | 5 | 1 | 5 | 1 |
| Foreign Affairs | 3 | — | 3 | 1 | 5 | 1 |
| Interstate Commerce | 5 | 1 | 4 | 1 | 4 | 1 |
| Judiciary | 5 | — | 4 | 1 | 3 | 1 |
| Post Office & Civil Service | 3 | 2 | 2 | — | — | — |
| Public Works | 4 | 1 | 3 | 2 | 3 | 2 |
| Science & Astronautics | 5 | 1 | 2 | — | 2 | — |
| **Nonexclusive** | | | | | | |
| District | — | — | — | — | — | — |
| Government Operations | 2 | 1 | — | — | — | — |
| House Administration | — | — | — | — | — | — |
| Interior | 4 | 2 | — | 1 | — | — |
| Merchant Marine | — | 2 | 1 | 1 | — | — |
| Un-American Activities | — | — | — | — | — | — |
| Veterans Affairs | — | — | — | — | — | — |
| Totals[c] | (55) | (14) | (38) | (13) | (34) | (11) |

[a] Major assignment was considered "semiexclusive or above" unless it included Post Office and Civil Service *plus* Interior. In the latter, Interior and Insular Affairs was considered the "major" assignment.

[b] The figures are calculated for members of the 89th who were still in the 90th or 91st. Thus, at the beginning of the 91st Congress, one Democrat and one Republican had moved to Appropriations, and one Republican had moved to Ways & Means. The reader should not add across.

[c] Totals are for the 69 freshmen who were interviewed during 1966.

gation wanted to move . . . most had advanced in their own committees by the high turnover. And then I really campaigned for it. I personally met every member on Ways and Means, and every subcommittee chairman on the committee I was seeking. In the case of the latter, I showed them I was interested and willing to learn by asking about the most minute details about their relationship to the House's operation, particularly problems in their own domain and so forth. Finally, our delegation drew up a series of propositions explaining why we felt our state should have a representative on Appropriations, and had letters from every member of the delegation, top to bottom, strongly supporting me. . .

It is impossible to definitively rank-order the factors that lead to success, but the above suggests something like the following: (1) a senior person within the delegation is not interested in the slot; (2) the representative is from a large, industrial state that doesn't have representation on a committee where geography is sometimes thought an important factor in seat allocations; (3) both the senior representative and other members of the state delegation are willing to work for the candidate's appointment; (4) the candidate has the necessary expertise and values to be considered a potentially "responsible" member;

## Table 6.3

### Committee "Switchers" and "Standpatters" Among Congressmen First Elected to the 89th Congress Who Were Still in the 91st Congress, 1965–70

| Three-session (89th-90th-91st) Movement on Committees | 91st Congress | | | |
|---|---|---|---|---|
| | DEMOCRATS | | REPUBLICANS | |
| | % | N | % | N |
| Remained on original major assignment[a] | 50 | (16) | 27 | (3) |
| Switched, but no change in formal committee status | 30 | (10) | 27 | (3) |
| Switched up from original nonexclusive to semi-exclusive status | 18 | (6) | 27 | (3) |
| Switched up to exclusive status | 2 | (1) | 19 | (2) |
| | 100 | (33) | 100 | (11) |

[a] Includes those who also added a second committee.

and (5) candidates campaign for the seat in a manner that impresses their future colleagues with their capacity to learn, their interest, their cordiality, ability to gain clientele-group support, etc.

Obviously, few freshmen are endowed with such a happy configuration of circumstance and skills. Time, however, is an important variable; the dissatisfied and electorally victorious were able to act on their frustration and shift to more felicitous committee environments.

Since formal assignments can be changed, deeper sources of potential frustration stem from the relationship of junior members to the ongoing operation of committees. As Fenno has observed, "... it is here, more than any other place, that the freshman will make or break his House career. Influence inside the chamber rests heavily on expertise, and expertise rests in turn on specialization in the field of one's committee or subcommittee."[17] The seniority system tends to reinforce both specialization and expertise as key House norms, a fact that impinges heavily on the freshman's behavior in, and reaction to, committee structure and performance.

All these newcomers seemed convinced of the value of both norms, and most were more than willing to make the commitment of time, interest, and hard work to gain the necessary technical abilities to become effective participants in the committee process. My horseback impression is that serious conflict and questioning is deferred among most congressmen until they have gained between four and six years' experience on a committee. Seniority then has the potential for conflict with a developing subject-matter expertise, a conflict usually resolved in favor of seniority. Freshmen are rarely leaders or even participants in revolts against committee oligarchs. Too much time must be devoted to simply learning the intricacies of House procedure, personalities, and power distribution. But some dissatisfaction had begun to surface after they had logged their first eight months in office.

As even a casual glance at the data in table 6.4 indicate, it was most frequently directed at the behavior and policy orientation of the chairman and, more importantly, heavily concentrated among members of the minority party. Among Democrats, only 14 percent (8 of 55) said they were "generally dissatis-

17. "Freshman Congressman," p. 24.

## Table 6.4

### Orientations Toward the Performance of Committees, and Comments on Strengths and Weaknesses, Freshmen in the House of Representatives, 89th Congress

| *General Orientation* | Democrats % | Democrats N | Republicans % | Republicans N |
|---|---|---|---|---|
| Committee performance | | | | |
| very satisfied | 39 | (21) | — | |
| generally satisfied | 47 | (26) | 57 | (8) |
| generally dissatisfied | 14 | (8) | 43 | (6) |
| very dissatisfied | — | | — | |
| | 100 | (55) | 100 | (14) |

| *Characteristics*[a] | Strengths DEM | Strengths REPUB | Weaknesses DEM | Weaknesses REPUB |
|---|---|---|---|---|
| *Attributes relating to the chairman:* | | | | |
| Procedural fairness | 3% | — | 3% | 7% |
| Legislative preeminence | 10 | — | 28 | 21 |
| Policy orientation | 23 | — | 8 | 42 |
| *Attributes relating to the committee:* | | | | |
| Relations with clientele groups | 3% | 14% | 10% | — |
| Organization (staffs, coordi- nation, scheduling, etc.) | 3 | — | 23 | 35 |
| Oversight of agencies | 39 | 7 | 8 | 21 |
| *Attributes relating to the members:* | | | | |
| Personal relations between majority/minority | 13% | 28% | — | — |
| Expertise of members | 39 | 28 | 7 | 7 |
| *Attributes relating directly to role of freshmen:* | | | | |
| Ability to participate | 12% | 35% | 27% | 67% |
| Ability for influence | — | 7 | 27 | 67 |
| N = | (55) | (14) | (55) | (14) |

[a] Percents add to more than 100 percent since members could indicate more than one strength or weakness.

fied" with committee performance, while almost half (6) of the Republicans felt this way. Compared to their Democratic colleagues, 39 percent of whom reported they were "very satisfied" with committee performance, none of the GOP freshmen was that sanguine. I'll return to the Democrats momentarily, since 4 of the 8 who were most critical were on the same committee.

Major sources of disgruntlement for Republicans were (1) lack of opportunity for minority freshman participation and influence (67 percent); (2) the chairman's programmatic dominance (42 percent); and (3) the lack of effective minority representation in the staffing of committees (35 percent). One comment, representative of this Republican group, captures these feelings nicely:

> Our chairman is impeccably fair ... runs the committee right out of Roberts Rules of Order ... and everybody respects him for it. But [and this is a large "but"] you know the old song and dance: freshmen, particularly Republican freshmen, should be seen and not heard. Not ask any questions in committee ... we never get the time anyway since the buzzers seem to ring about the time he's getting past the ten-year boys. And when it comes to legislation, he's an autocrat; autocrat, hell, he's a dictator. The other senior members don't seem to object, at least in committee. They're all scared of him, particularly the Democrats. He has absolute control over subcommittee chairmanships and appointments and any legislation they want. I've watched two or three cave in with little more than a stare. I'm exaggerating a bit, but not much. From our side of the aisle, it's even worse. The staff are stooges for the Democrats. I wouldn't rely on them for giving me the right meeting time, let alone more important matters. ...

While this representative was inclined to withdrawal ("at least temporarily") from active participation, another Republican responded to a similar situation in a more aggressive manner:

> Damn it, I do ask questions when I think they're necessary. I didn't come here to sit by and act innocent; I've spent my life in a business which handles some of these matters. One of my senior [Republican] colleagues once took me aside in the Rotunda [restaurant] and said he thought I should slow down a little bit, go a little slower, and while I took his advice seriously, I still feel it can be done in the right way, that is, courteously and cordially.

The irony of the Republican responses on freshman participation is contained in the fact that they were either inclined to

fault committee practices in this regard or find them an exceptional sign of positive strength. Democrats were less polarized—
both less enthusiastic and less critical concerning their opportunities in committee. Contrasting responses in table 6.4 show that
Democratic freshmen, contrary to Republicans, saw the chairman's policy-programmatic orientation as a distinct strength.
When they were critical, they tended to focus on (1) the chairman's *legislative* preeminence (28 percent); (2) freshman participation (27 percent); and (3) committee administration (23
percent). Most importantly, I suspect, the high levels of policy
output during the 89th Congress tended generally to depress
Democratic criticism. Much more than GOP dissatisfaction,
freshman criticism in the majority party was dependent on the
unique characteristics of a particular committee and/or chairman.

The bitterest struggle that Democratic freshmen confronted
occurred in one legislative committee long on the brink of open
warfare. Five freshmen had been added to the majority side, one
of whom departed for another committee in the aftermath of
eleven-months of internal haggling. His mid-term departure,
highly unusual during any Congress, was the only example of a
clear break with the more typical pattern of deferring such movement until the end of the first two years. Two direct quotes reflect
the very different individual manner in which freshmen perceived
and related to this committee's conflict:

> The first full meeting of our committee was devoted to a
> discussion of the rules by which the committee operates. A
> short time before that, a couple of the senior members had
> come to me, had told me the chairman was lousy, and had
> asked that I support them in helping to make the committee
> more democratic. Now the word democracy is a funny
> word . . . I like it, and I also like that it be used right. What
> these fellows really meant is that they wanted me to help
> them knock the hell out of the chairman. Well, we took
> about 18 votes and the chairman won on 16 of them. When
> he checked to see whether members had or had not gone
> along with him, he saw that I had voted with him not only
> 16, but 18 times. The next day he called me in and said,
> "———, I like a man who is loyal, which subcommittees
> are you interested in?" What did I know, a new member?
> So I said, if the chairman felt loyalty that important, he

ought to put me where he thought I would do the most
good. I was assigned to the ———— subcommittee, the most
important of the full committee. . . .

Most did not feel moved to articulate such an open and uncritical acceptance of the chairman's prerogatives, nor were they
apparently penalized for siding with senior members who were
in opposition:

We were talking about "rules of the game" earlier and I
said they don't mean as much to an older man, like myself,
as a younger one. Let me give you an example: take our
chairman, he seems like a real autocratic and arbitrary old
sonofagun and everybody on the committee, excepting two
or three of his stooges, feels the way I do. About midway
through the session, I got out of bed one morning and said
to myself, "————, you've just about put up with as much
crap as you're set to take." I had voted against him earlier,
although those votes were not anti-————, so much as they
were meant to give everybody a little more of an opportunity to participate. Anyway I called four of the other members
[two of whom were freshmen], told them we should go see
———— in person, and lay it on the line. They must have
been coming to the same conclusion, because all agreed.
We saw him later that morning in his office and told him,
politely but firmly, that if he was going to act the same way
with this bill now as he did last year, he was going to have
an open battle with us in committee. He responded to our
suggestions in a very cordial way, accepted the criticism,
and things have been going a lot smoother for all of us
since. . . .

Various factors tend to prevent more frequent eruptions of
such intense and potentially explosive conflict in committees.
Although committee chairmen are certainly powerful figures, few
exercise their leadership, particularly vis-à-vis other committee
members, in a manner designed to alienate rather than consoli-
date support. Wilbur Mills may be exceptionally astute in this
regard,[18] but most of the others are not far behind. From the
viewpoint of freshmen, the data also stress the integrative consequences of committee-level nonpartisanship (or at least the

18. On the extraordinary leadership ability of Mills, see Manley, *Politics of
Finance*, pp. 98–151.

muting of party differences), and the high value placed on committee members' expertise. None of the freshmen considered "majority-minority party relations" a weakness; 28 percent of the Republicans and 13 percent of the Democrats mentioned this factor as a strength in their committee's deliberations. Moreover, the greatest amount of freshman agreement across parties tended to be in their estimates of their colleagues' subject-matter expertise. This is an important counterpoint to the Republicans' clear hostility to much of the policy output of the committees. One other factor, clearly evident in the data, was a conviction among Democrats that their committee was doing a respectable job on executive oversight: 4 of every 10 Democratic freshmen cited this as an asset in the committee's operation. But, as with policy output, this opinion moved sharply along partisan lines. Among Republicans, 2 of 5 considered their committees deficient in this respect; only 1 of the 14 considered it a strength.

Increasing the new member's feeling of effective participation in the House depends on a variety of factors which impinge on the modalities of committee life.

It is important that freshmen feel they are assigned to appropriate committees and, when this proves impossible, that they can move to another relatively rapidly. Current procedures in the House seem to be encouraging for this important preliminary goal. Second, consultative rather than autocratic leadership by chairmen increases both the psychology and reality of committee power sharing (among freshmen as well as others) in the policy-shaping process. Few freshmen felt they should be given "equal time"; rather their expectations seemed quite modest: some chance to ask questions; to make minor corrections and/or additions to pending legislation; to be given, where possible, some role on the floor.

The fact that some frustration continues over these matters even after congressmen have gained seniority means that the House, by intent or accident, is simply not responding to some obvious needs. When such frustration gains momentum in committee, as in the extreme case discussed above, the incentive to revolt takes on substantial force. While most freshmen were not confronted with such a circumstance, the few who were did not cavil about "taking on the chairman." Indeed, those few who acted seemed rather to enjoy it.

Modest but important constraints on the behavior of chairmen were won at the beginning of both the 92nd and 93rd Congresses when leaders in both parties finally agreed to permit more serious party caucus challenges of chairmen.[19] Defeating a chairman in caucus will still be extremely difficult; most commentators are agreed that the more powerful constraints on autocratic chairmen must come from within the committee and from stronger party leadership outside the committee environment.

Finally, the Republican complaints about the inadequacy of minority staffing, certainly not confined to freshmen, were partially met through the provisions of the Legislative Reorganization Act of 1970.[20] This, and the increased need for more and better technical expertise when dealing with the Executive, seem clearly within the ability of Congress to rectify. Whether it will depends on a variety of factors beyond the control of any group of freshmen. But the impetus is clearly reflected in these early sources of frustration.

## Perceptions of the House

As one moves from the committee environs to the larger perspective of the House, two expressions occur with consistent regularity when new members are asked to describe their reactions: "labyrinthine" and "warm." More derogatory as well as more laudatory terms were frequently used, but these two underscore the paradox of life in the House. Although the House is usually more conservative, hierarchical, and impersonal than the Senate, freshman representatives still concede and are generally seduced by, the institution's tribal *gemeinschaft*-like qualities. Clubbiness is less "old boy" and ritualized than in the British

19. "Serious" is a matter of definition, of course. Both parties have had the formal power to vote on committee selections, including the annual reappointment of chairmen, for some time, but the rules recently adopted are somewhat tougher. Beginning in the 93rd Congress, both parties are using an automatic up—or—down secret vote on all potential chairmen and ranking minority members. If the person loses, the same procedure will be used for considering the next senior member.

20. Charles Jones notes that the standard minority complaints about staffing may be exaggerated since a Republican staffer, when checking with the Disbursing Office in 1966, found that one-half the House Republicans were *returning* clerk-hire funds each month. See his *The Minority Party in Congress* (Boston: Little, Brown, 1970), pp. 174–80.

House of Commons, but as Fenno remarks, ". . . a great deal of
what the freshman learns sums up to this—that the House is a little
world of its own and that legislative careers are shaped primarily by
what happens in that world."[21]

Conceding the impact of a generally favorable orientation
to the informal personal aspects of the institution did not preclude forceful criticism of many formal (and informal) practices.
Liberal Democrats, as one would expect, were particularly prone
to ambivalence in this regard. Said one:

> This is a great legislative body, every type of person
> imaginable is represented here. But many of the procedures
> are archaic, and the leadership is badly disorganized. I
> don't know what would have happened if the DSG had not
> been around. Some of these guys were born in the nine-
> teenth century, and still think you can make things happen
> by getting together with a small clique of friends. You
> see, Mr. McCormack is still living in a time when I guess
> that style worked, "You do this, Sam, and you do that, Joe,"
> but things have changed. We're a new breed of cats.

The function of elaborate informal norms of personal cordiality and tolerance for political differences—to soften the potentially divisive and disruptive character of policy disagreement—
was well understood and defended by most. For example:

> It's the way we get along with each other that's so different
> from the state legislature. People aren't so pushy, abrasive,
> headline-hunting. The members here are also much sharper
> and more honest. I can disagree with a man on every issue
> that comes down the pike, as I do with most of the Republi-
> can and southern fellows, but we still get along.

More systematic evidence on these themes is presented in
table 6.5. Whereas Republicans had been more critical of committee performance, here a small but significant minority of
Democrats emerges as the most dissatisfied with larger institutional practices: 26 percent generally disapproved of House procedures, believing that major structural reforms were necessary.
Majorities in each party, on the other hand, generally approved,
although they also felt "some" reforms were needed.

---

21. Fenno, "Freshman Congressman," p. 25.

Table 6.5

Orientations Toward Reforming the House of
Representatives, and Specific Comments on
Strengths and Weaknesses, Freshmen in the
89th Congress

| General Orientation | Democrats % | Democrats N | Republicans % | Republicans N |
|---|---|---|---|---|
| House as an Institution | | | | |
| little reform needed, approves | 12 | (7) | 21 | (3) |
| some reform needed, generally approves | 62 | (34) | 72 | (10) |
| major reforms needed, generally disapproves | 26 | (14) | — | |
| major reforms needed, greatly disapproves | — | | — | |
| not ascertained | — | | 7 | (1) |
| | 100 | (55) | 100 | (14) |

| Specific Characteristics[a] | Strengths DEM | Strengths REPUB | Weaknesses DEM | Weaknesses REPUB |
|---|---|---|---|---|
| Personal qualities of members (cordiality, honesty, etc.) | 57% | 85% | —% | —% |
| Party leadership (of own party) | 10 | 14 | 35 | 7 |
| Seniority system | 3 | — | 29 | 57 |
| Committee system for allocating workloads | 30 | 21 | 9 | — |
| Internal organization (staffs, scheduling, administration) | — | — | 38 | 28 |
| Amalgamate diverse interests through legislation | 46 | 14 | — | — |
| Constituency services | 21 | 28 | 3 | 7 |
| Oversight of agencies | — | 7 | 28 | 49 |
| Opportunity for freshman participation | 3 | 7 | — | — |
| N = | (55) | (14) | (55) | (14) |

[a] Percents add to more than 100 because members could name more than one characteristic.

Asked to indicate what were the greatest strengths and weaknesses in the body's operation, both party groups singled out the "personal qualities" of other members for strong approval. About one-third of the Democrats considered internal organization (e.g., scheduling, staffing), their own party leadership, and the excesses of seniority to be disasters. A minority also faulted the House on presidential oversight. This is somewhat intriguing since Democrats tended to see *committee* oversight procedures as a strength. The distinction between the corporate role of the House, and the more agency-specific oversight role of committees, was occasionally made during interviews. But minority freshmen were typically more consistent on this matter.

Compare these evaluations with those of the Republicans, one-half of whom agreed about the problems of seniority but who steadfastly cited the lack of executive oversight as the major weakness. The latter, as argued previously, was part of the GOP's general disapproval of the presidentially sponsored liberal legislation emanating from the House. Republican freshmen, unlike their Democratic colleagues, were almost unanimous in citing their own party's leadership as well organized. They reserved their criticism for factors controlled by Democrats.

As one asserted:

> The House has the worst organization I've ever been exposed to and I don't believe in the gospel of efficiency. They're just now beginning to introduce some automated procedures for handling the mounds of information we're expected to be familiar with. The interesting thing is how we manage to produce as much legislation as we have, but I doubt that fifty members know anything in detail about most of it. What can you expect given the age of the Speaker? Hell, he's living in the Thirties and doesn't realize— can't comprehend—the scope of the managerial revolution in this country.

Democrats who were dissatisfied generally reserved their strongest criticism for the Democratic leadership and the ubiquitous impact of seniority, seeing both as inextricably joined in the organizational problems of Congress.

> The leadership? It's lousy. They don't, and probably never will, understand some of us. Sure they're getting some good legislation through, and I think they've done a good job there, but they favor the status quo around here, that's how they got where they are. But we certainly could use some creative leadership that thinks beyond the immediate problems of how to get the budget passed. Have you read Dick Bolling's book? It probably hurts him with our more

senior colleagues, and I understand that some people around here don't trust him, but Bolling is at least thinking about some problems which the majority of the others have long since closed their minds to. I've often wondered whether things would have been different if he had been elected floor leader. . . .

However, most Democrats were less critical than the above, conceding here a strength, there a problem, arguing that various factors still made the House relatively responsive and efficient. One mountain state newcomer put it this way:

Sure I think the leadership has flaws, but they're getting the job done . . . some of the other men have had problems adjusting, but I think it depends on the individual. First, the [APSA] bipartisan orientation sessions were indispensable. I've heard it said that it used to take a member two-three years to simply be recognized, and that frequently senior men would ask, after that much time, who you were. That doesn't happen any more. Second, I haven't yet met a senior man who wouldn't sit down and talk rationally about whatever might be bothering you. We've beat the conservatives on every major issue in this Congress and the credit has got to go to the leadership.

Despite the adage, "The longer you're here, the more you'll like the seniority system," almost all felt it could be modified to give freshmen a slightly better batting average, whether in committee or elsewhere. For all the northern Democrats the greatest compensation came through identification with a domestic policy-making majority which many considered historic.

McCormick? Well, he's venerable. Albert? A nice guy. Boggs? Touchy and arrogant. But what the hell, they've been able to deliver . . . on education, medicare, civil rights, poverty programs, this is going to be the most productive Congress since FDR. So why complain? We rode over the southerners on Williams and Watson [who were stripped of seniority for supporting Goldwater], the DSG is functioning beautifully, and while we're a long way from solving many problems, at least we've started. The function of leadership is to get legislation passed and they've done it. I'm proud to be part of what's gone on.

The contrast with freshman Republicans could hardly have been sharper. Generally less critical of institutional procedures (excepting seniority), most were strongly unsettled by what they considered the "wholesale retreat of Congress in the face of Johnson's almost dictatorial powers." One particularly disgruntled Republican argued:

> You know what's happening in Congress, don't you? All we can do is rubber stamp or say No. I don't know whether the people are listening or not, but we're [the GOP] the only ones saying No around here—and I'm trying to make sure it's loud and clear ... the way Johnson has run roughshod over us has made this Congress very disappointing to me. The Democrats are in power and they just don't give a tinker's damn. They're going to spend this country into disaster.

Or, as another lamented:

> Elementary textbooks are always discussing the separation of powers in our national institutions. As far as I can tell, there hasn't been any during the 89th Congress: "Johnson proposes and Johnson disposes." Gerry Ford and the others have done a fine job, but how can you compete with the Johnson legions? They've got the resources, such as information—we're suffocating under the tons pouring out of the agencies—they've got the votes on the Democratic side, there's little we can do. . . .

Gertzog's intensive examination of minority freshmen in the 89th Congress stresses the importance of party as an organizing mechanism in reinforcing freshman Republican sentiment against Great Society legislation. As a group, they were more cohesively antiadministration than their veteran fellow Republicans, apparently feeling a greater need "to build a party record of strenuous opposition to the programmatic and political taunts of the majority."[22] I will return to this phenomenon since freshman Democrats tended to be *more proadministration* then did their senior northern colleagues. Both freshman groups achieved remarkable polarity on the major social-economic issues facing the United States in 1965–66. Psychologically, newcomers in the

---

22. Gertzog, "Frustration and Adaptation," p. 19.

House appeared to come to grips with their virtual exclusion from the policy-making process by moving toward consistently opposed ideological blocs on major roll-call votes.

Socialization in the House, however, is not solely a function of the representatives' reactions to existing norms, byways, and problems encountered in the institution. Wahlke and others have argued that important roles and orientations are probably shaped by a variety of prelegislative factors and that each legislator thus enters the institution with some degree of "role potential."[23] Three factors were critical in their emergence as opposition candidates the year before and will be examined here: ideology, political careerism, and levels of ambition. One additional "external" variable, district marginality, will also be considered.

## Sources of Institutional Discontent

Of the four variables, ideology in the guise of reform liberalism is perhaps the most frequently cited "explanation" of dissatisfaction with procedures in the House of Representatives. I place "explanation" in quotes since standard critiques of the House rarely formalize such matters, relying rather on a commonsense perception of who's doing what by way of reform activities.[24] Stereotypically the model critic is a liberal northern young Turk, disproportionately found in the Democratic party but occasionally popping up in suspect Republican circles like the Wednesday Club. Like many stereotypes, the image carries substantial truth: liberals have provided most of the combat troops in the continuing struggle to gain major internal reforms. But consider the data presented in table 6.6.

23. Wahlke et al., *Legislative System*, pp. 21–3. The work of Charles Bell and Charles Price on California legislators is probably the largest ongoing project which seeks to explore the effects of prelegislative experience on legislative role behavior. See their "The Impact of Pre-Legislative Experience on Legislators' Role Orientations" (Paper delivered at the 1969 annual meeting of the American Political Science Association). For a variety of reasons, I have decided against utilizing concepts stemming from role theory in the above analysis, preferring instead to stick with manifest attitudes toward life in the House.

24. Exceptions would include Roger Davidson, David Kovenock, and Michael O'Leary, *Congress in Crisis: Politics and Congressional Reform* (Belmont, Calif.: Wadsworth, 1966); and Richard Bolling, *House Out of Order* (New York: Dutton, 1965).

Table 6.6

Precongressional Ideology and Orientations Toward
Reform of Congress, Freshmen in the House
of Representatives, 89th Congress[a]

(*In Percent*)

| Item | Democrats | | Republicans | |
| --- | --- | --- | --- | --- |
| | LIBERALS | MODER-ATES | MODER-ATES | CONSER-VATIVES |
| House as in institution | | | | |
| greatly approves | 24 | — | 25 | 10 |
| generally approves (some reform needed) | 55 | 67 | 50 | 90 |
| generally disapproves (major reforms needed) | 21 | 33 | — | — |
| greatly disapproves (major reforms needed) | — | — | — | — |
| n.a. | — | — | 25 | — |
| | 100 | 100 | 100 | 100 |
| Committee performance | | | | |
| very satisfied | 41 | 33 | — | — |
| generally satisfied | 48 | 46 | 50 | 60 |
| generally dissatisfied | 11 | 21 | 50 | 40 |
| greatly dissatisfied | — | — | — | — |
| | 100 | 100 | 100 | 100 |
| N = | (28) | (24) | (4) | (10) |

[a] Only those candidates who responded to the original questionnaire *and* were subsequently interviewed are included above. The question, posed in a questionnaire which reached candidates within one week of the election in November, 1964, was: "On most issues today, do you think of yourself as Liberal, Middle-of-the-Road, Conservative, or what?" Moderate and middle-of-the-road are being interchangeably throughout this book. The few Democratic conservatives and Republican liberals have been omitted from the above.

The classification is based on *precongressional* ideological orientations. Among Democrats who thought of themselves as "moderate" before entering Congress, one-third felt major reforms were needed in the House as an institution, as contrasted with only one-fifth of the self-identified "liberals." More strikingly, an additional one-fifth of the liberal Democrats believed the House needed little change, while none of the moderates were that sanguine. As one would expect of middle-of-the-roaders, 67 percent of the moderates generally approved while still opting for some reform, whereas "only" 55 percent of the liberals selected this option. The numbers, of course, are tiny and the between-group differences should not be overemphasized. The more impressive factor is the extent of agreement across ideological groups within *both* parties.

While such a finding may seriously challenge the accuracy of the stereotype, there are a number of important caveats. The inadequacy of subjective positioning, discussed earlier, is also apparent here. Some check is provided later in this chapter (see table 6.12) where ADA roll-call voting scores are presented. Challengers who thought of themselves as liberal prior to entering the House generally behaved in a manner consistent with that belief: 86 percent gained ADA scores above 70 whereas only 38 percent of the Democratic moderates did so. Consistency is difficult to impose on any ideology, but there is some shred of it in the "Class of 89." Among the eight challengers who considered themselves liberal prior to entering Congress, and who scored 90 or above in ADA roll-call rankings, five thought major reforms in the House necessary. The remaining liberal internal reformer had a score of 60 on the ADA ratings. Conversely, four of the self-identified moderates who believed major reforms necessary scored under 70, two scored in the 70s, and two scored 80. To the extent freshmen are representative of their House parties, antiestablishment reform coalitions are possible, indeed absolutely necessary, among representatives who differ in their attitudes on other major issues. The threshold for freshman Democrats, and I would imagine this is equally true for their senior colleagues, is somewhere around 60 percent on the typical ADA roll-call voting records.[25]

One other hypothesis would hold that Democratic challengers, although liberal when they enter, rapidly become more conservative on procedural issues after spending a short time in the House. I have no way of directly testing this, but such an assertion fails to explain the findings for moderates. Surely it seems

25. Davidson and his colleagues found that both seniority *and* support for the Conservative Coalition increased a member's hostility to institutional change. See their analysis, *Congress in Crisis*, pp. 86–88.

questionable to argue that liberals are more susceptible to rapid internal socialization than are moderates. However, long-run (six terms plus) processes of socialization do operate, and powerfully so. Davidson, Kovenock, and O'Leary aptly demonstrate this: independent of ideology, congressmen with six or more terms rarely scored high on their reformism index while a substantial minority (41 percent) of those with less than six years were intensely concerned with internal reform.[26]

Excluding the five "pure" liberals noted above, institutional dissatisfaction among freshmen is not coterminous with precongressional ideological positions. And, excluding as well demands for *major* structural change, these data undercut the idea that the reform impulse is monopolized by the Democratic party: eight of the eleven GOP freshmen were inclined to urge some changes in House procedure, mainly directed toward majority party "abuses" of seniority.

Perhaps these findings cannot be generalized. But they support the idea that a larger institutional reform dimension functions somewhat independently of congressional attitudes toward other major policy issues in American life. Strategically, congressional reformers can count on picking up support from a pool of potential allies that is broader than the "100 percent ADA-type" argument would imply. Conversely, antireform coalitions in the House will usually be composed of individuals who part company (and party) on other domestic and international issues. The diverse support provided many of the proposals recommended by the Joint Committee on the Organization of Congress (1965) supports this contention, as does the coalition which finally produced the Legislative Reorganization Act of 1970.[27]

To be sure, the latter act focused on incremental change designed to improve the efficiency and openness with which individual members conduct their business, rather than provide for a fundamental redistribution of power in the House. But those changes relating to the potential power junior members can now bring to bear in party caucus and in their committees—if

26. Ibid., p. 88.
27. See *Congressional Quarterly Weekly Report*, 25 December 1970, pp. 3061–64, for a brief summary.

Table 6.7

District Marginality and Orientations Toward Reform
of the House, Freshmen in the 89th Congress
(*In Percent*)

| Item | Democrats | | Republicans | |
|---|---|---|---|---|
| | MARGINAL[a] | SAFE | MARGINAL | SAFE |
| *House as an institution* | | | | |
| greatly approves | 11 | 13 | 16 | 25 |
| generally approves; some | | | | |
| reform needed | 67 | 59 | 84 | 50 |
| generally disapproves; | | | | |
| major reforms needed | 22 | 28 | — | — |
| n.a. | — | — | — | 25 |
| | 100 | 100 | 100 | 100 |
| *Committee performance* | | | | |
| very satisfied | 44 | 35 | — | — |
| generally satisfied | 44 | 44 | 50 | 37 |
| generally dissatisfied | 12 | 21 | 50 | 63 |
| | 100 | 100 | 100 | 100 |
| *N* = | (41) | (14) | (6) | (8) |

[a] See chapter 4 for a discussion of the measures of marginality.

they are so inclined—are not meaningless.[28] "The test of the
effectiveness of this reform measure," *Congressional Quarterly*
observed, "is the extent to which these new procedures are implemented." This in turn depends on sustaining a vigorous reform-
oriented coalition in each of the House party organizations.

Moving to the next variable, district marginality (table 6.7),
one finds few surprises in the data. On both institutional and
committee evaluations, whether a freshman competes in a safe

28. Commentators generally argue that the two most important provisions of
the 1970 legislation centered on the options of recorded teller votes and recorded
committee votes. Here, however, I'm referring to the following (all subject to
committee majorities to become operative): require that committee meetings and
hearings be open to the public; permit broadcast and televised hearings; bar
proxy voting; require committees to announce hearings at least one week in advance. Left untouched, unless individual committees operate under such a rule,
is the power of chairmen to decide which bills will be considered. The most
significant change in party caucus rules, is the option of voting down party nominees
for committee chairmen.

or marginal district seems to exert little influence on his basic attitudes toward reform. Gertzog arrives at a very different conclusion, arguing that it is the marginal Republican "who experiences the greater frustration since he is less certain about his return, less certain that he will be able to make a contribution to public policy, and more insecure about his performance in the eyes of his constituents."[29] The dissimilarities in our findings are probably a function of the somewhat different independent variables under consideration, but I found little evidence of significant divergence among GOP freshmen on the basis of district competitiveness. Much of the influence Gertzog attributes to marginality could more properly be attributed to regional distinctions. Of nine marginal Republican freshmen, seven were newcomers from the Old South (I interviewed six of the nine). My interviews suggested a deep sense of mutual suspicion between these southerners and their northern colleagues during their first two years together, particularly since the southerners were from states (Alabama, Georgia, Mississippi) which had not sent Republicans to Congress since Reconstruction. Said one:

> Yes, there's a lot of talk about these things, and I've tried, but damnit, some of these people just won't let things be. Particularly after that speech by _____ during the Selma-Montgomery march [an unusually vicious attack on civil rights workers intimating that blacks and Catholic nuns were engaging in sexual intercourse]. It wasn't a very good speech, admittedly, but some of the folks back home had let him down on the facts. He's apologized countless times . . . but ever since, I've gone over to the floor, or in the cloakroom, and tried to be friendly and cordial with *all* my colleagues—arguing that our state was in a period of transition and that you had to have patience—and then one of those rascals would be takin' the floor and denouncing our state. I just couldn't sit back and take it, so we've probably stepped on some toes. I think in time things will heal. . . .

Whatever the effects of district marginality on other attitudes —a greater reliance on party leaders, for example—these data suggest that it has little impact on evaluations of House and committee performance.

29. Gertzog, "Frustration and Adaptation," p. 21.

Nor, somewhat more surprisingly, do the freshmen's precongressional attitude about a political career seem particularly germane for these evaluations. Most of the literature on Amateurs in politics, scholarly and otherwise, leads one to expect them to be substantially more critical of "business as usual" in the House. Conversely, Careerists are typically thought to be more realistic about the necessary steps involved in successfully moving up the ladder of political power; hence less prone to seek transformative change in existing political practices. A glance at the data in table 6.8 confounds that expectation.

To be sure, Amateurs were slightly more likely to fault the performance of their committees (27 percent) than were either the Transitionals (20 percent) or Careerists (6 percent). But the similarity of evaluations among the three groups when they considered the House as an institution is surprising.

One other variable, one that I believe is also formed prior to entering Congress, needs consideration. The index of political careerism, used above and developed to tap a generalized commitment to the political vocation among candidates, does not measure the future office ambitions of politicians after they have begun to score some degree of success. Ambition theory would predict that freshman legislators with a drive to move beyond the confines of the House would emerge as the most critical of ongoing procedures; not from any idealistic sense of what is right, although that may be a part, but from the need to calculate the effect of lack of change on emergent career possibilities.[30] Congress, as Joseph Schlesinger rightly observes, is procedurally conservative because the internal career structure is compatible with "static" ambitions, i.e., making a long-run career out of one particular office. Table 6.9 provides a direct test of the following predictions: those who are most anxious to build a career outside the House should have the least stake in adapting to existing procedures and will be the most dissatisfied; those whose career paths are geared to inching their way up the ladder in the House have the most to lose by sustained and combative criticism and will be the least dissatisfied.

Freshmen were classified as "externally" or "internally" ambitious on the basis of responses to an open-ended question

30. Joseph A. Schlesinger, *Ambition and Politics: Political Careers in the United States* (Chicago: Rand McNally, 1966), p. 209.

## Table 6.8

### Perspectives on the Political Career and Orientations Toward Reform of the House, Freshmen in the 89th Congress

(*In Percent*)

| Item | Democrats | | | Republicans | | |
|---|---|---|---|---|---|---|
| | CAREERIST | TRANSI-TIONAL | AMATEUR | CAREERIST | TRANSI-TIONAL | AMATEUR |
| *House as an institution* | | | | | | |
| greatly approves | 13 | 10 | 13 | 33 | 25 | — |
| generally approves; some reform needed | 61 | 45 | 74 | 67 | 75 | 100 |
| generally disapproves; major reforms needed | 26 | 45 | 13 | — | — | — |
| | 100 | 100 | 100 | 100 | 100 | 100 |
| *Committee Performance* | | | | | | |
| very satisfied | 36 | 60 | 33 | — | — | — |
| generally satisfied | 58 | 20 | 40 | 50 | 50 | 75 |
| generally dissatisfied | 6 | 20 | 27 | 50 | 50 | 25 |
| | 100 | 100 | 100 | 100 | 100 | 100 |
| N = | (31) | (10) | (14) | (6) | (4) | (4) |

[a] See chapter 3 for a discussion of the Index of Political Careerism.

Table 6.9

"Progressive" and "Static" Office Ambitions and Orientations Toward Reform of the House, Freshmen in the 89th Congress[a]

| Item | Democrats | | | | Republicans | | | |
|---|---|---|---|---|---|---|---|---|
| | PROGRESSIVE AND EXTERNAL OFFICE AMBITIONS | | STATIC AND INTERNAL OFFICE AMBITIONS | | PROGRESSIVE AND EXTERNAL OFFICE AMBITIONS | | STATIC AND INTERNAL AMBITIONS | |
| | % | N | % | N | % | N | % | N |
| *House as an institution* | | | | | | | | |
| greatly approves | 17 | (3) | 12 | (4) | 22 | (2) | 25 | (1) |
| generally approves; some reform needed | 34 | (6) | 78 | (26) | 88 | (7) | 75 | (3) |
| generally disapproves; major reforms needed | 51 | (9) | 10 | (3) | — | | — | |
| | 100 | (18) | 100 | (33) | 100 | (9) | 100 | (4) |
| *Committee performance* | | | | | | | | |
| very satisfied | 34 | | 40 | | — | | — | |
| generally satisfied | 44 | | 48 | | 55 | | 50 | |
| generally dissatisfied | 22 | | 12 | | 45 | | 50 | |
| | 100 | (18) | 100 | (33) | 100 | (9) | 100 | (4) |

[a] Congressmen were classified on the basis of responses to an open-ended question probing their future political plans. Progressive/External Office Ambitions were inferred where they were (1) a candidate for another office in 1966; (2) indicated they definitely would be in the near future; or, (3) were "open to the possibility" if a "good" opportunity presented itself. Static/Internal Office ambitions were inferred where they were either (1) definitely or probably remaining in the House; or, (2) unsure about the future except to be reelected to the House.

probing their future office-seeking behavior.[31] Among Democrats, this variable is the single most powerful predictor of institutional dissatisfaction of the four under consideration: 51 percent
of those with progressive and external office ambitions believed
major reforms necessary while only 10 percent of their more
House-oriented colleagues so argued. The impact of external
ambition, however, is muted by the very different findings shown
for Republicans, none of whom were predisposed toward major
reform. Parenthetically, GOP members were more frequently
externally ambitious (by a margin of 2–1) but did not apparently
view major overhaul in the institutions of Congress as a mechanism
for advancing those ambitions. While progressive ambitions magnify the imperfections of existing procedure, party affiliation obviously serves to screen the scope of demands for change.

     Unlike Everett G. Burkhalter, a sixty-seven-year-old freshman
who resigned his seat in the House in 1964 because he considered
the role of junior members intolerable, none of these respondents
suggested they were moving outside the House *because* they
were deeply unhappy with procedures. For most, I would argue,
external ambitions preceded entrance into the House and their
visible lack of clout during the first two years simply intensified
the desire to continue moving on. Evidence for this supposition,
I readily concede, is hardly overpowering. In fact, no way of
directly testing it can be developed with these data. But the
remarks of one freshman, who later ran for the Senate, are consistent with the argument and I believe not atypical:

> The House *is* frustrating and I hope that I can help change
> many of the reasons that make it so. But it's going to take a
> long time, too long to satisfy me. So much in this business is
> fortuitous . . . simple luck. If you're in the right place at the
> right time, you can go for the Senate, or perhaps the gover-
> norship. You have to plan and organize, however, so that you
> can take advantage of opportunities when they arise. That's
> how I got here. . . .
>
> [*Interviewer:* You seem to have a larger staff than many of the
> others I've talked with. Any particular reason?]
>
> [*Member, grinning rather shyly:*] Sure. I'm aiming for the
> Senate and their duties are to make sure luck keeps moving in
> the right direction.

31. See table 6.9 for the exact items.

Table 6.10

Electoral Outcome of the 1966 Election
as It Affected the Distribution of Members
Committed to Reforming the House of
Representatives, Freshmen in the
89th Congress
(*In Percent*)

|                                | Democrats[a] | |
| House as an Institution        | WINNERS | LOSERS |
| ------------------------------ | ------- | ------ |
| Little reform needed           | 12      | 14     |
| Some reform needed             | 58      | 66     |
| Major reform needed            | 30      | 20     |
|                                | 100     | 100    |
| N =                            | (34)    | (21)   |

[a] Republicans are excluded since only one lost.

Still, not all of those with external office ambitions were uniformly committed to major reform. Schlesinger, although generally correct, exaggerates the consequences of intense ambition when he argues that such drives force men to "guide" and "develop" rather than "reflect" current policy issues.[32] The bulk of these freshmen, Democratic or Republican, considered some change necessary, independent of variations in ambition. Their staying power over the five years preceding adoption of the 1970 reform bill was critical.

Despite substantial Democratic setbacks in 1966, reform-oriented Democrats and Republicans were not disproportionately defeated (see table 6.10). Increasing pressure on the House leadership was sustained precisely because most of these men and women were committed to remaining in Congress, mounted effective reelection campaigns, and hence were able to continue the struggle. Of course they were only part of a broader coalition involving more senior members; indeed with each successive term they themselves were gaining the necessary expertise, coalitional skills, and, need I add, seniority to be effective.

The 1970 act, modest as it was, addressed itself to two major problems most new members considered important: placing

32. Schlesinger, *Ambition and Politics*, p. 209.

greater *potential* control over chairmen by determined majorities within committees, and greater *potential* control over the selection of chairmen by equally determined majorities within each party.[33] Unlike many reform proposals, the bill does not divert legislative power to sources outside Congress, nor does it further centralize control in the party leadership inside the House. Implementing its provisions will require a strong commitment to building a career in the House of Representatives in a manner that enhances both the individual and collective aspects of congressional life.

Reform coalitions outside (and inside) the House which propose measures whose impact is perceived by most members as further reducing their power vis-à-vis the president and bureaucracy will certainly confront more substantial barriers. Proponents of the "executive-centered" and "responsible-party" models will always have enormous difficulty developing broad support inside Congress. This is not because most congressmen are nineteenth-century antiquarians (although some are) but rather, as one study suggests, because "of the sharp divergence in goals between reformists *outside* and *inside* Congress."[34]

Ralph Nader is surely correct when he argues that Congress is a perennial underachiever. From the view point of new members, correcting that problem is a matter of expanding the power resources available to each congressman. Utilizing these resources, on the other hand, will require both individual imagination and institutional flexibility.

## Ideology and Policy Response

Despite the low probability of a large membership turnover during any single Congress, a factor normally acting to foreclose the possibility of dramatic changes in policy output from session to session, three forces operated to make the 89th a remarkably productive and innovative exception.

33. The second change was not created by the bill, but adopted by each of the party caucuses. All the problems which bear on how determined a "determined" majority must be to achieve success are also implicit in the Legislative Reorganization Act. Only time will permit an evaluation of whether these changes, like some of their counterparts in 1946, are symbolic rather than real.

34. Davidson et al., *Congress in Crisis*, p. 89.

First, a subtle but significant redistribution of internal power favoring northern Democrats had been underway for fifteen years prior to the 1964 election. The preeminence of the "conservative coalition," seemingly invulnerable before the 89th Congress, was anchored in the 1946 northern electoral sweep by Republicans and the continuing Democratic dominance in the South. The joint impact of both had been in a long-run process of decline: liberal Democrats were regaining northern districts and gradually accumulating the necessary seniority to recapture powerful committee positions from their southern colleagues.[35]

Second, the development of Johnson's domestic legislative program, incorporating proposals which had been on the labor-liberal back burner for years, was aggressively defended and pushed during both sessions. While empirical research[36] has been unable to document that conditions were met for a "national mandate," both the Johnson Administration and the prestigious media acted *as though* such conditions were operative.

Third, and most important for this book, the liberal ideological commitment of most freshman Democrats before they entered Congress was activated on a variety of critical roll-call votes. As other studies have found, Democratic freshmen moved as a "phalanx" in supporting liberal programs even though 41 of the 66 were from districts that had previously elected Republicans.[37] GOP freshmen moved just as cohesively—in the opposite direction.

Few groups could better meet the assumptions of responsible party government theorists than did these freshmen—particularly

35. While southern Democrats were heavily overrepresented in powerful committee positions during the 1950s, this had been significantly reduced by 1969. Constituting approximately one-third of the Democratic delegation, southerners in 1969 held 8 of 17 chairmanships (down 5 since 1956); 37 percent of subcommittee chairmanships (down from 53 percent in 1964); and 34 percent of the top three positions on congressional committees (down from 49 percent in 1964). Moreover, the number of northern "safe" seats had increased substantially over the past twenty years while the number of southern safe districts declined. For data and extended analysis of the implications of this transformation, see Raymond Wolfinger and Joan Heifetz Hollinger, "Safe Seats, Seniority, and Power in Congress," in *Readings on Congress*, ed. Raymond Wolfinger (Englewood Cliffs, N.J.: Prentice-Hall, 1971), pp. 36–59.

36. Marvin E. Weinbaum and Dennis Judd, "In Search of a Mandated Congress," *Midwest Journal of Political Science* (May 1970): 276–302.

37. Ibid., pp. 301–2; and Thomas P. Murphy, "Political Ethics in a Coattail Congress," *Ethics* (1966–67): 291–96.

as those assumptions bear on how opposition candidates, once in power, ought to behave. The concept of a critical minority is a slippery numerical device when applied to roll-call voting in the House,[38] but Democratic freshmen certainly provided the winning margins on a variety of progressive legislative proposals. As Weinbaum and Judd conclude, ". . . freshman Democrats in 1965 provided about twice the support for all administration bills and almost three times the support for Larger Federal Role items than would have their Republican predecessors."[39] Their votes were critical for:

—changes in House procedures which permitted readoption of the 21-day rule, a device permitting floor action on any bill tied up by the Rules Committee 21 days (224–202: D., 208–79; R., 16–123);

—passage of the Housing and Urban Development Act (217–184: D., 208–66; R., 9–118);

—defeat of efforts by anti-civil rights forces to delete the open-housing provision of the 1966 Civil Rights Act (222–190: D., 172–104; R., 50–86);

—defeat of a motion that would have killed Rent Supplements for the poor (208–202: D., 204–72; R., 4–130);

—defeat of efforts by anti-OEO forces to cut funding by approximately 40 percent (227–178: D., 214–57; R., 13–121);

—passage of legislation repealing Section 14B (situs-picketing) of the Taft-Hartley Act (221–203: D., 200–86; R., 21–117).

In addition, overwhelming majorities of freshman Democrats supported, and their Republican cohorts opposed, major changes in federal responsibility for education and medical care. The former, the Elementary and Secondary Education Act of 1965, broke ten years of opposition to massive federal aid to

38. Selection of blocs providing "the winning margin" might almost as easily focus on farm Democrats, western Democrats, Democrats from the "Class of 86" (1959–60), or the 82nd Congress (1949–50), but crediting freshmen in the 89th Congress who replaced Republicans from the 88th Congress seems reasonable. See Murphy, "Political Ethics," for a detailed presentation of voting data on these freshmen.

39. Weinbaum and Judd, "Mandated Congress," p. 300.

education (263–153: D., 228–57; R., 35–96); the latter, Medicare, was passed following a twenty-five-year struggle to create a compulsory health insurance program for persons sixty-five and over (313–115: D., 248–42; R., 65–73).

Any doubt about the relatively greater degree of liberalism among freshman Democrats, and conservatism among Republicans, should be dispelled by a glance at table 6.11. Freshmen in both parties are at the polar ends of the distributions on both administration support scores and federal role scores. Congressmen who thought of themselves as liberal, middle of the road, or conservative *before* entering the House generally behaved in a manner consistent with common sense expectations about those orientations. Data are presented in table 6.12. Twenty-two of the twenty-eight self-identified liberals scored in excess of 70 on ADA ratings for the 89th Congress; nine of twenty-four moderate Democratic freshmen scored that high. The average for liberals was 80, for moderates, 57. As I will show later, Democratic cohesion on economic issues, and divergence on noneconomic issues, does not disappear over time, even though the problems of the late 1960s increasingly outpaced the original dimensions of the Great Society.

Interpreting the lack of *intraparty* differences for Republican freshmen is somewhat more difficult. Twelve of the fourteen who were interviewed received ADA scores during 1965–66 of zero, even though four had thought of themselves during the 1964 campaign as middle of the road. For those who would object that ADA scores do not sufficiently tap dimensions of Republican "liberalism," I might add that embedded in this ADA index was a test of civil rights commitment. Thirteen of the GOP freshmen, including three of the four self-styled moderates, voted to support Representative Arch Moore's (R.-W.Va.) motion to recommit the Civil Rights Act of 1966 with instructions to delete Title IV, the open-housing title. The motion was defeated 222–190 with, incidentally, the assistance of fifty veteran "moderate" Republicans.

On other measures, presidential support scores for example, three of these moderate Republican freshmen did score higher than the majority of their self-identified conservative brethren.[40] Among these few GOP freshmen, however, party was a better predictor of

40. Republicans ranged from a high of 59 (Conable) to a low of 16 (Martin). See Gertzog, "Frustration and Adaptation," p. 21.

Table 6.11

Freshman Congressmen and Their Veteran Colleagues in the 89th Congress, 1965–66.
Average Administration Support and Larger Federal Role Scores[a]

| | Freshman Northern Democrats | Veteran North Democrats | Freshman Southern Democrats | Veteran Southern Democrats | Veteran Republicans | Freshman Republicans |
|---|---|---|---|---|---|---|
| Administration support | 85 | 79 | 64 | 55 | 42 | 37 |
| Federal role | 95 | 93 | 57 | 49 | 36 | 24 |

[a] Adapted from Marvin G. Weinbaum and Denis R. Judd, "In Search of a Mandated Congress," *Midwest Journal of Political Science* (May 1970): 289.

Table 6.12

Precongressional Ideology and ADA Roll-Call Voting
Scores of Freshmen in the 89th Congress,
1965–66 (*In Numbers*)[a]

| ADA Score[b] | Democrats[c] | | Republicans | |
|---|---|---|---|---|
| | LIBERALS | MODERATES | MODERATES | CONSERVA- TIVES |
| Session average (%) | *80* | *57* | *3* | *00* |
| 100–90 | 8 | — | — | — |
| 89–80 | 7 | 5 | — | — |
| 79–70 | 7 | 4 | — | — |
| 69–60 | 3 | 3 | — | — |
| 59–50 | 2 | 6 | — | — |
| 49–40 | 1 | 4 | — | — |
| 39–30 | — | — | — | — |
| 29–20 | — | 1 | — | — |
| 19–10 | — | 1 | — | — |
| 9–1 | — | — | 2 | — |
| 0 | — | — | 2 | 10 |
| *N* = | (28) | (24) | (4) | (10) |

[a] Only those candidates who responded to the original questionnaire and were later interviewed are included above.

[b] This ranking is based on the ADA's summated index for the second session, January to November 1966.

[c] Two self-classified conservative Democrats were omitted from the above. Congressmen were classified as liberal, moderate, and conservative on the basis of a self-anchoring question in a questionnaire which reached them one week after the election of 1964.

roll-call voting than was ideology.[41] This changes slightly for moderates over time, as the data on their behavior between 1966 and 1970 will show. But as Gertzog has argued, their solidarity in the 89th Congress seems to be a reflection of the somewhat more intense need for minority freshmen to use "party as an organizing force to resolve their frustrations when having to deal with majority party control, domination, and contempt."[42]

Despite countervailing pressures stemming from the diversity of political life in the United States, each cadre of party freshmen

41. On many Great Society economic issues, the same statement applies to Democrats; southern freshmen who were Democratic scored higher on both federal role and administration support scales than did Republicans.

42. Gertzog, "Frustration and Adaptation," p. 21.

redeemed in remarkably consistent fashion the *domestic* platform promises of Republicans and Democrats in 1964. Certainly, roll-call votes are imperfect measures of "real" attitudes toward public policy. Options for subtle influence or evasion are available throughout the legislative process. Rare is the legislator who, in response to imagined or real pressures from either inside or outside Congress, has *never* voted against his beliefs, preferring to live to fight another day. "Congressmen," wrote one observer, "are running for public office, not canonization." But the move from outside to inside Congress did not undercut most of these challengers' basic commitment—whether liberal or conservative— to act in a way they deemed essential, despite the popular folklore which suggests American party politicians are obsessed with little else than reelection and personal gain.

Although not representative in his estimate of the constituency problems associated with ideological consistency, the following comment from a midwestern Democrat is typical of how freshman Democrats perceived their responsibilities on roll-call votes:

> Let me tell you a story. Of course I'm more liberal than my district, but I've been a lifelong liberal Democrat and I didn't come down here to simply play games with a bunch of people back home whom I wouldn't fart with—so to speak— normally. I've done a better job, I'm sure, than my predecessor, servicing my constituency, but I'm appalled by the war and the poverty programs are absolutely necessary. When I go back I tell them exactly that and many obviously don't like it. So what? I'm here to help with the President's program and I intend to do it . . . except the war . . . things have got to change, and change soon, in Vietnam. . . .

If one were to substitute the code words "conservative," "Republican," and "oppose," in place of "liberal," "Democratic," and "support," the essence of the statement could easily have been articulated by a Republican freshman. The dilemmas of an essentially negative oppositional role, as Charles Jones has argued, were clearly apparent among Republican freshmen during 1965–66; both their junior status and the fledgling character of the GOP's House leadership under Gerry Ford combined to prevent them from responding in more creative ways to a determined and innovative majority. One year later, following a substantial comeback during the 1966 mid-term elections, Jones' data show that House Republicans experienced a sharp increase in positive and constructive opposition strategies.[43]

Other forms of opposition were emerging, however, as the Great Society increasingly focused on expanding one war in Vietnam and preventing another from occurring in the urban streets at home.

43. Jones, *Minority Party*, pp. 182–83.

# 7

# BEYOND
# THE 89TH CONGRESS

The 89th Congress focused the domestic congressional policy-making agenda in a sharp and highly productive manner. Whether the four major areas of achievement—poverty, education, health, civil rights—were legislated with appropriate wisdom and foresight is a judgment I shall leave to the value premises of the reader. Importantly, such productivity certainly challenged the previous image of Congress as structurally incapable of responding to (some) widely perceived deficiencies in the American social system. That this response was rapidly followed by a further deepening crisis in foreign and domestic policy should not be surprising.

James Sundquist, among others, has suggested the 89th Congress was the finale of a fifteen-year struggle to act on the policy agenda of the late 1940s and 1950s.[1] The lag in institutional responsiveness, for some not enough, for me too much, is a familiar feature of American political history. Sundquist summarizes the problem astutely, arguing "... when the climactic congressional session of 1965 adjourned, a decade of ardor had finally produced a battery of measures that brought the country, in some respects, abreast of the major social problems of the times ... but much of

1. In his *Politics and Policy: The Eisenhower, Kennedy, and Johnson Years* (Washington, D.C.: Brookings, 1968), pp. 506–37.

the legislation fell short of the hopes ... and boasts ... of those
who sponsored it ... from the activist standpoint, the country's
problems were mounting faster than they were being met. ..."[2]

Three events were hastening the reopening of yet another
cycle in the policy-making process:[3] the Watts insurrection and
the wave of similar protests in northern urban areas, intensifying
the political mobilization of blacks and other minorities; the Johnson Administration's escalation of American involvement in Vietnam; and, of course, the Free Speech Movement and the subsequent six years of intense student political activism.

Congress, like other institutions, reflected a variety of different, sometimes conflicting, responses to these changes in environmental cues. Individually and collectively, those members of the
Class of 89 who survived the 1966 and 1968 elections confronted
a number of issues which were outside the usual shape of the
liberal-activist/conservative-restrictionist continuum. While methodologically rigorous longitudinal analysis of the policy behavior
of the Class of 89 outruns both my data and the intent of this
chapter, some attempt to sketch their general response seems useful.

## Ideological Patterns: 1966–70

Various commentators have asserted over the past six years
that the "old politics" are dying,[4] that liberals and conservatives
by the standards of the New Deal or even Great Society, have all
become equally conservative under the impact of the turbulent

2. Ibid., p. 536.

3. Cyclical thinking about the development, response, and implementation of
policy demands can be misleading since it frequently assumes an automatic response to "disturbances" in the environment. While I believe the American political system has been able to respond to some demands, simultaneously ignoring
others, such a conclusion about the future seems (1) unduly optimistic, and (2) need-
lessly deterministic.

4. The term "new politics" is highly imprecise, sometimes referring to technological changes in campaign management, other times referring to the coalition
that opposed Johnson and supported McCarthy, Kennedy, or McGovern. Here the
"death" of the "old politics" is used to summarize the assorted hopes, predictions,
commentaries, and fantasies of those who saw the New Deal coalition disappearing
in 1967–68.

forces of the late 1960s.[5] Such a judgment has considerable intuitive appeal: early (1964–68) opposition to the Vietnam war and differences over how to respond to the demands of mobilized blacks, Chicanos, Indians, women, antiwar protesters, radical youth, Wallace sympathizers, and a host of post-New Deal issues badly fractured the activist structure of both major parties. *Congressional Quarterly* wrote that ". . . the 1961–70 decade saw a significant shift in voting behavior by a large bloc of senior House Democrats whose early New Deal liberalism yielded to a conservative stance on Civil Rights and foreign policy issues."[6] Changes in issue content and emphasis, plus some of the normal spin-offs of seniority, have quite obviously had a conservative impact on *some* veteran Democratic and Republican congressmen.[7] It would be surprising if this weren't the case.

Of more direct concern here is how far such changes reached into the ranks of those men and women first elected during the early part of the Johnson years and who remained in the House. All first competed before the emergence of newer patterns of conflict; few had difficulty thinking of themselves as liberals, moderates, or conservatives within the context of the Great Society; most had to face up to the conflicting demands of the 1966–70 period.

Two types of evidence will be used to explore change and continuity: voting on four critical issues during 1966–70; and the ADA's summated index of liberalism for each session. I've retained the ADA's roll-call index for both the 90th and 91st Congresses

5. Perhaps the most persistent assertion of critics in and around the New Left. The statement may be true or false, depending on one's ideological benchmarks, but it certainly is inaccurate as a comparative generalization focusing on dominant values associated with either the New Deal or Great Society. From the viewpoint of serious radical alternatives, periods of American reform have always been "conservative," i.e., designed to conserve political institutions while opening them to new and/or different constituencies. Among the more persuasive on this pattern of institutional response is Theodore J. Lowi, *The End of Liberalism* (New York: Norton, 1969), pp. 101–286. His prescription is less convincing.

6. *Congressional Quarterly Weekly Report*, 12 March 1971.

7. The opposite (more liberalizing effect) also appears to be the case with some Republicans inside the House: Charles Mosher, Charles Whalen, Paul McCloskey, Donald Riegle; and outside: Wally Hickel, Charles Goodell, William Saxbe, and that infamous former non-Republican Republican, John Lindsay. A similar argument could be made concerning Democrats, especially, governors in the so-called New South such as Reuben Askew or Jimmy Carter.

since Americans for Democratic Action shifted position in response to the events of the last decade and theirs is the most sensitive index to the newer dimensions of conflict. In 1961, 7 of 10 ADA votes dealt with increasing the scope of government activity in economic aid and social welfare issues; in 1970, 13 of 25 selected votes focused on civil rights/civil liberties and foreign aid/defense policy.

Consider the data presented in table 7.1. Despite shifts in both public issues and the ADA index, members of the Class of 89, Democrat and Republican, remained remarkably consistent over the four-year period 1966–70. Indeed, both Democratic and Republican moderates during the early days of the Great Society became slightly more liberal as they gained more seniority. The average ADA support percentage for Democratic moderates during the 89th was 57, rising to 68 in the 90th and 66 in the 91st Congresses. Liberal Democrats and conservative Republicans, as groups, were virtually unshakable. The former started with an average ADA score of 80 during the 89th Congress, increased to 90 for the 90th, and returned to 80 for the 91st; the latter refused to budge, scoring perfect anti-ADA ratings in each of the three terms.

Clearly this challenges the argument that the late 1960s witnessed a uniform shift to the Right, at least among these pre-"new politics" congressmen. Individual shifts, among veterans and among a minority of these representatives, were noticeable. Typically such behavior received the most coverage from the popular press. Two examples among this group, representing the divergent push and pull within the Democratic party, are Frank Annunzio, a Chicago Democrat, and Eligio de la Garza, an organization Democrat from Texas. Annunzio, like most of Cook County's inner-city delegation, is a classic New Deal labor-liberal. His ADA score during 1965–66, 100 percent, had dropped to 40 by 1969–70. On the other hand, consider de la Garza. Identified with the Connally wing of the Texas Democratic party, his ADA score went from 29 during the 89th Congress to 37 in the 90th and 40 in the 91st. Of Texas Democrats, de la Garza's ADA ratings in the 91st Congress were third highest, below only Bob Eckhardt (87) and Henry Gonzalez (67).

Or ponder individual shifts among some of the Republicans. J. William Stanton, entering the House from a district in the eastern Cleveland suburbs (Lake County), joined most of his fresh-

Table 7.1

Precongressional Ideology and ADA Roll-Call Voting Scores of the Class of 89 in the 90th Congress, 1967–68, and the 91st Congress, 1969–70

(In Numbers)

| ADA Index[c] | 90th Congress[a] | | | | 91st Congress[b] | | | |
|---|---|---|---|---|---|---|---|---|
| | Democrats | | Republicans | | Democrats | | Republicans | |
| | LIB-ERAL | MOD-ERATE | MOD-ERATE | CONSER-VATIVE | LIB-ERAL | MOD-ERATE | MOD-ERATE | CONSER-VATIVE |
| Session average (%) | 90 | 68 | 18 | 00 | 80 | 66 | 12 | 00 |
| 100–90 | 10 | 3 | — | — | 6 | 2 | — | — |
| 89–80 | 1 | 4 | — | — | 5 | 3 | — | — |
| 79–70 | 3 | 1 | — | — | — | — | — | — |
| 69–60 | 1 | — | — | — | 1 | 2 | — | — |
| 59–50 | 2 | 1 | — | — | — | 1 | — | — |
| 49–40 | 2 | 2 | 1 | — | 2 | 1 | — | — |
| 39–30 | — | 2 | — | — | 1 | 2 | 1 | — |
| 29–20 | — | — | 1 | — | — | — | 1 | — |
| 19–10 | — | — | 1 | — | — | — | — | — |
| 9–1 | — | — | 1 | — | — | — | 1 | — |
| 0 | — | — | — | 9 | — | — | — | 8 |
| N = | (19) | (13) | (4) | (9) | (15) | (11) | (3) | (8) |

[a] ADA summated liberalism index for the second session, 12 votes, January to November 1968.
[b] ADA summated liberalism index for the first session, 15 votes, January to November 1969. In both, failure to vote lowers the member's score.
[c] The index represents the percentage of votes the member cast which supported the ADA's position.

man colleagues in the 89th with a perfect record of opposition
(.00), but subsequently raised that average to 42 percent support
during 1968 and 27 percent during 1969. Stanton's COPE record
also increased, and more dramatically, from 8 in the 89th to 80 in
the 91st. During this same period, Barber Conable (R.-N.Y.),
generally conceded a GOP moderate, moved upward in his ADA
ratings more cautiously: from 6 to 17 to 27 percent support.

The significant finding, however, is how *atypical* each of the
above are; neither collectively nor individually did a majority of
these original challengers begin to vote in a manner that differed
substantially from what could have been expected as the older
points of liberal-conservative tension gave way to new and conflicting issues. Democratic and Republican members of the Class
of 89 still distribute in a fashion that is highly differentiated. More
important, most self-identified liberals and conservatives from the
early 1960s were still voting in the late 1960s in a way that readers
of the *New Republic* or *National Review* would find highly
comprehensible.

## Critical Issues: 1966–70

Issue conflict had shifted, however, and it is therefore important to push this analysis further by examining their behavior
on four critical policy areas, each of which came to the floor for a
vote during 1968 or 1969. Specific votes involved: (1) efforts to
retaliate against the waves of student protest activity during 1967–
69; (2) legislation designed to reverse the Warren Court's decisions on defendants rights, generally increasing the power of
police and law-enforcement authorities to move against crime,
and disproportionately aimed at groups within the black communities and at white radicals; (3) legislation directed against large-
scale antiwar protest activity in Washington, whether nonviolent or
violent; and (4) efforts to secure bipartisan congressional endorsement for Nixon's policy of sometime demobilization in Vietnam.
The ADA formally opposed each of the legislative measures I've
selected for this period.[8]

8. Material for the discussion which follows has been culled from a variety of
sources, but primarily the *Congressional Record* and *Congressional Quarterly Al-
manacs, 1968, 1969, 1970.*

In the aftermath of increasingly violent confrontations between protesting students and police during 1967–68, first at Berkeley, then at San Francisco State, Wisconsin, and finally Columbia, the House approved an amendment to the Higher Education Bill of 1968 requiring universities to withhold federally backed aid or scholarships from students "who willfully refused to obey a lawful regulation of a college," when that refusal was of a "serious" nature or "disrupted" the "normal" operations of an institution.

The Columbia strike, igniting in April 1968, galvanized anti-protest forces in the House around Representative Louis Wyman's (R.-N.H.) approach to the "problem" and they managed to beat back attempts by opponents to modify his amendment. Ultimately Wyman's amendment was opposed by most university administrations as cumbersome, vague, perhaps unconstitutional. Bob Eckhardt (D.-Tex.), one of a small number of House members who voted against the Wyman provision, observed that during his university days at Texas, a critical student news editorial was considered "disruptive" and that the Wyman provision placed few restraints on the ability of determined and hostile administrators to withdraw federal support whatever the situation. His argument apparently went unheeded; the House buried Wyman's opponents, 306–54.

How much symbolic posturing was involved in the actual vote by members who otherwise agreed with Eckhardt is difficult to ascertain. The Wyman provision was later deleted by Senate opponents in conference and a subsequent bill passed carrying very different provisions (e.g., guaranteeing hearings, requiring that the students must have committed legally criminal acts, giving universities more latitude rather than mandating the withdrawal of support). The possibility of constituency window dressing is obvious. But the data still provide a useful comparison of congressional response. Breakdowns are provided in table 7.2.

Within the Democratic party, northern members clearly *favored* the Wyman amendment (63 percent voted aye), but the distribution among northern Democrats from the 89th Congress is almost reversed (54 percent voted nay). Among those who considered themselves liberal in 1964, and who survived the 1966 mid-term elections, 13 voted against and 6 for; among Democratic moderates, the ratio was 2–11. Republicans from the 89th were

## Table 7.2

### Critical Issues and the Response of the Class of 89 in the 90th Congress, 2nd Session, 1968

| Voting Groups | Student Protest Legislation[a] | | | | Omnibus Crime Legislation[b] | | | |
|---|---|---|---|---|---|---|---|---|
| | PRO-ADA[c] | | ANTI-ADA | | PRO-ADA | | ANTI-ADA | |
| | N | % | N | % | N | % | N | % |
| All Democrats | 51 | | 151 | | 53 | | 153 | |
| northern Dems | 49 | 37 | 83 | 63 | 50 | 40 | 76 | 60 |
| southern Dems | 2 | 3 | 68 | 97 | 3 | 5 | 77 | 95 |
| 89th northern Dems[d] | 15 | 54 | 13 | 46 | 13 | 48 | 14 | 52 |
| 89th southern Dems | — | — | 8 | 100 | — | — | 8 | 100 |
| All Republicans | 3 | | 155 | | 7 | | 165 | |
| 89th Republicans | — | — | 14 | 100 | — | — | 14 | 100 |

[a] Amendment by Louis Wyman (R.-N.H.) to the Higher Education Bill of 1968 requiring universities to withhold aid from students "who willfully refuse to obey a lawful regulation of the institution" when the refusal was of a "serious" nature or "disrupted" the "normal" operations of the university. Wyman's amendment passed (306–54) but was dropped during conference. A very different amendment later found its way onto an education appropriations bill.

[b] Omnibus Crime Bill of 1968, containing provisions reversing Supreme Court decisions such as *Miranda* v. *Arizona* and giving Justice and local police increased latitude in wiretapping and bugging operations. Vote was on a Celler motion mandating a conference committee in the hope Senate-added provisions could be eliminated. Celler lost. 318–60.

[c] "Pro-ADA" position was a vote against the Wyman amendment, for the Celler motion.

[d] Only those congressmen who were interviewed are tabulated above.

unanimously anti-ADA on this vote, as well as the other three selected issues. Although there are a few individual surprises in regional distributions, most of the second-term Democrats voted as one would expect: all the southern contingent, including some moderates, voted with Wyman; border-state Democrats like Machen (Md.), Kee (W. Va.), and Hungate (Mo.) joined their southern colleagues, as did an occasional northeastern or western liberal (Brock Adams of Washington, for example). Still the core of opposition sprang from the traditional sources of ADA support in the House—the Northeast and urbanized Midwest and Far West.[9] Even the two Cook County members from the 89th (Annunzio and Dan Ronan) joined their usually more liberal colleagues and parted company with the rest of the Chicago delegation, in opposing Wyman's amendment.[10]

On a second component of what Richard Scammon and Ben Wattenburg call the Social Issue, crime, 1968 provided a critical test of different approaches to the problem. The Omnibus Crime Bill of 1968 is a collection of both good and bad elements from the viewpoint of the ADA. It is widely conceded to be the most sweeping crime legislation developed and passed over the last twenty years. Reluctantly signed by Johnson during the summer, the final legislative product bore little resemblance to his original Safe Streets Act of 1967, or to the first bill approved and sent to the Senate by the House in early 1968.

Senator McClellan's Judiciary Subcommittee on Criminal Laws and Procedures had added three major provisions, all of which were opposed by the Johnson Administration and most Senate liberals. They were (1) the use of block grants for assisting states and communities to develop "anticrime" programs including the purchase of "antiriot" hardware; (2) the reversal of three Supreme Court decisions involving defendant's rights, including *Miranda v. Arizona,* by allowing confessions to be admissible in evidence if they were taken "voluntarily," even if the defendant

9. John Culver (D.- Iowa), the only remaining member of five Democrats elected from his state to the Class of 89, is an exception to this rule. Culver voted pro-ADA (against the Wyman amendment), as he did on two of the three other selected issues. On the other hand, Culver was widely regarded as hawkish on the war prior to 1968 and his vote on the Vietnam issue covered later reflects this tension. He voted with the doves on a procedural question, against them on the substantive issue.

10. This excludes Sidney Yates, who also opposed the Wyman amendment.

had not been warned of his Constitutional right to remain silent; and (3) the granting of new and broader prerogatives to police and the Justice Department in the use of bugging and wiretapping for a variety of issues beyond "national security." Despite disclaimers, it is difficult not to believe that each of these could be used as not very subtle forms of political repression.

Other provisions—a limited gun-control measure and manpower funds for police training and criminology research, for example—increased the coalitional base supporting the bill. "Who," asked one member, "could vote against the police, against gun controls, and 'for' crime in the summer of 1968?" Two months after Martin Luther King, Jr., was assassinated, and twelve hours following the shooting of Robert Kennedy, the House defeated a move by Emanuel Celler to change the McClellan provisions. Celler had moved to disagree to the Senate amendments to the bill and force a conference with that body to resolve differences. Proponents of the Omnibus Crime Bill effectively used the modest gun-control provisions, and the powerful immediate impact of Kennedy's death, as one tactic in riding over Celler's objections. Kennedy (and one would predict, King) had been a vigorous opponent of the three provisions added by McClellan's subcommittee. Such inconvenient facts were ignored by those defending the legislation. The names of King and Kennedy were constantly invoked as symbolic testimony to the need for rapid action. Celler and his allies were simply overwhelmed, 318–60.

Compare again the behavior of Democrats from the 89th and other Congresses: as a group northern second-termers were slightly more likely to support the Celler motion than were their more veteran colleagues, but the margin is reduced from the earlier vote on students. Among liberals, the ratio was 12–7 in support of Celler; among moderates, 1–12. Again southern Democrats and all the Republicans from the 89th were united in opposing the ADA position. Some individual shuffling again occurred among the Class of 89: Representatives Annunzio and Ronan rejoined the moderate-conservative majority in control of the House; Brock Adams returned to the pro-ADA liberal opposition; border-state second-term members continued in unanimous support of the then working majority. But, importantly, northern Democratic members from the 89th were still providing a significant share (27 percent) of the shrinking, but highly liberal minority while their Republican cohorts were steadfastly not adding to the tiny number of GOP mavericks.

Five months and the "Siege of Chicago" later, Richard Nixon entered the White House and a slightly diminished but increasingly senior number of third-term members (43, down 5 Democrats and 1 Republican from the previous session) returned to open the 91st Congress. Nixon's narrow victory was reflected in minuscule party shifts in the House as Republicans managed a net gain of only four seats.

Two issues seem important as further measures of continuity and change among this group of congressmen. First, despite (because of?) a marked shift in public and elite opinion concerning the Vietnam war,[11] a small number of senior House members were determined to retaliate against what they considered the excesses of antiwar protest activity over the past two years. These protests not only converged on Chicago during the summer of 1968, and were sustained throughout the campaign, but dramatically increased (in terms of national planning and ultimately number of participants) *after* the 1968 election. Following the victory of Nixon and preceding by many months the actual Vietnam Moratorium in October and the Student Mobilization D.C. Demonstrations in November 1969 (drawing, as the reader might recall, 400,000 persons), Mendel Rivers and his allies on the House Armed Services Committee had begun angling for adoption of "antipicket" legislation designed to restrict the scope and focus of antiwar protests. These efforts were brought to successful fruition in an August 1969 vote.

The second issue developed partly in response to the fall antiwar planning activity in Washington, partly as an initiative to give Nixon some congressional sanction for his Vietnam war policy. House leaders agreed on the necessity of a joint resolution "expressing support for the President in his efforts to negotiate a just

11. See John D. Mueller, "Trends in Popular Support for the Wars in Korea and Vietnam," *American Political Science Review* (June 1971): 358–76; Harlan Hahn, "Correlates of Public Sentiments About War: Local Referenda on the Vietnam Issue," *American Political Science Review* (December 1970): 1186–98; and Philip Converse and Howard Schuman, " 'Silent Majorities' and the Vietnam War," *Scientific American* (June 1970): 17–25.

peace in Vietnam. . . ." The so-called Peace with Justice in Vietnam Resolution passed in December 1969. Both issues tap dimensions relating to the conflicting currents generated by the Vietnam
war.

The first vote, coming on a motion to recommit and delete
the antipicket provisions of the Military Construction Authorization Bill of August 1969, found an overwhelming majority of
House members willing to support Rivers and opposed to the re-
committal move of Charles Whalen (R.–Ohio). Two factors should
be noted concerning the motion: a small but vocal bipartisan minority within the committee (Whalen, Robert Leggett (D.-Calif.),
Lucien Nedzi (D.-Mich.), and Otis Pike (D.-N.Y)) were willing to
publicly oppose Rivers; and, it provided House doves an opportunity to express opposition on a bill that raised fundamental
questions about the direction of institutional response to previous
and upcoming Washington demonstrations. Since the provisions
were later killed in conference, more cynical readers may dismiss
such a test as another example of constituency posturing by
otherwise opposed members (". . . the Senate will take care of us
. . .").

The question, however, is which constituencies were various
members responding to? If, as I'm attempting to suggest, the Class
of 89 was somewhat more responsive to the changing demands of
the late 1960s, simultaneously more liberal *and* more conservative,
then such a vote seems an important indicator.

The Rivers provision would have prohibited "picketing" and
"undue harassment" of civilian and military employees in the Department of Defense and "surrounding areas," providing penal-
ties of up to one year in prison and/or $1,000 fine for anyone con-
victed of such offenses. The bill was particularly inspired by the
antiwar demonstrations of November 1967 when 40,000 people,
primarily young, but abetted by the likes of dangerous oldsters
such as Norman Mailer, Robert Lowell, Dwight MacDonald, and
the remnants of the Abraham Lincoln Brigade, converged on the
Pentagon. Rivers defended the provision with his usual gift for
reasoned understatement:

> It is almost two years since we had these dirty, filthy demon-
> strations at the Pentagon. . . . The Constitution says that
> your Congress should provide for the military and make rules
> for the government thereof. The Congress has appointed

the Armed Services Committee to discharge this responsibility and we are, therefore, here on our Constitutional grounds. . . . You can do what you please about this. If you want to protect your very existence [this Fall] support the Committee. I have talked all I'm going to talk.

Leggett, who spoke against the provision, had earlier argued:

If the Pentagon is in danger—and sometimes I think it may be—they can construct a fence around it . . . they can do all kinds of things to protect security, but they have to do it in a Constitutional way. . . .

To which John E. Hunt (R.-N.J.) later replied:

If some of the bleeding hearts who now resemble the babbling of inbred parrots had gone over there to examine the motives of the demonstrators and what they were doing I am quite sure they would have a different tune to sing today.

Leggett first attempted to amend the bill, but lost by teller vote, 145–43. Whalen later moved to recommit on a roll-call vote, losing handsomely also, 323–87. But examine the voting data provided in table 7.3. For the first time on my measures, a slight majority (51 percent) of *all* northern Democrats emerged in favor of the ADA position; more important, 75 percent of the northerners from the Class of 89 voted for the Whalen amendment. For Democrats who considered themselves liberal or moderate in 1964, the ratios on the Whalen motion were 12–3 and 4–5 respectively. Their Republican and southern Democratic classmates unanimously supported Rivers. Ironically, perhaps understandably, the only Democrat from the 89th on Rivers' committee, Floyd Hicks, voted with the chairman. His three colleagues from the Washington delegation, Adams, Foley, and Meeds, all of whom also entered in 1965, supported the Whalen motion.[12]

12. The trade-offs for Hicks not to oppose Rivers on this issue—even if he were so inclined—are suggested in the following anecdote by Thomas Murphy: "In one of his first speeches to the House, [Hicks] spoke out against Chairman Rivers; yet in September, Rivers was in Tacoma with Hicks. When a skeptical reporter asked [Rivers] if he wasn't really there to help Hicks, Rivers replied, 'Well, you could say I'm not here to hurt him.'" Reported in Murphy, "Political Ethics," p. 294. Lewis Anthony Dexter's study of Armed Services also underscores the reasons for avoiding a direct and public challenge of the chairman on issues that go beyond committee members' perceptions of what Armed Services is actually about: in Dexter's words, the main concern of the committee is the location of installations, and related trans-

Table 7.3

Critical Issues and the Response of the Class of 89 in the 91st Congress, 1st Session, 1969

| | Vietnam Protest Legislation[a] | | | | Nixon Vietnam Policies[b] | | | |
| | PRO-ADA[c] | | ANTI-ADA | | PRO-ADA | | ANTI-ADA | |
| *Voting Groups* | N | % | N | % | N | % | N | % |
|---|---|---|---|---|---|---|---|---|
| All Democrats | *75* | | *156* | | *54* | | *162* | |
| northern Dems | 74 | 51 | 72 | 49 | 54 | 38 | 89 | 62 |
| southern Dems | 1 | 1 | 84 | 99 | — | — | 73 | 100 |
| 89th northern Dems | 18 | 75 | 6 | 25 | 13 | 55 | 11 | 45 |
| 89th southern Dems | — | — | 7 | 100 | — | — | 7 | 10 |
| All Republicans | 12 | 7 | *167* | 93 | 1 | | *172* | 100 |
| 89th Republicans | — | — | 12 | 100 | — | — | 12 | 100 |

a A motion by Charles Whalen (R.-Ohio) to strike a provision in the fiscal 1970 Military Construction Authorization which would have prohibited "picketing" and "undue harassment" of civilian and military employees in the Department of Defense and "surrounding areas." This provision was widely regarded as retaliation against the antiwar protest activity at the Pentagon in 1967. Whalen's motion was defeated, 323–87, but the provision was later killed in conference.

b The Nixon Administration's 1969 Vietnam resolution: "Toward Peace with Justice in Vietnam." Adopted 334–55.

c "Pro-ADA" position voted for Whalen's motion, against the Vietnam resolution.

During the Johnson Administration's expansion of American involvement in Vietnam, a tiny number of House opponents had been regularly focusing on military appropriations bills as a method to force a vote on the president's Vietnam policy. Predictably such efforts never resulted in a representative sample of antiwar sentiment in the House. On December 2, 1969, the House for the first time voted on a substantive measure bearing on U.S. policy.

The vote followed by two weeks the November demonstrations in Washington and reflected, as such votes always do, a complex set of partisan, procedural, and ideological considerations. One day before the final vote, administration supporters and the House leadership succeeded in beating back efforts (325–132) to challenge the four-hour, no-amendment rule under which the Peace with Justice in Vietnam resolution (H. Res. 613) was reported to the floor. Ninety-nine Democrats—all but five from the North—and 33 Republicans voted to oppose the rule. Many simultaneously indicated they would support the final resolution, as the rule itself encountered substantial opposition because of the speed and circumstances surrounding its introduction. Some members objected to the way the resolution had been handled in Foreign Affairs and/or Rules; some Democrats found it a political gain for a Republican president; some members of each party saw the resolution as a "carte blanche" endorsement of a war policy which they opposed. Others (James O'Hara, for example) considered it lacking in any substance and therefore "silly" to vote it down.

Despite this, the vote on the final product seems the best test of intense antiwar sentiment, at least for Democrats. Only one Republican, Paul McCloskey (Calif.), voted against H. Res. 613. Perhaps, however, it should be stressed that Nixon's policies were deeply opposed by other Republicans in the House (although never by more than 10–15) despite the eventual vote. Said Donald Riegle (R.-Mich.), "I support what is contained in the resolution, but feel a great sadness for what is not contained there." As the data show, an overwhelming majority of his party colleagues and a

---

fer, purchase and sale of properties. Providing one of the most famous quotes from committee research, he cites one member as bluntly stating, "Our committee is a real estate committee." Curiously, in a recent revision of his study, Dexter does not deal with the impact of Vietnam-related issues on the behavior of committee members. See his revised contribution, "Congressmen and the Making of Military Policy," in *Readings on Congress*, ed. Raymond Wolfinger (Englewood Cliffs, N.J.: Prentice-Hall, 1971), pp. 371–87.

substantial majority of northern and southern Democrats, for whatever reason, supported the resolution. Again, northerners from the 89th contradict the pattern: a slight majority (55 percent) voted *against* the resolution. The figures for liberals, 10–5; for moderates, 3–6. Among GOP members from the 89th, none, of course, voted against the final resolution; more significantly, none voted for earlier efforts to change the rule on debate and amending procedures.

Roll-call voting in the House is hardly a perfect measure of the ebb and flow of either collective or individual response to the policy demands of any given historical period. Too many other variables impinge on the way the House of Representatives conducts its business. But the data reviewed here are certainly suggestive of one source of institutional continuity and change.

Successive waves of new members, tiny as these waves might be, help to prevent Congress from becoming a "House without windows."

Electoral staying-power is an important political commodity, however, both as a predictor of policy continuity as well as a guarantor of policy change. Personal ambition, electoral circumstance, fortuitous events, all ultimately contrived to focus the attention of most members on the perennial problem of reelection—and reelection in 1966 clearly was a more risky business for these representatives than for their more senior colleagues.

## Electoral Fortunes: 1966–70

Three months after the landslide 1964 Democratic victory, Richard McGuire, then treasurer of the party's national committee, announced the creation of two "massive" fund-raising programs whose major purpose would be "to assure" the reelection of Great Society Democratic congressmen in 1966. By December 1965, McGuire had been ousted, one program was moribund while the other was in serious trouble,[13] the DNC's staff had been cut

---

13. The funds raised from one, the notorious political advertising book, *Toward an Age of Greatness*, were still tied up in 1972, resting uncomfortably in a special bank account in Boston. This book featured 68 pages of full-page advertising by corporate government contractors at a cost of $15,000 per page. It raised close to $1 million, but the ensuing publicity led the DNC to reject using the money for its operating expenses. Sen. John Williams called it a "shakedown" and successfully persuaded the Senate Finance Committee in 1966 to add a provision to John-

from 100 to 45, and the Democrats' highly publicized Congressional Support Program was rapidly fading.[14]

Various forces worked against the ability of the DNC to follow through on what had been an ambitious mix of cash and service programs for freshman congressmen—instrumental were a lingering carryover deficit of $2.5 to $3 million from the presidential campaign, the long-standing skepticism of the congressional campaign committees about the DNC's ability and/or intention when it came to fund-raising efforts for congressional races, and the usual kinks associated with all comprehensive assistance programs formulated by the national committee. Perhaps the most obvious example of the latter form of difficulty is the DNC's attempt to computerize a personalized mailing list for 70 House members, most but not all of whom were freshmen. Ultimately, 5 million names were loaded on magnetic tapes. The most charitable judgment of the DNC's admirable effort is that experience with it was highly mixed. The program was temporarily disbanded after the 1966 elections, but has reappeared in different and more sophisticated guises since.[15] On the Republican side, an intense and vitrio-

---

son's tax bill prohibiting tax deductions for advertisements in political magazines. The provision cleared both houses and was later signed into law. Although there was early discussion of giving the funds to the American Heritage Foundation such generosity has subsequently evaporated. The other McGuire fund-raising idea involved staging a series of movie premieres in the districts of willing Democratic incumbents, mainly freshmen. Two hundred affairs were planned; a net profit of $2 to $3 million predicted. Only three, to my knowledge, were ever held. They were such dismal failures (the steller feature in one was *Heroes of Telemark*) that the DNC scrapped plans for others.

14. Impetus and leadership for the program came from the DNC's news and information director, Wayne Phillips, during the 1964 congressional campaigns. Phillips organized a series of very imaginative automated TV-radio programs for freshmen using "audio press releases" transmitted directly via phone to home stations and newspapers. Other services—regular trips with cabinet members to congressional home districts, expanded research and ghosting services tied to the particular needs of freshmen—had receded in 1966 to about 40 percent of what the DNC had committed during 1965. The change in priorities was symbolized by Phillips' resignation in March 1966 when he shifted to the public affairs division of HUD. A good background account can be found in *Congressional Quarterly Weekly Report*, 27 May 1966, pp. 1074–80.

15. Both hardware and software problems plagued the DNC's system; ultimately its utility was confined to three or four mass mailings for about 24 of the 66 Democratic freshmen. More recently, the Research Division has moved to develop district voter profiles which will permit tailored mailings to specific demographic subgroups within each district. This program is now in the testing stage.

lic struggle over control of the national committee was in progress; none of the GOP freshmen looked to the committee for any meaningful assistance.

Democrats had other institutional resources in the major agencies—via the expanding pork-barrel of the Great Society—but the scope and electoral clout of such activity has been impossible to ascertain. Midway through the 89th Congress, the Liberty Lobby published a reasonably detailed account of the types of district projects some Democratic freshmen were scoring with. Further evidence, claimed the lobby, of a Johnson plot "to control the voters and perpetuate Me-Tooism in the hallowed halls of Congress . . . widespread areas are involved in this fiscal spree [to undercut] resurgent Republicanism." The lobby's sample, based on responses to a letter from a "freelance writer" (one Clifford Sandahl, who later turned out to be public relations director of the lobby), was restricted to ten freshmen since the Democratic Study Group circulated a warning in time to prevent further responses. None of the ten appeared particularly concerned about the disclosures. Said Richard White (D.-Tex.), "I'm sure there are many reasonable Republicans who have been successful in attending to the needs of their districts, too."[16]

Whatever the scope of Democratic efforts, the lobby's alarm about undercutting "resurgent Republicanism" was quite groundless. In November 1966 Republicans managed a net increase of 47 seats, 9 more than the Democrats had gained in 1964, and an unusually high off-year gain in congressional elections (the average mid-term switch since 1950 has been 25). Of these GOP victories, 23 were over freshman Democratic incumbents, 24 at the expense of veteran members. Of the 47 Democratic freshmen who had unseated Republican incumbents in 1964, 24 returned to the 90th Congress. Data are shown in table 7.4.

Freshman congressmen are always more vulnerable than their senior colleagues. This factor declines radically as they begin to log even a few years in office. Among Democrats, 63 percent were victorious in 1966, 74 percent in 1968, and 97 percent in 1970. The vulnerability rate is actually lower than these figures suggest since included here are members of the Class of 89 who were defeated in 1966 but returned to challenge Republicans in 1968 and 1970.

16. Sources for this episode came from interviews and an amusing account by George Lardner, Jr., in the *Washington Post.*

Table 7.4

Electoral Fortunes of Members First Elected to the 89th Congress, 1966–70

| | Democrats | | | | | | Republicans | | | | | |
|---|---|---|---|---|---|---|---|---|---|---|---|---|
| | 1966 | | 1968 | | 1970 | | 1966 | | 1968 | | 1970 | |
| | % | N | % | N | % | N | % | N | % | N | % | N |
| Total winners | 63 | (39) | 74 | (34) | 97 | (31) | 93 | (14) | 92 | (12) | 85 | (10) |
| Total losers | 37 | (23) | 26 | (12)[a] | 3 | (1)[b] | 7 | (1) | 8 | (1) | 10 | (2) |
| not House candidates: | — | (4) | — | (20) | — | (34) | — | (3) | — | (5) | — | (6) |
| Electoral margins: | | | | | | | | | | | | |
| won, 61% plus | 27 | (17) | 41 | (18) | 70 | (22) | 86 | (13) | 61 | (8) | 85 | (10) |
| won, 56–60% | 8 | (4) | 10 | (5) | 15 | (5) | 7 | (1) | 24 | (3) | — | — |
| won, 50–55% | 27 | (11) | 24 | (11) | 12 | (4) | — | — | 8 | (1) | — | — |
| lost, 45–49% | 31 | (19) | 17 | (8) | — | — | 7 | (1) | — | — | 5 | (1) |
| lost, 44–40% | 8 | (4) | 4 | (2) | — | — | — | — | — | — | — | — |
| lost, 39% or less | — | — | 4 | (2) | 3 | (1) | — | — | 7 | (1) | 5 | (1) |
| | 101[c] | (62) | 100 | (46) | 100 | (32) | 100 | (15) | 100 | (13) | 100 | (13) |

[a] Loser figures include, for 1968 and 1970, incumbents and candidates who were defeated in 1966 but ran again in 1968 or 1970.
[b] Clair A. Callan, a member from Nebraska during the 89th Congress, was defeated in 1966, regained the nomination but lost the general in 1968, lost the nomination in 1970, but still ran as an independent in the general election—and lost.
[c] Because of rounding.

If one excludes these "non" incumbents, the proportion who are successful rises even more dramatically (91 percent in 1968, 100 percent in 1970). Moreover, their victory margins as incumbents with increasing seniority also improve: 27 percent of those who won reelection in 1966 did so with 55 percent or less of the vote; in 1970 this had declined to 12 percent (four candidates).

Once unseated, Democrats from the 89th found it virtually impossible to regain their seats: eight who lost in 1966 challenged Republicans in 1968 and lost. Only John Dow (D.-N.Y.), who survived the 1966 Republican resurgence to be defeated in 1968, contradicts this pattern. He rechallenged his 1968 opponent in 1970 and regained the seat by a narrow (51 percent) victory. Further, the longer a candidate is out of office, the harder it becomes to regain the seat, or even the nomination. Three Democrats from the 89th who lost in this period—Matson O'Neal (Ga.), E. S. "Johnny" Walker (N. Mex.), and Clair Callan (Neb.)—were defeated in the 1970 House primaries. Callan subsequently ran as an independent in the general election, pulling 15 percent of the vote. The 1968 attempted comeback campaigns ended, for most, serious attempts to reenter the House.

The six-year period also worked to the advantage of those freshman Republicans who remained in the House. Only two, Glenn Andrews (Ala.) in 1966 and Chester Mize (Kan.) in 1970 have been defeated. The rest who left did so to seek other office. The two GOP attempts shown in the table to return to the House were unsuccessful—Andrews in 1970, Prentiss Walker (Miss.) in 1968.

How much of the pattern of growing invulnerability is a reflection of the enormous resource advantages incumbents usually enjoy over challengers? While the data are hardly conclusive, the overwhelming burden of evidence suggests incumbency, per se, is not the most powerful determinant. Robert Erikson, in an ingenious test, estimates the average "incumbency advantage" at about 2 percent.[17] Rather the structural makeup of the district— the pattern of party dominance and constituency characteristics— is far more significant. His data are subject to certain limitations, being time bound (1954–60) and prone to problems of "regression

17. "The Advantage of Incumbency in Congressional Elections," *Polity* (1971): 395–405.

### Table 7.5

### The Demography of Victory and Defeat for Democrats
### First Elected to the 89th Congress, 1966–70

| | Composition of Congressional Districts[a] | | | | | | | |
| | Rural | | Urban | | Surburban | | Mixed | |
| Year | WON | LOST | WON | LOST | WON | LOST | WON | LOST | |
|---|---|---|---|---|---|---|---|---|---|
| 1966[b] | 15 | 10 | 10 | 1 | 7 | 4 | 7 | 6 | (60) |
| 1968[c] | 14 | — | 10 | — | 5 | 1 | 5 | 2 | (37) |
| 1970 | 14 | — | 10 | — | 4 | — | 3 | — | (31) |

[a] District composition as of 1963 estimates by *Congressional Quarterly*. Figures are for incumbent officeholders only.

[b] Excludes those who ran for another office, retired, or losers (2) in the 1966 elections whose district composition could not be established.

[c] Does not include candidates who sought another office.

effect,"[18] but they are corroborated by data presented in table 7.5. There is a clear tendency for Democrats who survived the three elections following 1964 to represent the same types of districts— urban *and* rural—which have undergirded the Democratic coalition since the New Deal.

Comparatively, trade-offs benefiting Republicans have also come in their traditional centers of strength, particularly in the suburbs. The ten rural districts which returned to Republican control, disproportionately located in the Midwest, will probably continue as occasionally vulnerable to Democratic challengers.

Of the 47 seats which switched to Democrats in 1964, the GOP retook 24 in 1966, 2 in 1968, and 2 in 1970. On the other hand, they lost 3 of their 1964 gains in 1966 (all in the South) and 1 in 1970 (Mize of Kansas).

I do not mean to imply that the nineteen Democratic challengers who defeated Republican incumbents in 1964, and who are still in the House, are simply pawns in an otherwise deterministic universe. Certainly the skill and imagination with which incumbent resources have been used by a John Culver in Iowa, Henry Helstoski in New Jersey, John Dow in New York, or a Lee Hamilton in Indiana count for something; precisely how much

18. The tendency of measures taken over time to "regress toward the mean" in a way that distorts accurate estimates. Erikson's data may be subject to underestimating the average incumbency margin because of exceptionally high initial winning margins. He adjusts for this problem in a variety of ways, but especially at pp. 401–3.

is a question on which these data are silent. The same applies for some of the Republicans: Jack Edwards, John Buchanan, William Dickinson, all of whom held their own against Wallaceites and National Democrats in Alabama.

The electoral resurgence of congressional Republicans during the past six years (bringing the party ratios in 1972 to 254–178 with 3 vacancies) reflects an almost perfect reinstitution of party strength in the House circa late 1963. Now, as in 1963, House Democrats stand in little danger of becoming an instant minority. The "emerging" Republican majority is still an artifact of Kevin Phillips' wistful imagination, despite Nixon's impressive gains in 1972.[19] Nor, if my earlier data are accurate, was there any massive movement by voters to punish through defeat strongly liberal congressmen in the House. Most of those who were defeated in 1966 were beaten, not because they were perceived to be *liberal* Democrats, but simply because they were Democrats. Likewise, I would argue, for those who have resisted efforts to defeat them during the past three elections. (The reader should review the evidence on this score presented in chapter 4.) Given the normal boundaries of American ideological alternatives, each member has substantial control over how "liberal" or "conservative" his voting record can become before he need fear widespread voter hostility. Other constituency constraints, to be sure, are important (e.g., financial backers, well-organized minorities), but they should not be confused with the general dispositions of most voters. If there are other constituency pressures, they apparently are disproportionately focused on Republicans. Among this group, research has shown a clear and steady decrease in vote-pulling power as the congressman's roll-call behavior becomes more *conservative*. This finding does not hold for Democrats, who are not penalized when moving toward the liberal end of the ideological continuum.[20]

Building the perennial base "back home" (for Democrats) cannot be achieved on the sole basis of identifying with a "moving center" and voting accordingly. Too many "moderate" north-

19. The distinction between a temporary majority for the presidential candidate and a stable majority among the electorate is a difference that is ignored by Phillips and others who see the GOP as the dominant party in the 1970s.

20. Robert S. Erikson, "The Electoral Impact of Congressional Roll-Call Voting," *American Political Science Review* (December 1971): 1018–33.

ern Democrats paid the price for this illusion in 1966, as did "liberals" who believe they were defeated because they were not more "moderate." Single issues in particular districts or regions can become powerful determinants of electoral outcome, but the more typical linkage between voters and candidates seems to allow the latter considerable range.

For some of these candidates, however, the question was not so much reelection as how to parlay a successful House campaign into something larger.

The House is one of two major institutional stepping stones to the Senate. Approximately 26 percent of the postwar Senate has been composed of men and women who entered directly from the House.[21] But the move is highly risky, as the data in tables 7.6 and 7.7 show. Since 1966, six Democrats and one Republican from the Class of 89 have sought senatorial seats. Only one, John Tunney (Calif.), was successful. Two of the six Democratic losers, Joseph Resnick and Richard McCarthy, both of New York, failed to gain their party's nomination. Both had been forced into considering the Senate because of substantial changes in the makeup of their districts. Of the remainder who have sought other office, only Robert Sweeney's contest for attorney general in Ohio during 1966, and the multiple office thrusts of Gilligan, resulted from "forced" exits. For the rest, the campaigns represented calculated efforts to move beyond the House. Compared to those who initially expressed such willingness (18 Democrats and 9 Republicans were classified as progressively ambitious), this group comprises approximately 50 percent.

Perhaps the most interesting electoral career of the outwardly mobile members from the 89th is that of John J. Gilligan. Narrowly beaten by Robert Taft, Jr., in a 1966 House reelection bid, Gilligan then scored a stunning primary upset over Senator Frank Lausche during 1968. He lost the general election to William Saxbe but, underterred, came back in 1970 to win the Ohio governorship. Three other candidates, all Republicans and all from the South, have been beaten in attempts to gain their state governorships.[22] Of the five GOP outwardly mobiles, only Ed

21. Schlesinger, *Ambition and Politics*, p. 93.
22. Howard "Bo" Calloway actually won a plurality of the popular vote in the Georgia governor's race (Lester Maddox was the other major candidate) but lost when the decision went to the state legislature and the Democrats backed Maddox.

Table 7.6

Office-seeking Activity and Electoral Outcome
Among Freshmen in the 89th Congress, 1966–70
(In Numbers Only)

|  | Democrats | | | Republicans | | |
|---|---|---|---|---|---|---|
|  | 1966 | 1968 | 1970 | 1966 | 1968 | 1970 |
| Reelected to House | 39 | 34 | 31 | 14 | 12 | 10 |
| House candidate; lost primary | — | — | 3 | — | — | — |
| House candidate; lost general | 23 | 12 | 1[a] | 1 | 1 | 2 |
| U.S. Senate candidate; won | — | — | 1 | — | — | — |
| U.S. Senate candidate; lost | 1 | 2 | 2 | — | 1 | — |
| Gubernatorial candidate; won | — | — | 1 | — | — | — |
| Gubernatorial candidate; lost | — | — | — | 3 | — | — |
| Other state office; won | — | — | — | — | — | 1 |
| Other state office; lost | 1 | — | — | — | — | — |
| Not a candidate for public office | 2 | 18 | 27 | — | 4 | 5 |
| N = | (66) | (66) | (66) | (18) | (18) | (18) |

[a] One candidate, Clair Callan (D.-Neb.), lost both the Democratic primary and the general election (running as an Independent).

Reinecke, now lieutenant governor of California and in all probability will be a gubernatorial candidate in 1974, has been successful.

The collective odds, as these data attest, are against those who do take the chance, either in quest of a governor's chair or the U.S. Senate. Not surprisingly, the Senate continues to oppose any proposal (the four-year term, for example) which would reduce the structure of risk for externally ambitious House members. Just as the electoral environment provides great risk, so the advantages of seniority for the forty-one who are left should make alternatives to the House increasingly less attractive. This tension helps ex-

Table 7.7

Freshmen in the 89th Congress who Have Sought
Other Elective Offices, 1966–70

| Candidate | Office Sought | Outcome |
|---|---|---|
| *1966* | | |
| Teno Roncalio (D.-Wyo.)[a] | U.S. Senate | lost general election |
| Robert Sweeney (D.-Ohio) | Attorney General | lost general election |
| Howard B. Calloway (R.-Ga.) | Governor | lost[b] |
| James Martin (R.-Ala.) | Governor | lost general election |
| Prentiss Walker (R.-Miss.) | Governor | lost general election |
| *1968* | | |
| John J. Gilligan (D.-Ohio) | U.S. Senate | lost general election |
| Joseph Y. Resnick (D.-N.Y.) | U.S. Senate | lost nomination |
| George V. Hansen (R.-Ida.) | U.S. Senate | lost general election |
| *1970* | | |
| John J. Gilligan (D.-Ohio) | Governor | won |
| Richard D. McCarthy (D.-N.Y.) | U.S. Senate | lost nomination |
| Richard L. Ottinger (D.-N.Y.) | U.S. Senate | lost general election |
| John V. Tunney (D.-Calif.) | U.S. Senate | won |
| Edwin Reinecke (R.-Calif.) | Lt. Governor | won[c] |

[a] Roncalio returned to the House in 1971.

[b] Calloway won a plurality of votes in the Georgia contest with Maddox but lost when the legislature then selected the governor.

[c] Reinecke was appointed to fill the vacancy of Robert Finch, who left to join the Nixon Administration. Reinecke won his first election for lieutenant governor in 1970.

plain both sources of change and continuity within the House of Representatives.

Lamenting his loss to Hale Boggs in a spirited contest over the majority leadership at the opening of the 92nd Congress, Morris Udall recently observed:

> . . . in the House, yesterday's revolutionaries become tomorrow's elitists . . . if you believe, as some of us do, that time is running out, that the country's problems are accumulating and our society is in crisis—well, then you have to think

about restructuring your career possibilities and your life . . .
What can you do? Run for the Senate and hope it's a little
better over there? Teach? Write? Practice law? Where can
you be more useful? [23]

One hopes that luck, skill, and circumstance will continue to
make the House a credible alternative for the forty-one who
seven years ago "seen their opportunities and took 'em."

From the perspective of the writer's own values, Plunkitt's wisdom about the withering away of reformers is yet another example
of *bubeleh* political science[24]—most of these representatives have
looked as good during the Great Reaction as they first did in the
morning glory of the Great Society.

23. Larry L. King, "The Road to Power in Congress: the Education of Mo Udall
—And What it Cost," *Harper's* (June 1971): 39–63.
24. Daryl J. Bem first alerted me to the persistence of this type of knowledge
in the social sciences. *Bubeleh:* Yiddish for grandmother. Everyone's *bubeleh* knows
that reformers don't last in Congress. Regrettably for grandmothers, my data suggest otherwise.

# 8

# OPPOSITION AND AMERICAN PARTIES

*Longer boats are comin' to win us,*
*Hold on to the shore,*
*They'll be takin' the key from the door.*
*I don't want no god on my lawn,*
*Just a flower I can help along,*
*'Cause the soul of nobody knows*
*How a flower grows.*

*(Cat Stevens, 1971)*

Party organizations in democratic societies are shaped by their ability to command and capitalize effectively on resources: manpower, issues, money, leadership, organizational skills, and ultimately, votes. Parties in power almost always hold considerable advantage over their opposition when faced with the task of pyramiding resources in politically useful ways. Providing the necessary incentives to compensate for this imbalance is a particularly complex task for opposition parties.

Whether the drive to gain and hold office is the most distinguishing characteristic of American major parties has long been disputed.[1] Congressional elections would be one-person affairs in all but 25 percent of the districts if other incentives did not play a powerful role. Serious competition for office need not preclude the simultaneous operation of other inducements to candidacy; the five broad incentives examined in this book are highly interrelated. Both parties confront other electoral competitors—from the Left and Right—with a limited but impressive

---

1. More recently, see M. Margaret Conway and Frank Weigert, "Motivation, Incentive Systems, and the Political Party Organization," *American Political Science Review* (December 1968): 1159–74.

array of organizational incentives. A comprehensive summary of the findings on this score will not be undertaken here. Walter Dean Burnham and others may be correct in their belief that the public's psychological identification with either party is in a process of long-run decline, but there is little evidence that major party monopoly over the electoral route to power is equally threatened. More important is the constellation of factors which undergird *one*-party dominance in most districts and the implications for electoral opposition at the congressional level.

Under what conditions would changes in the existing resource base affect the scope and consequences of electoral opposition outside Congress? This chapter focuses on some possible answers.

## Competition and Its Problems

Assume for a moment an outrageously improbable outcome of the 1972 election. Every incumbent in the House is defeated by the major party opponent. Would it make any difference for the broad programmatic orientation of members in this contrived Congress? A direct test of this assumption was undertaken by two researchers who compared the policy orientation of all incumbents with all opponents in the 1966 elections. The findings were predictable. Both the existing and projected Congresses were interchangeable on major issues.[2] On the other hand, selectively defeating 100 incumbents could have profound impact on the programmatic direction of the House. Perhaps the point is obvious. Generating the resources to change (or sustain) the policy output of political institutions requires stability as well as turnover among those who staff critical positions. This applies to any elite structure, whether it be revolutionary, liberal, middle-of-the-road, conservative, reactionary, or simply beyond ideology altogether.

Evaluating the merit of proposals designed to increase the competitive position of congressional challengers vis-à-vis incum-

2. John L. Sullivan and Robert E. O'Connor, "Electoral Choice and Popular Control of Public Policy: The 1966 House Elections," *American Political Science Review* (December, 1972): 1256–68. This generalization depends on two assumptions: southern Republicans will not contest more districts; southern Democrats are more "liberal" than their GOP replacements.

bents depends on a variety of factors, including: (1) the probable impact on other participants in the electoral arena; (2) the probable impact on participants in the congressional arena; (3) the probable impact on participants in other policy arenas; (4) the conception articulated by the analyst concerning how participants in all these arenas *ought* to act; and, (5) the reliability and validity of the information base (data and predictions) for making such prescriptions. Based on past performance, political scientists should well be modest men, for they have much to be modest about.[3]

Consider a typical formulation about the impact of increasing competiveness:

> ... a more competitive two-party system in most congressional districts should result in improved quality of debate and should produce a campaign that is more strongly directed toward issues. It is also possible that a greater degree of competition will attract candidates of higher quality.... Men of true ability are more likely to run in contests where there exists some hope of winning....[4]

The authors are admirably cautious about qualifying each of these predictions. But to my knowledge, there is not one whit of evidence supporting any of them, even assuming common agreement on what constitutes "quality" and "ability."

Three of the major incentives discussed in this study—open career possibilities, social representativeness, and programmatic development and articulation—are not fundamentally altered by variations in district competitiveness. Candidacies are open to a very small number of articulate ideologues, as well as other mavericks in districts that are heavily oriented toward the opposite party. This should not be overstressed since the burden of my data demonstrates the absence of any large systemic effect. If these data can be generalized, increasing competition will have little impact on the types of candidates churned up in congressional elections.

Strong party competition, though, has been shown to have other important correlates. David Leuthold notes that competi-

3. Comparing the innovative policy of British government under Clement Attlee and Winston Churchill (who directed the original version of this barb at his Labour opponent), Attlee might have retorted that Churchill *should* have been a modest man, for the Tories had much to be modest about.

4. Robert J. Huckshorn and Robert C. Spencer, *The Politics of Defeat* (Amherst: University of Massachusetts Press, 1971), p. 232.

tive districts in the San Francisco area attracted more voters than did noncompetitive races (by a margin of 4 percent), more campaign workers (800 to 250), and caused more information-seeking behavior on the part of candidates. Most of the important theoretical questions about district competitiveness are not of the either-or variety, but rather:

1. *How much?* Is the present proportion of competitive congressional districts (25 percent) too little? Too much? In terms of what assumptions, stemming from what components of democratic theory? Should it be increased to 35 percent? 45? 75? 100? Could any changes in the way resources are allocated actually bring about such change?

2. *How frequent?* Are districts which experience a change in party representation once every ten years competitive? Every six years? Are districts which consistently return 45 to 49 percent of the vote to the challenger "competitive" even though one party manages to retain the seat?

3. *What type?* Large pockets of one-party dominance in congressional districts cohabit with highly competitive electoral environments elsewhere. Industrial states such as Pennsylvania, New York, California all contain safe congressional seats while supporting consistently competitive state arenas. Party competition and stable opposition *inside* Congress is guaranteed because a sizable number of districts are safe for one or the other party. Should this be changed? If so, how?

Political science frequently reduces questions of this sort to operational and/or definitional problems, but the issues raised go beyond operational matters. From the viewpoint of habitual reformers (like the author), or democratic theorists who place great stress on the importance of a competitive struggle for votes—Schumpeter or Sartori, for example—such questions do not suggest obvious answers. Specific proposals for change should be couched in terms of these considerations as well as a set of working assumptions about what groups or individuals ought to benefit from reallocating the costs and benefits of the existing electoral arena.

## Changing the Arena Outside Congress

Political money is almost universally conceded to be a primary resource from which others are derived. Nelson Rockefeller notwithstanding, voters are not bought in the United States; at least in the sense that increasing units of land may be acquired by investing increasing increments of cash. Too many Norton Simons have floundered in politics by assuming the polity was analogous to the economy. In a recent call for campaign finance reform by the Twentieth Century Fund Task Force,[5] their report cited a variety of highly questionable practices associated with financing congressional races. Prominently featured were the enormous increases in money being spent during campaigns. One challenger admitted spending $2 million for a 1970 House race. Less conspicuously carried in the Task Force report was a simple fact: he *lost* the election. Still, all congressional candidates need some form of cash down-payment. Financial thresholds certainly exist. Serious campaign probes, most commentators estimate, now require an initial investment of between $20,000 and $25,000.

Incumbent congressmen begin campaigns with this minimum well assured. The cash value of a governmentally financed field staff, and the franking privilege, are easily worth $35,000. Hence the recurring popularity of proposals for federally subsidized campaigns, for challengers and incumbents, through either direct (cash payments, tax credits) or indirect methods.[6] Transfers in cash would clearly assist challengers, but subsidies in kind are also frequently recommended. Two of the most common—"free" television/radio time and access to the franking privilege—have been kicked around in various guises and proposals for fifteen years.[7]

The considerable array of direct and indirect subsidy schemes, embracing a variety of different assumptions, plans, and components, can be organized under three simplified but

5. *Electing Congress: The Financial Dilemma* (New York: Twentieth Century Fund, 1970).

6. The best recent examination of various methods can be found in David Adamany, *Financing Politics* (Madison: University of Wisconsin Press, 1969), particularly pp. 246–72.

7. Discussion of some of these can be found in *Electing Congress*, pp. 76–80.

convenient models: (1) party-centered; (2) candidate-centered; and (3) mixed, combining elements of both.[8]

Proponents of direct subsidies where the political party is the major organizational conduit typically defend their proposals by arguing that public financing will protect parties from dominance by economic interests, strengthen their organizational base, and create more competitive districts where they do not now exist. Dropping the second element, proponents of candidate-centered proposals have usually based their arguments on the same claims.

The first and third assertions are highly suspect for both models, particularly on empirical grounds. Experience with public subsidies in Puerto Rico, and in West European systems such as West Germany, provides little evidence that parties or individuals are liberated from reliance on major economic constellations simply because public funding is available. As David Adamany carefully documents, money is a highly convertible resource.[9] Economic groups like COPE or BIPAC[10] could divert their funds into other political activities (media campaigns, direct lobbying operations, get-out-the-vote drives, etc.) whose effects are designed to benefit one or the other party. The same caveat applies to candidate-centered subsidy plans, like the presidential one contained in the Revenue Act of 1971. Unless government is prepared to assume almost total financial support for the campaign process—in the primaries and in the general election—public subsidies will most likely add to, or redirect, rather than substitute for, individual and group spending.

Party-centered subsidy plans which emphasize their utility for correcting the "erosion" of parties over the past two decades must also contend with a host of problems. First, even if one concedes there has been substantial slippage in the dominance of the two major parties, survey data suggest that it is occurring in

8. More radical proposals, involving the comprehensive restructuring of the electoral or party systems, will not be examined. Utopia building can have great utility, indeed is essential for a critical social science. But working out the difficulties of reshaping institutional arrangements for electing congressmen (replacing single-member, simple-majority districts, or writing "New" American Constitutions) are activities I will gladly leave to others. Examining the ways in which resources can be used to defeat, or reelect, existing congressmen seems to me a more compelling task.

9. Adamany, *Financing Politics*, pp. 108–72.

10. Businessmen's Independent Political Action Committee.

the psychology of voters' attachment to these groups. Organizational transformations since the turn of the century, reflected in the rise of a professional campaign management industry, or the emergence of issue-oriented mass groups outside the party system, are a response to the rapidity and complexity of social and technological change in the United States. I remain skeptical that public subsidies for party operating costs can (or should) ever restore the earlier monopoly of parties over the issues, skills, and manpower associated with electoral politics. Dealing with the first problem—increasing cynicism, decreasing partisanship—will not be helped by having the government pick up the tab for the Democratic and Republican national, state and/or local committees. Or, for that matter, the Peace and Freedom or American Independent party operations in various states.[11]

On the other hand, direct subsidies to candidates, or their personal committees, would continue to sustain candidate independence from formal party organizations. The compromise provision on tax check-offs of the Revenue Act of 1971, which if implemented will provide public financing for presidential candidates in 1976, bypasses the RNC and DNC. Money will go directly to candidates or their committees.

Extrapolating some of these arguments to congressional districts leads to even greater difficulties. Most party-centered proposals would channel direct subsidies through either the House campaign committees or county party committees. Assuming adequate guidelines for how direct cash subsidies might be spent, it is difficult not to believe the same pressures that killed Senator Russell Long's bill in 1966 (which targeted the national committees as recipients) would not again be generated. Most incumbents are as yet unwilling to accept the *potential* loss of control over their own campaigns which these procedures might permit. Providing direct payments to congressional candidates, like the earlier candidate-centered proposals, would also reinforce financial autonomy from the local party. I presume this is not an outcome compatible with the preferences of those committed to a party-centered solution.

11. Russell Long's original public finance bill would have given minority parties (defined as 5 to 25 percent of the vote) a higher amount per vote than the major parties. Under his formula, the AIP would have been the only minor party to receive a subsidy in 1968. The others did not get enough votes to make the 5 percent minimum.

Congressmen apparently feel more comfortable risking the vagaries and nuances of the private finance system over adopting one with an uncharted, perhaps hostile, terrain. Challengers might benefit, but they must be willing to accept dealing with the Eastlands as well as McGoverns of either party.

The obvious impasse has led numerous observers to urge a mixed strategy, one that would send cash payments directly to candidates *and* provide public subsidies for operating expenses of parties.[12] The rationale of a mixed model seems persuasive where one is committed to incremental change because:

1. With appropriate disbursing formulas, it would not alter existing power relationships between parties and candidates, or between different levels of party operation; and

2. It would make the recruitment of candidates in one-party districts somewhat easier, although it is certainly not clear they would be very different—programmatically or otherwise—than under the existing finance system. Whether or not this is true of races other than congressional contests is even more conjectural.

Justification for public financing in congressional campaigns, using a mixed party-candidate format, should not rest on any large claims about its consequences on the internal structure of Congress or the external environment of House elections. Although the data are hardly conclusive, public subsidies are not likely to alter the existing short-run balance of (non)competition in most congressional campaigns.[13] Nor would it prevent other groups from utilizing their muscle in ways designed to give some candidates an advantage over others; or fundamentally circumvent the "onward march of party decomposition"; or eliminate "the rigidity and sterility in Congress at a time that demands flexibility and new blood"; or any of the other immodest claims frequently marshaled to support changes in the financial base of congressional races. From the viewpoint of the congressional challenger, and the opposition party, a public finance scheme should be justified simply on grounds of marginal equity.

12. Adamany, for example. See his comments, *Financing Politics*, at pp. 256–71.

13. Unless they are massive in scope, approximating full campaign costs. Still, other factors (party voting patterns) are equally important.

There are no strategic incentives for incumbents to adopt a program that radically alters their current advantage in converting federal subsidies to campaign resources. A plan that generated $20,000 for general election expenses of major-party incumbents and challengers, and earmarked $2,500 to serious third-party candidates,[14] might stand a chance of reducing current opposition in the House to public financing. This would cost approximately $18 million every two years. I shall leave the details of specific formulas, such as an automatic "campaign cost ratio," guidelines for disbursal, etc. to the imagination of any reader who might consider this worth pursuing.

The proposal would not give challengers equal footing with incumbents. It would provide each challenger a small base once he won the nomination. I suspect it would be most useful in only the most hopeless districts. For incumbents, it would ease (but not eliminate) whatever pain they might encounter when working their normal money circuits. The relatively small amount of money involved might also reduce incumbent anxiety over more ambitious efforts to equalize the financial clout of their competitors. Officeholders, as Adamany points out, realize that political money is subject to a principle of diminishing returns; where all campaigns are well financed, the advantage of investing more money has less impact. But as of 1972 and despite the new restrictions on media use in congressional elections, a direct $20,000 subsidy will hardly provide a "well financed" campaign for a challenger. Nor will a modest candidate-centered subsidy such as this one have much impact on the role and function of opposition parties; it would simply make recruitment of candidates easier.

Most of these men and women are currently performing the primary function of opposition candidates in congressional campaigns—presenting programmatic alternatives for voters—and this proposal would guarantee that the financial burdens of continuing to do so are not always overwhelming. No more, no less. Adoption would be a small but important lug in shoring up the opposition arena outside Congress.[15] It would strengthen the short-run incen-

14. Using Long's formula of 5 percent, third parties would have to garner 5,000 votes in a typical 100,000-vote district. Equal payments to both majority and minority parties is the only way challengers could be assured a minimal cutting edge.

15. The strategic barriers outlined above are further compounded by persistent public hostility to direct public subsidies. Tax credit methods have been adopted to avoid this problem. Their major deficiency stems from the tough collection problem parties will have using tax credits, even given the opportunity. The Uni-

tives parties need in order to capitalize on long-run changes in issues, the districts' dominant party orientation, historic constituency voting patterns, and so forth. Engineering policy change in Congress requires that parties be able to mesh short-run incentives with long-run opportunities, as I believe the output of the 89th Congress demonstrates.

If my analysis is correct, the two groups having maximum stake in supporting modest subsidies are the Republicans in the House, and the majority within the majority, the Democratic Study Group. Civil rights legislation is not the only area in which Republicans and liberal Democrats can find something of mutual benefit.

Many of the same problems are evident as one moves from cash to indirect subsidies like free television/radio time or cost-free postage. Two additional considerations are added. Congressional candidates frequently make little use of television in dense urban areas. TV is inefficient for reaching single-district voters compared with other alternatives, and it is expensive, despite the lower rates available under the Federal Election Campaign Act of 1972. Opposition to suspending the equal-time provision has been long and consistent. Incumbents do not trust local station owners, nor are they (as yet) willing to risk giving challengers additional exposure, even where it is inefficient from the viewpoint of electoral payoffs.[16]

Harry Ashmore and others can continue to denounce the use of spot political advertising, demanding "educational" formats of longer duration, but one suspects few congressmen are seriously listening. In my judgment, spot advertising usually *is* abominable. Suspending the equal-time provision without simultaneously mandating that stations provide good chunks of time for extended presentations would hardly lead to drastic revision in present

---

versity of Michigan's Survey Research Center has consistently shown large majorities (71 percent in 1964) opposed to a direct subsidy for presidential candidates. There is little reason to believe this would be any less true for congressional races. Political leaders sometimes do lead (*run* might be a better description) as congressional approval of public subsidies for presidential contests attests. The melancholy conclusion of the struggle over presidential financing seems inescapable: congressmen must first be so distraught over the rising costs of campaigning, apparently in a way that leaves one major party almost bankrupt, that they're willing to risk all the unknowns in an effort to do something realistic about it.

16. See Robert L. Peabody et al., *To Enact a Law: Congress and Campaign Finance* (New York: Praeger, 1972), pp. 201–17.

coverage. Mandating time for congressional candidates alone seems undesirable. A good case could be made for mandated time (politically, not legally) for all other "significant" candidates, including presidential, senatorial, state senators, state assemblymen, county commissioners, city councilmen, mayors, boards of education, and county party figures.

Objections to various schemes in the equal-time/mandated-time theme have been put most simply by David Rosenbloom in the Twentieth Century Fund's Report: ". . . they do not give candidates what they feel they need . . . a campaign finance system that helps candidates communicate in only one way might create unfair advantages."[17] And, of course, they are proposals which are uniformly candidate-centered. Their enactment would do little to improve the collective role of parties.[18]

Other indirect subsidies, free postage for a specified number of mailers, or banks of computer time, seem reasonable, but they still beg some of the same questions.

*Seriously* regulating media rates, and providing congressional candidates modest direct cash subsidies, seems the least complicated and most efficient method of correcting some of these distortions. I'm not suggesting television and radio stations should be permitted to avoid a broader, expanded role in public affairs reporting. Rather, by encouraging the use of consumers choice among candidates, subject to appropriate regulation, one employs a simpler device for reallocating some of the costs and benefits of congressional campaigns. Political economists of the Milton Friedman school may have at least one useful idea in their otherwise shifty arsenal of unregulated capitalism.

Subsidy proposals involving even minimal political feasibility (a suspect term, I concede) will have only marginal impact on the current distribution of power in Congress, or the lack of competition in many districts. Subsidy proposals which might make possible the total transformation of Congress, by throwing *all* the rascals out, would not change the broadly liberal, moderate, or conservative shape of any session's typical policy output. They would undermine the stability essential for sustaining major

17. *Electing Congress*, pp. 78–80.
18. Unless stations provided time to party organizations, as Larry O'Brien and the DNC have been pushing the networks to do for purposes of counteracting President Nixon's sophisticated use of national television.

power blocs, liberal or conservative. Such stability is one of a number of essential conditions for nonviolent change in the American political system.

Redirecting national priorities requires another strategy for groups interested in maximizing the impact of opposition outside Congress on the behavior and composition of those inside.

## Changing the Arena Inside Congress

Political scientists frequently reach for complex solutions when simple ones seem uncomfortably persuasive. There is a character in an early play by Edward Albee, *The Zoo Story*, who spends three hours on stage, and a lifetime before that, setting up the necessary conditions for an acceptable suicide. On the way, he observes, "What I'm going to tell you has something to do with how sometimes it's necessary to go a long distance out of the way in order to come back a short distance correctly." This analysis seems in an embarrassingly similar situation.

Depending on the particular election, and the observer's criteria, there are usually 100 to 125 "vulnerable" seats in the House. Groups interested in maximizing their electoral investment during the short-run should do what groups so interested have always done: go where the ducks are. This applies to both primaries and general elections. What to do when you get there requires another type of analysis than the one developed in this book. For those who share my own value preferences, a good place to begin is the Movement for a New Congress's *Vote Power*.[19]

Some hint that the number and type of vulnerable incumbents may be undergoing small but significant increase is implied by a variety of emerging data. The impact of an increasingly better educated electorate (approximately 38 percent had some college in 1970, compared to 20 percent in 1950), plus the potential clout of younger voters, makes the issue-oriented, volunteer-based style of an MNC more feasible now than ten years ago.[20]

19. Englewood Cliffs, N.J.: Prentice-Hall, 1970.
20. "Potential" is a term to be emphasized here. A preliminary evaluation of the impact of the Movement for a New Congress will be found in William T. Murphy, Jr., "Student Power in the 1970 Election," *P.S.* (Winter 1971): 27–33. The MNC was active prior to ratification of the Constitutional amendment giving

Consider the remarkable number of Democratic House chairmen who have been defeated in primaries over the past four years by young, and for the most part progressive, challengers:

—George H. Fallon, 68, Public Works, by Paul S. Sarbanes in 1970;

—Samuel N. Friedel, 72, House Administration, and ranking majority member on Interstate and Foreign Commerce, by Parren J. Mitchell in 1970;

—George P. Miller, 78, Science and Astronautics, by Fortney P. Stark in 1972;

—Wayne N. Aspinall, 76, Interior and Insular Affairs, by Alan Merson in 1972;

—Emanuel Celler, 84, Judiciary, by Elizabeth Holtzman in 1972;

—John L. McMillan, 70 plus, District of Columbia, by James W. Jenrette in 1972.

The forced exit of this many chairmen via electoral defeat in two successive elections, almost one-third of the House's total chairmen, is unparalleled during the past twenty years.

Cohesive voting by blacks and other minorities, when joined by broader coalitions, *may* also continue to nudge upward the number of minority congressmen and challengers. Two-party competition in southern congressional districts, god willin' and the GOP crick don't recede, should begin to produce a larger number of southern Republican House members. Earlier retirements by senior members, either voluntarily or through a mandatory system, would immediately open 15 to 25 seats and a small number each election thereafter.[21]

---

persons 18–20 the vote. An analysis of this voting bloc's possible future behavior, running counter to the implications of much socialization research during the 1950s and 1960s, can be found in Louis M. Seagull, "The Youth Vote and Change in American Politics" (Paper delivered at the 1971 annual meetings of the American Political Science Association, Chicago).

21. Based on the number of members sixty-five and above. Mandatory retirement at age seventy has been advocated by a variety of persons. Nelson Polsby recently observed that "if on college campuses these days thirty years of age seems about right [for retirement], perhaps for Congress the age seventy is suitable." See his "Strengthening Congress in National Policy Making," *Yale Review* (Summer 1970): 481–97.

None of these shifts will have a dramatic, immediate impact on policy output, on the increasing professionalization of the House, or on the continuity of party-based opposition within Congress. The latter two features are important assets, in my estimation, in a historical epoch of presidential hegemony over critical decisions. The fact that it took so long, and so much, to reinforce and increase the few in Congress who were willing to challenge Johnson on the Vietnam war underscores the limitations built into the American congressional and electoral process.

On balance, I remain unconvinced that alternative legislative or electoral systems would have processed antiwar demands in a more effective way. The misguided premises of American foreign policy in the cold war, of which the war in Vietnam is still (1972) a logical deduction, run too deep to assume constitutionally different legislative or electoral arrangements would correct them. To be sure, the French did liquidate the Indochina war by relying on the no-confidence voting powers of a modern parliament. Four years later, deciding on the same strategy in Algeria, they faced an invasion by their own army. DeGaulle averted that catastrophe and ended the Algerian involvement. Few democrats were pleased by what happened to the Chamber of Deputies in the process.

If the Javits-Fulbright bill on curbing presidential warmaking powers is any indication, then the U.S. Congress may still be sufficiently vigorous to generate some self-correcting measures. If not, Congress will need a little nonviolent help from its friends— at the ballot box and in the streets. The two are not mutually exclusive. Absolutists may object; but *each* has a long, durable, and generally honorable history in the politics of American opposition.

Altering the outcomes in a critical number of congressional district elections can have significant, if limited, policy consequences. The data presented earlier document this assertion. Other studies reinforce it, pointing to different consequences in different issue areas.[22]

Elections, presidential or congressional, are still imperfect mechanisms for linking citizens, decision makers, and public policy. Strategies of political change will require, I believe, the creation of "extraparliamentary" organizations which can de-

22. Sullivan and O'Connor, "Electoral Choice."

velop and allocate resources to congressional candidates *and* which can operate effectively outside the electoral arena during the interim. Direct action by nonparty groups, through lobbying, litigation, issue development and research, community organizing, and unconventional forms of protest, have proved essential ingredients in the struggle for representative government.

Political parties are but one form of collective power useful for large-scale opposition in the United States. While the major parties are hardly "disappearing," they must increasingly compete with other groups for distinctive functions and clienteles. This competition need not be zero-sum; an absolute gain for one form of political organization need not be matched by a similar loss for another.

American parties have survived because of their enormous adaptive capabilities. New issues, new constituencies, and new historical periods have led parties in the past to different modes for dealing with the flow of social change. Whether they will continue to do so in the future is a question more profitably left to astrologers.

# Appendix

## Strategies of Research

Any research project stretching over a six-year period inevitably leads one into a set of problems rather similar to those confronted by Alice:

> "Would you tell me, please, which way I ought to go from here?" asked Alice. "That depends a good deal on where you want to get to," replied the Cat. "I should see the garden far better," said Alice to herself, "if I could get to the top of the hill, and here is a path that leads straight to it— but no, it doesn't do that. This goes straight back to the House. Well, then, I'll try it the other way."[1]

Typically, textbook descriptions of social science research emphasize a process that is based on (1) methodically formulated and explicitly replicable goals; (2) an equally well defined and exhaustive search of alternatives for reaching those goals; (3) precise weighting of probable consequences; followed by, (4) selection of the "best" (value-optimizing or suboptimizing) choice. But just as the Comprehensive Rational Model does not fit actual behavior in human organizations, so too most research proceeds along a course of (more or less) successive, limited comparisons. Planning and precision *are* important, yet the demands of pinching here, grabbing there, and resurfacing in entirely unexpected ways inexorably forces one to part company with comprehensive rationality. My own research is no exception.

---

1. Apologies to John Kemeny, *A Philosopher Looks at Science* (Princeton, N.J.: Van Nostrand, 1959), for pirating one of his selections from Lewis Carroll.

Three types of data dominate the analysis in the book—mail survey items, derived from a questionnaire sent to all candidates, and timed to reach them two days after the election in November 1964; open-ended but structured interviews with 69 of the 83 challengers first elected during that campaign;[2] roll-call and electoral information for the entire period, 1965–70. Less systematic and periodic reinterviews with some of those who have survived since 1966 also provided useful background data. Each has distinctive problems of reliability and validity; each generates different problems in collection and analysis. This appendix examines some of the more common difficulties associated with collecting and analyzing these data.

## Using Mail Surveys

Selection of a mail questionnaire as one of the primary research instruments was based on the conviction that carefully administered questionnaires can be almost as efficient as direct interviewing (in terms of overall response rate), are usually mandatory when an individual researcher is confronted with considerable geographical dispersion of target groups, and are infinitely cheaper if one is interested in securing data on a large number of respondents.

Others have shown[3] that mail techniques are not subject to abnormally high nonresponse rates where the population sample is skewed away from the normal adult population in terms of education, income, and occupation (depending on the occupation, as is shown below). While "mailers," scholarly and otherwise, have become a burden in most congressional offices, the same judgment does not apply to other highly active types in American politics. Properly conducted, mail survey research is still an underutilized technique in political science.

2. This figure excludes those freshmen who entered the 89th Congress after January 1965, and challengers who were former incumbents and won again in 1964.

3. William J. Crotty, "The Utilization of Mail Questionnaires," *Western Political Quarterly* (March 1966): 44–54; Stanley Bachrack and Harry M. Scoble, "Controlled Reduction of Non-Response," *Public Opinion Quarterly* (Summer 1967): 265–72; Alan R. Andreasen, "Personalizing Mail Questionnaire Correspondence," *Public Opinion Quarterly* (Summer 1970): 273–74. A detailed discussion of various techniques is provided in Parker M. Holmes, *Marketing Research: Principles and Readings* (Chicago: Southwestern Publishing, 1966).

The study was originally designed to include both incumbents and challengers. Paired comparisons, more recently examined by Sullivan and O'Connor,[4] would have provided some obvious advantages. Incumbent response was so low, however, that it seemed wise to drop them and concentrate on challengers.

Of 822 major-party nominees,[5] 56 percent (432) eventually completed and returned the questionnaire; of these, 428 provided usable and codable data sets. Response rate, by party, incumbency, and time of mailing, is shown in table 1.

Since I was attempting an enumeration of both congressional challengers and their incumbent opponents, statistical tests for partially and comparatively measuring nonresponse

Table 1.

Response Rate, by Party, Incumbency and Time of Mailing, Congressional Candidates, 1964

| Categories | Number | Percent | |
|---|---|---|---|
| Total questionnaires mailed | 822 | | |
| First mailing response | 270 | 32% | (of 822) |
| Second mailing response | 157 | 27 | (552) |
| Third mailing response[a] | 5 | 50 | (10) |
| Total response | 432 | 56 | (822) |
| Total Democratic questionnaires mailed | 434 | | |
| Total Democratic response | 215 | 45% | (434) |
| Democratic incumbents | 70 | 32 | (230) |
| Democratic nonincumbents | 145 | 72 | (204) |
| Total Republican questionnaires mailed | 388 | | |
| Total Republican response | 217 | 56% | (388) |
| Republican incumbents | 59 | 37 | (160) |
| Republican nonincumbents | 158 | 70 | (228) |
| Total incumbent response | 129 | 33 | (390) |
| Total nonincumbent response | 303 | 71 | (432) |

[a] Includes only those challengers who won.

4. John L. Sullivan and Robert E. O'Connor, "Electoral Choice and Popular Control of Public Policy: The Case of the 1966 House Elections," *American Political Science Review* (December 1972): 1256–68.

5. Democrats nominated a candidate in every district but the First of Massachusetts. Republicans nominated 388 candidates in 1964. Almost all vacancies were in the South.

error could not be utilized.[6] A third mailing was then prepared and sent exclusively to winning challengers. Only one-half responded to this third effort, but the combined three-wave response rate (71 percent) does not seem inefficient when compared to SRC's national election studies (85 to 86 percent),[7] and is higher than many other similar efforts.

Broadly speaking, two kinds of error tend to characterize all survey research: sampling and nonsampling. Although some aspects of sampling theory could be applied to the population under consideration (assuming Hubert Blalock's "infinite universe"), I prefer not to do so. This point is developed in more detail later. The immediate problem here, operating on assumptions of enumeration, is two areas of nonsampling error (random and constant).

Two techniques are available to increase the researcher's confidence that results from a mail questionnaire will not be unduly biased by nonresponse. First, as others have suggested, one should anticipate resistance and design procedures (advance mailings, personalized appeals, special delivery postage, diversified appeals in follow-up) in advance to overcome it.[8] Although an advance mimeographed letter under university letterhead had been planned, problems in timing prevented using this ice-breaking device. Hence the first packet mailed consisted of the questionnaire, a separate mimeographed letter under university letterhead, and a self-addressed, prepaid envelope. The letter outlined the purpose, scope, sponsorship, and financing of the study. The name and address of each of the 822 candidates was typed on the envelope, but the letter used in the first mailing was not personalized. Airmail postage was used. An attempt to obtain formal endorsement of the chairmen of both national committees

6. Statistical tests of this kind seem clearly inaₚpropriate unless one is attempting to generalize inductively from a sample to a finite population. See Harry M. Scoble, "A Study of Contributors to the National Committee for an Effective Congress" (Department of Political Science, University of Wisconsin, 1961), pp. 24–32. Mimeographed.

7. For some problems in the University of Michigan's Survey Research Center national samples, see Aage Clausen, "Response Validity in Surveys: Vote Report," *Public Opinion Quarterly* 32 (Winter 1968–69): 588–607.

8. Researchers have devised a number of clever tests to measure the impact of different techniques. Generally, the results show that each is only slightly additive in producing greater response. Where one is interested in high response, as many should be used as is feasible. See Holmes, *Marketing Research*.

failed (Dean Burch, then chairman of the GOP, did provide a computerized mailing list with home addresses for candidates, as did John Bailey, his Democratic counterpart, but neither group would at that time extend endorsement).[9] Of the original 822 first mailings, 32 percent of the candidates responded.

Approximately one month after the first mailing, a second attempt was made to reach those candidates who had not responded to the first query. A new letter, also under university letterhead, was mailed along with a second copy of the question-naire and another stamped, self-addressed envelope. This time the candidate's name and address was personally typed on *both* letter and envelope. This second-wave mailing netted a 27 percent return from the 552 candidates receiving it.

On the basis of correspondence, resistance to this type of research seems to be a reflection of three different factors. The first, at least overtly a clear minority, came from those who are self-consciously hostile to survey research (perhaps any kind of research). The attitude is best conveyed by the following, a Republican who had lost his seat after ten years in the House:[10]

> I do not mean to be impolite or a complete boor, but I'm simply tired of being dissected and cross-sectioned by every political science group in the country and afterwards these results being used all over the United States to defeat many, good solid Republicans. . . . I suggest your group ascertain its leadership answers by climbing down off the ladder and file for a major office. After that, and after you undergo the rigors of primaries, fund raising, compromises and final elections, I'm sure you will be able to answer your own questionnaire with much more exactness than will ever be possible by sub-mitting it to candidates.

And, from another, this time a Democrat:

> After considering your "questionnaire" with some care, I

9. Official support, due to pressures of time, was never seriously pursued with either Burch or Bailey. National committee endorsement may have led to higher incumbent response rates had I invested the time and energy.

10. Ironically, this response was sent by one of the sixty-two congressmen who, six days before the opening of the Republican National Convention, signed a full-page *New York Times* ad declaring, "We are convinced that the nomination of Senator Barry Goldwater will result in substantial Republican increases in both Houses of Congress." Of the 62 who signed, 57 competed for office, and 20 were defeated; 3 of the 5 who retired had their seats taken by Democrats.

conclude that it was framed on a series of false assumptions and that my reply could not possibly serve any useful purpose. In fact, I cannot imagine why such an inquiry would be sponsored by your university or the Falk Foundation. In fact, I'm writing the Falk Foundation and strongly urging them to utilize their money (which is tax-exempt) in the future in a wiser way.

More typically, most who actively refused either noted the press of time or indicated that congressmen receive so many requests, from so many sources, that it necessitates a policy refusing all such requests.[11] Replied one, "I deeply regret that because of the large number of questionnaires I have received similar to yours . . . I can no longer answer any such questionnaires."

Still, most of the correspondence received was favorable to the idea (about thirty of forty-five letters) even when it was felt immediate response was impossible. Said one who was under particular stress:

Unfortunately, I was in a serious automobile accident two days before the election and am still in traction in the hospital. However, I think your research potentially very valuable and will be happy to comply when I can devote some undivided time and thought to these matters. I will look forward to seeing the results.

Like Lewis Anthony Dexter and others,[12] I'm nevertheless convinced that mail surveys with congressmen, no matter how carefully planned or designed, will ultimately destroy access for other kinds of necessary research. Former sinners may be the worst kind of believers, but a moratorium on mail surveys of Congress is long overdue. No such conclusion now seems reasonable for other important subgroups in American politics.

A second feature associated with systematically treating the problem of nonresponse is to introduce a procedure for keying

11. Someone should collect and publish a selection of oddball letters received during the course of mail surveys. One congressman, citing the burdens of time and saturation as an excuse for not returning the questionnaire, nevertheless proposed that if I would write the president urging "no reduction in feed grain price support rates for 1965," he might find time to complete the questionnaire. I did and he did.

12. See the general discussion on this and other matters in Earl M. Baker, "Research on Congress," *P.S.* (Summer 1969): 361–65.

each questionnaire to sampled individuals in the population. Where sampling procedures are used, this will permit the analyst comparatively and partially to estimate the probable bias created by nonresponse. Ultimately, however, the biasing effects of nonresponse are probably not measurable. But even where sampling techniques are not used, a procedure like the above has distinct payoffs.

The advantages and disadvantages of anonymity were considered, but the case for serialized identification was strong enough to override any of the (largely unestablished) claims made for complete anonymity. Keying each questionnaire to individual candidates permitted inclusion of district and census data for all candidates, data that were absolutely necessary to construct independent variables in the analysis. It also permitted the creation of two critical baselines by which to compare those who responded with those who did not: party and region. Differences between these two groups, as the data in table 2 show,

Table 2.

Differences in Distribution of Response and
Nonresponse on Selected Factors Available for
Both Categories, Congressional Challengers, 1964
(In Percent)

| Categories | Response | Nonresponse | Difference |
|---|---|---|---|
| Party | | | |
| Democratic | 47 | 45 | −2 |
| Republican | 53 | 55 | 2 |
| Region[a] | | | |
| New England | 6 | 4 | −2 |
| Mid-Atlantic | 23 | 25 | 2 |
| Border | 5 | 5 | — |
| South | 11 | 10 | −1 |
| Midwest | 31 | 29 | −2 |
| Southwest | 8 | 9 | 1 |
| Mountain | 2 | 4 | 2 |
| Pacific | 13 | 12 | −1 |
| Not available | 2 | — | — |
| | $N$ = (303) | (129) | |

[a] Regional classification follows the format of the Survey Research Center, University of Michigan.

do not exceed 2 percent, an encouraging if not completely reassuring finding.

Moreover, informing the respondent, particularly if he is a public figure of some sort, that his questionnaire is numbered for response checks (but that confidentiality will be maintained) may even increase the reliability of the information gained; particularly if he feels reasonably certain such information will be treated only statistically. Scoble reports that the only obvious misinformation provided in his mail survey of the NCEC was from those who, on a third mailing, were sent anonymous questionnaires.[13]

The other sources of nonsampling error were dealt with (but not eliminated) in a variety of ways. Random error in processing survey data is always a question of reliability and can be handled through replication using identical (or similar) instruments, or equivalent (but different) instruments, for measuring what is presumed to be the same characteristic.[14] Obviously, this is not possible in the context of a single study, although some impressions were gathered in the later interviews with sixty-nine respondents.[15]

Constant error probably occurred most frequently in the process of question-framing and coding. The most useful device for reducing ambiguity in questions, a pretest, was impossible given the time and financial resources available. Other surveys were thus consulted in organizing some of the questions finally used. It was clear after the first return that two questions should have been reworked or scrapped. Neither was used in generating

13. Scoble, "Study of Contributors," p. 31.

14. The best single discussion is still Claire Selltiz, Marie Jahoda, et al., *Research Methods in Social Relations* (rev. ed.; New York: Holt, Rinehart & Winston, 1962), pp. 146–86. The Institute for Social Research at the University of Michigan has published a long-overdue volume providing clear and useful summaries of a variety of political attitudinal measures including the actual questions, reliability information, etc.: John Robinson, Jerrold G. Rusk, and Kendra B. Head, *Measures of Political Attitudes* (Ann Arbor: Survey Research Center/Institute for Social Research, 1968).

15. The congressional interviews began with the question, "Last year you indicated that the (national/state/local) party gave you (considerable/some/etc.) help in the campaign. Could .you elaborate on that?" Only one of the sixty-nine specifically took issue with the judgment rendered fourteen months prior. This can be misleading, of course, but it provides a modicum of evidence on the accuracy of the original judgment. The one exception is worth quoting: "Considerable help, did you say? I must have been drunk or asleep when I filled that thing out. The only help I got from the National Committee was a letter of congratulations on getting nominated and some canned crap about what a great help for the country Lyndon Johnson would be as President."

data for the analysis. Coding did not raise substantial problems since most of the questions were of the closed, fixed-choice variety. A large codebook was prepared and all the data transferred to standard card format and then to tape.

Other problems of reliability and validity involving specific measures derived from the questionnaire were dealt with where they constituted a major component of a particular chapter.

## Interviewing in Congress

Given the verbal beating Congress has taken from the intellectual community over the past twenty-five years, and the occupational suspicion many members are thought to harbor about interviews with "outsiders," most neophyte researchers arrive expecting a wall of resistance. Walls there were, but the overwhelming majority I sought in the 89th Congress were open, accessible, and candid.

The plea made by another scholar to an earlier group of congressmen had apparently been internalized by these men and women: "I hope that when someone comes around, knocking on your door asking for an interview, engaged in research, that you will be able to scrounge up five minutes to help them carry on."[16] Sixty-nine of the eighty-three I interviewed found much more time than five minutes. Average interview time was one hour and fifteen minutes; the range was from thirty minutes to five hours.

Two factors, I believe, explain what appeared to be the increasing receptivity of Congress to political science field research in the mid-1960s. One is peculiar to my project and obvious—the interviewees were freshmen and hence easier to deal with—while the other is more subtle, quite difficult to prove, and belongs in the realm of the sociology of knowledge.

The Study of Congress Project, organized under the direction of Ralph K. Huitt and Robert L. Peabody with the active assistance of key members inside the House, focused research on Congress in a fundamentally different manner than had been true of most earlier work. I was once startled to hear a prominent critic of the House say that he made a policy of *never* interviewing any member with whom he was in substantial disagreement. At

16. H. Douglas Price in *Transcript of Seminars for New Members of the 88th Congress* (Washington, D.C.: Congressional Quarterly Service, 1965), p. 52.

the risk of belaboring the obvious, it is clear that Huitt and Peabody, their associates, and most other political scientists doing research on Congress over the past ten years have started with different assumptions. "Until these tasks [understanding how Congress actually functions] are completed," Huitt and Peabody once wrote, "our lists of congressional reforms are little more than statements of personal preference."[17] Such a commitment seems bound to generate a more positive reception from any group invaded by field researchers. Congress, like all social institutions, tends to be more receptive to outsiders who arrive as something other than precommitted saboteurs. The fact that a small but significant number of congressmen have consistently felt otherwise, providing an inside alliance partner for outside critics, simply served to reinforce the separation between reform-oriented political scientists and the development of empirically based theory that was acceptable to both reformers and non-reformers. It is clear that recent research has made its greatest contribution in working on the empirical side of the equation. Accordingly, the tone and style of political science literature on Congress has become less combative and critical about the institution's supposed malfunctioning.

Of course the opposite problem now dogs those who have minimized their commitment to subversive aims, as attacks on everything from the discipline's "bourgeois pluralism" to the APSA Congressional Fellowship Program underscore.[18] I would argue that field researchers, independent of how they feel about problems of institutional change, should ultimately come to regard their role vis-à-vis Congress in about the same manner Conrad saw Axel Heyst in *Victory*:

> Heyst was not conscious of either friends or enemies. It was the very essence of his life to be a solitary achievement, accomplished not by hermit-like withdrawal with its silence and

17. In a joint foreword to Lewis A. Froman, Jr., *The Congressional Process* (Boston: Little, Brown, 1967), p. viii.

18. For a constructive critique of the research generated by The Study of Congress Project, avoiding the imprecision of blanket condemnation or the paranoia about political scientists losing their intellectual virginity by participating in the fellowship program, see Donald R. Matthews, "The APSA Committee on Congress (1945) and the APSA Study of Congress (1965–1969) Studies" (Paper delivered at the Annual Meeting of the American Political Science Association, Los Angeles, 1970).

immobility, but by a system of restless wandering, by the de-
tachment of an impermanent dweller amongst changing
scenes . . . invulnerable because elusive.

Or so it seemed to me when I arrived in the early part of 1966,
very green and somewhat bemused at the prospect of facing up
to the dictates of Conrad. I shared most of the assumptions and
biases of Richard Bolling's *House Out of Order*— and still do—
but successful field research requires that such baggage be at least
temporarily jettisoned.

Others had been plying the hallways long before me, and
their knowledge, experience, and insights proved extraordinarily
useful. [19] The interview schedule followed the open-ended but
structured format, incorporating questions from various sources,
developing others that were unique to the project.[20] A copy is
provided on pages 230–35.

Functioning as a guest scholar at The Brookings Institution
permits one to use the institution's considerable prestige in
Washington as an added inducement for cooperation. Indeed only
one of the interviewees raised any questions about institutional
sponsorship; when he demanded to see some piece of "official"
identification, the only thing I had beyond a California driver's
license (Brookings was then quite casual about supplying anything to nonpermanent staff) was a door pass to the office on
Massachusetts Avenue. He examined it, apparently decided I
was not an enemy agent, and the interview went rather well
thereafter. I later discovered the public relations director of the
Liberty Lobby had sent letters and questionnaires to freshman
Democrats, posing as a freelance researcher collecting information
about the Class of 89. Whatever the source of this member's

19. Charles O. Jones, "Notes on Interviewing Members of the House of
Representatives," *Public Opinion Quarterly* (Fall 1959): 404–6; James A. Robinson,
"Survey Interviewing Among Members of Congress," *Public Opinion Quarterly*
(1960): 127–38; and the methodological appendix of John Wahlke, Heinz Eulau,
William Buchanan, LeRoy C. Ferguson, *The Legislative System* (New York: John
Wiley, 1963), pp. 435–65. Subsequently, Lewis Anthony Dexter codified long years
of experience in various milieus in his *Elite Interviewing* (Evanston: Northwestern
University Press, 1970). The reader may also wish to consult a volume written by a
social anthropologist, Raymond L. Gorden, *Interviewing: Strategy, Techniques, and
Tactics* (Homewood: Dorsey, 1969).

20. Three major sources were: Wahlke et al., *Legislative System;* James D.
Barber, *The Lawmakers* (New Haven: Yale University Press, 1965); and the interview schedules of Dwaine Marvick and Samuel J. Eldersveld on party activists.

reluctance, resistance was clearly the exception rather than rule. Credible institutional affiliation in Washington, unless the researcher is well known, is an important commodity for gaining access. I suspect this is even more important now than it was in 1966.

Of the fourteen who were not interviewed, only three were active resisters. The remainder were willing but elusive. After a number of broken appointments, I decided to drop them, focusing on other problems in the development of the project.

Open-ended interviewing, no matter how structured, requires more time than most researchers initially budget. Unless the interviewer is a machine, indifferent to what the respondent has to say, unconcerned about his own psychology in the interviewing situation, or operating under impossible time constraints (in which case another project should be considered), "knocking off" sixty-plus congressional interviews in less than five months is impossible. I spent seven months, working rather consistently on other aspects of the project while also taking an average of three interviews each week. Others may consider this an outrageously small average. The reason is simple: ten interviews were completed during the first two weeks of active research and I had become simultaneously bored and clumsy during the process. Asking repetitive questions of different members, as structured interviewing requires, tends to generate repetitive answers—no matter how unique each respondent and his experience might be. Yet it is precisely *patterns of response* that make structured interview data superior to "backgrounders" as evidence in social science. One either hires other interviewers, or reduces the frequency of repeating the process. The latter seems eminently more sensible for relatively small projects, particularly where the researcher can both gain insights that are unique as well as gather comparable information across the sample population. Structured interviewing should be a learning experience for the interviewer, despite the repetition, and reducing the frequency of interviews is the only way to maximize both learning and data-collecting payoffs. In any event, interviews for this phase of the project were completed in October 1966, a completion date that represented an investment of about twice the time initially planned.

Overt resistance by the three congressmen who actively refused interviews took the normal route of hostility to survey-based social science research. One of the three, however, seemed exceptionally neurotic on this score. Since Congress is thought to be somewhat representative of the adult population, one out of eighty-three does not seem an unusually distorted ratio. Which figure belongs on what side of the ratio is a judgment I shall happily leave to the reader's own value premises. In this instance, the congressman prohibited his staff from even discussing the *possibility* of an appointment until additional correspondence had been exchanged (letters explaining the project and discussing sponsorship were sent prior to calling each office to arrange an interview). Four additional letters and a copy of the interview schedule failed to convince him. The other two congressmen simply refused indicating they saw little point in such research. Still, whether passive or active, nonresponse did not appear to introduce bias along any visible partisan, ideological, or regional axis. Four Republicans and ten Democrats were ultimately missed.

Brief notes were taken during all the interviews, using mimeographed copies of the schedule as a guide for questions. At the close of an interview, I retreated to one of the cafeterias and attempted a word-for-word reconstruction of the entire exchange. Obviously this process leads to considerable information loss. Only tape recordings correct such problems; their use was considered but rejected since I had neither the stature nor confidence to use them effectively. Occasionally I found myself heading for the nearest corner, or simply stopping outside the member's office, to record what the interviewer always believes is a superb quote, or particularly insightful paragraph. Most of the interviewing was done in the member's office, although a few interviews were completed in the dining room, the Speaker's Room, or (in two cases) in a local bar. All coding was undertaken by the author.

Congressional cooperation seemed remarkably good since as someone observed with only slight exaggeration, there were almost as many political scientists interviewing freshmen in the 89th Congress as there were new members. During the same period, three other researchers were collecting data on this particular freshman class: Irwin Gertzog, with special interests in the adaptation of minority members; Stephen Wasby, examining their relationship with Democratic party funding organizations;

and Thomas P. Murphy, who was interested generally in the policy implications of their arrival.

Most freshmen still proved to be gracious if somewhat overinterviewed respondents.

## Data Analysis

The strategy of analysis followed throughout this book should cause few problems for readers with even minimal quantitative training. Cross-tabulation requires only that the analyst be able to add to one hundred, think (more or less) logically, and have some theoretically defensible notions about independent and dependent variables. Developing a "good" analysis, while avoiding some common problems of inference and interpretation, is somewhat more complex, but the paths along which sensitive cross-tabulation has traveled are well marked in the social sciences.[21]

More bothersome to statistically conscious readers, I suspect, are two omissions: tests of significance and statistics measuring the strength of association between variables. The two are frequently confused, as the continuing controversy about their use suggests. [22] Neither is used in this book.

Although it is still a matter of controversy among statisticians, tests of significance like chi-square seem theoretically pointless unless one is making inferences to finite universes from systematic samples. My data are based on an attempted enumeration of a universe. Hubert Blalock suggests that even when an enumeration has been undertaken, statistical tests are still legitimate because "... one may be interested in developing generalizations which could apply to other as yet *nonexistent* [universes]" (my emphasis).[23] The strongest objection to this line of reasoning comes from Johan Galtung when he argues that "... if we are free

21. The best single source using cross-tabulation as the dominant technique is Morris Rosenberg, *The Logic of Survey Analysis* (New York: Basic Books, 1968).

22. See Johan Galtung, *Theory and Methods of Social Research* (New York: Columbia University Press, 1967), pp. 358–90. A useful brief discussion can be found in Thomas J. Duggan and Charles W. Dean, "Common Misinterpretations of Significance Levels in Sociological Journals," *American Sociologist* (February 1968): 45–47.

23. Hubert M. Blalock, *Social Statistics* (New York: McGraw-Hill), p. 270.

to construct hypothetical universes, we are also free to construct several hypothetical super-universes for each universe we have data about [but without experimentation] we cannot turn back to 1810 and begin generating Latin American nations again, a circumstance that makes the hypothetical universe not only hypothetical but operationally empty."[24]

I preferred to remain conservative on this issue and to restrict any generalizations about congressional challengers to the built-in restrictions of a universe existing in concrete time and space; hence no significance tests were used. As an alternative, I followed those conventions suggested by Heinz Eulau in *The Legislative System*, [25] treating differences of 10 percentage points or more as "large," less than that, "small." Differences of this magnitude, by definition, are "real" (not due to sampling error) although they are subject to the normal problems of spuriousness where small *N*s prevented multiple controls.

The case for moving from percentage comparisons with ordinal and nominal data to a single summarizing measure of association is quite simple and usually compelling. A summarizing measure should enable the researcher and reader to *compare* relationships more easily from table to table. Given the speed with which computer technology processes data, the availability of a variety of good statistical packages, and the seemingly strong logic of moving beyond cross-tabulation, I dutifully generated a large number of nonparametric bivariate statistics, mainly Kendall's tau and Goodman-Kruskal's gamma. Neither measure greatly increased my ability to comparatively examine relationships with these data; indeed, after using gammas throughout one chapter, I found the entire analysis bogging down in repetitive statements about the strength of association, here a .32, there a .26, and so forth. For better or worse, straightforward cross-tabulation seems to force the researcher (at least this one) into a process of elaboration and qualification about the theoretical meaning and/or utility of one's data that was lacking in correlational analysis. Perhaps the problem is bivariate correlational operations, independent of the technique used,[26] but that is a

24. Galtung, *Theory and Methods of Social Research*, p. 368.
25. Pp. 461–62.
26. This is frequently argued for other social sciences. For political science, see Edward R. Tufte, "Improving Data Analysis in Political Science," *World Politics* (July 1969): 641–54.

problem that must wait for correction in another book. Summarizing measures of association, as with tests of significance, proved of little utility and were dropped.

Distinctions between "good" and "bad" social science research rest on a set of canons about the intelligent allocation of scarce resources. Decisions affecting this allocation should increase the probability that the study (1) will yield theoretically interesting and replicable results; (2) provide a mechanism for reducing and measuring the inevitable errors which are part of all empirically based research; and, (3) will be completed in a reasonable amount of time.[27]

This book, failing in some respects, hopefully succeeding in others, is a product of the usual struggle to balance all three.

## MAIL QUESTIONNAIRE FOR CONGRESSIONAL CHALLENGERS

UNIVERSITY OF CALIFORNIA, LOS ANGELES            NUMBER_____
DEPARTMENT OF POLITICAL SCIENCE
LOS ANGELES 90024

### *CONFIDENTIAL*

*Instructions for completing this questionnaire.*[28]

1. Your cooperation in this research endeavor is sincerely requested. Please complete the following questions by placing a check-mark or filling in the blank which best describes your opinion.

2. The serial number at the top right-hand corner of this page, to repeat, *is a mechanical device only* which will be used to determine the rate of response. Once checked, the number *will not* be further associated with your name.

3. Again, if you wish to receive a preliminary copy of the

27. One definition of "reasonable" suggested by a colleague: before the researcher or subject(s) expire.
28. A covering letter spelled out the rationale more thoroughly.

report, please make the appropriate check on the last page of the questionnaire.

4. Because the data provided herein will be analyzed in quantitative form only, we specifically request that you DO NOT SIGN the questionnaire. Your cooperation will be of incalculable assistance in helping all those interested in political life to develop a more accurate picture of the qualities of political leadership. Thank you.

---

First, we would like to know something about your estimation of the local, state, and national party organizations as each related to your campaign. In the *general* election how much help (campaign literature, financial contributions, staff assistance, etc.) did you receive from the *local* party organizations?

_____Considerable   _____Some   _____Not much   _____None

How much help did you receive from the *state* party organization?

_____Considerable   _____Some   _____Not much   _____None

How much help did you receive from the *national* party organization?

_____Considerable   _____Some   _____Not much   _____None

How did you first become interested in running for office in this election?

_____Pretty much my own idea   _____Suggested by party leaders

_____Suggested by friends   _____Other (specify)

In your opinion, would you say that your party's candidate for president helped, harmed, or didn't materially affect your own chances for victory?

_____Helped   _____Harmed   _____Didn't affect   _____Don't know

When you were nominated to run, how did you assess your chances of winning?

_____Very likely   _____50–50 chance   _____Not very likely

Which of the following best characterizes your district?

_____Mainly rural    _____Mainly urban    _____Mainly suburban
_____Mixed (specify)

Which of the following political groups were you the nominee of?

_____Democrat    _____Republican    _____Independent
_____Other (specify)

Regardless of which group nominated you, or how you voted in the last few elections, how have you usually thought of yourself—as a Republican, a Democrat, or what?

_____Republican    _____Democrat    _____Independent
_____Other (specify)

If either "Democrat" or "Republican" would you consider yourself a *strong* party member or *not so strong* a party member?

_____Strong    _____Not so strong

The following reasons are often given in explaining why persons become candidates for public office. How important, in your own case, do you consider each of the following:

|  | VERY IMPORTANT | SOMEWHAT | NOT VERY IMPORTANT |
|---|---|---|---|
| Politics as a way of life | _____ | _____ | _____ |
| Make social contacts and friends | _____ | _____ | _____ |
| Strong sense of party loyalty | _____ | _____ | _____ |
| Chance to serve community | _____ | _____ | _____ |
| Build future in politics | _____ | _____ | _____ |
| Make useful business contacts | _____ | _____ | _____ |
| Enjoy campaigning | _____ | _____ | _____ |
| Influence public policy | _____ | _____ | _____ |

In your view, how important is each of the following campaign activities to the outcome of an election?

|                                         | VERY IMPORTANT | SOMEWHAT | NOT VERY IMPORTANT |
|-----------------------------------------|----------------|----------|--------------------|
| Endorsement from community leaders      | _____          | _____    | _____              |
| Endorsement from *state* party leaders  | _____          | _____    | _____              |
| Visits to factories and offices         | _____          | _____    | _____              |
| Appearances before small groups         | _____          | _____    | _____              |
| Appearances on television               | _____          | _____    | _____              |
| Newspaper support                       | _____          | _____    | _____              |
| Billboards                              | _____          | _____    | _____              |
| Door-to-door canvassing                 | _____          | _____    | _____              |
| Other (specify) _____ |

Next, we would like some idea about how you feel on certain policy-issues often discussed around the country today. On most issues, would you consider yourself *liberal, middle of the road,* or *conservative*?

_____ Liberal    _____ Middle of the road    _____ Conservative

On most issues, would you consider yourself *more* liberal, *about the same,* or *more* conservative than each of the following:

|                      | MORE LIBERAL | ABOUT SAME | MORE CONSERVATIVE |
|----------------------|--------------|------------|-------------------|
| Your *local* party   | _____        | _____      | _____             |
| Your *state* party   | _____        | _____      | _____             |
| Your *national* party| _____        | _____      | _____             |

Much of what the federal government does can be judged in terms of whether it should do *more,* just about the *same,* or *less.* Please check the following to indicate your judgment about each of these policies or program areas:

|                          | THE FEDERAL GOVERNMENT SHOULD DO... | | |
|--------------------------|------|------------|------|
|                          | MORE | ABOUT SAME | LESS |
| Work for disarmament     | _____ | _____     | _____ |
| Give foreign economic aid| _____ | _____     | _____ |
| Assist public education  | _____ | _____     | _____ |
| Keep up farm prices      | _____ | _____     | _____ |

| | VERY IMPORTANT | SOMEWHAT | NOT VERY IMPORTANT |
|---|---|---|---|
| Work for minority and Negro rights | _____ | _____ | _____ |
| Support the United Nations | _____ | _____ | _____ |
| Help the poverty-stricken | _____ | _____ | _____ |
| Regulate big business | _____ | _____ | _____ |
| Cooperate with Russia | _____ | _____ | _____ |
| Provide the elderly Medicare | _____ | _____ | _____ |
| Regulate labor unions | _____ | _____ | _____ |

This concludes the questions on politics. The remaining are routine biographical items and are indispensable for meaningful statistical analysis of the data which you have already supplied.

What is the *highest* level of *party* office you have ever held?

_____ National _____ State _____ County _____ City _____ None

What is the *highest* level of *public* office you have ever held?

_____ National _____ State _____ County _____ City _____ None

What is your age: _____ (years)   Sex: _____   1964 income? _____
(annual)

Are you married? _____ Number of children _____ Your religion? _____

What is your occupation?_____ (specify)

Did you win your election? _____ Percent of vote received _____ %

Were you an incumbent? _____ How many years had you held this office? _____

How active are you in groups concerned with community affairs?

_____ Very active _____ Somewhat _____ Not very active

How active was your father and/or mother in political affairs?

_____ Very active _____ Somewhat _____ Not very active

What was your father's occupation when you were growing up? ____

Your father's political party?

____ Republican    ____ Democratic    ____ Independent
                   ____ Other

Please check last school year completed:

____ Grammar school    ____ Some high school _____ High school
                                                        Graduate
       ____ Some college    ____ College graduate    ____ Postgrad;
                                                          professional

Please check size of community in which you grew up:

       ____ Farm    ____ Under 25,000    ____ 26,000–50,000
____ 51,000–99,000    ____ 100,000–249,000    ____ 250,000
                                                  and above


If you would like a copy of the preliminary study of this data, please make a check in the following slot ____ . Thank you again for your patience and cooperation.


## INTERVIEW SCHEDULE FOR CONGRESSMEN


## I.    CAMPAIGN ACTIVITIES

    1.    First, I would like to ask you some questions about the election coming up next fall. Will you be a candidate for reelection?

        Yes, definitely        ____
        Not sure                ____
        No, definitely          ____

    1a.    IF NO:    Why Not?

    2.    How do you rate your chances? Are you anticipating any stiff opposition in a primary or party convention?

3. In the questionnaire, you indicated that your local party organization gave you _____ help. Would you say things will be about the same this fall, different, or what? How is that?

3a. Specifically, what kind of activities would you say the local party performs best? Worst?

4. Now, what about the state party organization? Last year you seemed to feel it was _____ help. Do you expect any changes next fall?

4a. Again, what types of activities does the state party seem to undertake which are the greatest assistance? the least?

5. What about the various offices of the national party? You indicated it was _____ last year. Do you anticipate any changes this year? In what way? How would you compare the Democratic/Republican Congressional Campaign Committee with its counterpart in the opposition? Are there any changes which you would like to see undertaken in the operation of this committee?

6. What would you consider the major strengths of your party, as a whole, considering all three levels of party organization as they relate to your campaign?

6a. And what are the major weaknesses?

## II. RECRUITMENT

7. Now I would like to ask some questions about the events which led up to your candidacy in 1964. Had you been a candidate for the House before?

    Yes _____
    No _____

7a. Any other public elective office? Which one(s)?

7b. What other governmental or party position—local, state, national—had you held before coming to Congress? Do you hold any of these positions now?

7c. Could you describe the principal events which led to your

candidacy? In the questionnaire, you indicated it was
_____. Could you elaborate on that?

8.    In making up your mind about running, what factors did
      you take into account? What were some of the pros and
      cons as you saw it then?

8a.   What were some of the reactions (attitudes) of your
      family and friends about this?

8b.   If you had to decide, which of these factors you've men-
      tioned would you say had the most to do with your final
      decision?

9.    How long would you say you've been interested in
      politics? (Earliest recollection.)


### III.   CONGRESSIONAL SOCIALIZATION

10.   Turning now to your work as a congressman: Would you
      say that your impressions of the operation of the House
      have changed a great deal or very little since the day you
      were sworn in? How is that, or Why, etc.

10a.  What impressions stand out in your mind regarding your
      first year here? What brought about this feeling of
      _____?

10b.  IF NOT COVERED: How would you describe the job of
      being a legislator? What are the most important things
      you should do here?

10c.  Do you think these viewpoints will change as you gain
      seniority?

11.   Are there any important differences between what *you*
      think this job is and the way some of *your constituents*
      see it? What are these differences?

12.   It seems to be generally accepted that both the House
      and the Senate have certain unofficial rules of the game—
      certain things members should do and should not do if
      they want the respect and cooperation of their colleagues.
      What are some of these things—these unofficial rules—
      that a member should observe to hold his fellow member's
      respect and cooperation?

12a.  How do other members make things difficult for people who seem to constantly flaunt these unofficial rules? How would you compare the House and Senate in this respect?

13.   Now, let's turn to your work on committee(s). What is your general reaction to committee work so far? How have things been going for you there?

14.   You were assigned, I believe, to _____ committee(s). Was that your first, second, third choice, or what?

14a.  Could you describe briefly the steps by which you finally secured this assignment? (Who talked, any letters of support, etc.)

14b.  Tell me about your initial impressions at the first meeting of your committee(s).

14c.  How would you evaluate the job of Chairman _____ so far? Are there any things he does do but shouldn't, or doesn't do but should?

14d.  How would you say the committee members get along with one another? Do you think party is important in this regard?

14e.  Generally speaking, is there anything in the present operation of your committee which you would like to see changed?

14f.  Anything else about its work which stands out in your mind?

15.   Now, let's move over the general operation of the House. What role ought the Speaker and his staff take in order to be most effective?

15a.  What about the Minority leadership, what role should they play?

16.   And what about some of the other party leaders here in the House. What should they do in order to be effective?

16a.  What have been your own relationships with the party leadership? (Causes, etc.)

16b.   Have you ever felt pressured by the leadership?

16c.   Is it your impression that others—freshmen *and* more senior members—have or have not felt this way?

16d.   IF YES: What forms does this take?

16e.   Would you suggest any changes in the way the party leadership now operates?

17.    Thinking back to some of your first impressions of activity on the Floor: How would you describe the general session? (Impressions of others there, how other members feel about the sessions, improvements, etc.)

18.    Have you delivered what you would consider a relatively major speech on the floor yet? (What was your feeling about speaking then, reactions by others, etc.)

19.    How often do you get together with other congressmen outside of committee and normal office activities?

       Regularly, sometimes, rarely, or never?

19a.   Who are some of your closest personal friends in the House—I mean the members you see most often outside the Chamber, at lunch, dinner, parties, or other social gatherings?

19b.   What about your state delegation: How often does it caucus as a whole, what issues seem to be particularly hard to win general agreement on?

19c.   Would you say that you meet socially more often with other members of your state delegation or not? (If relevant, what about the city delegation?)

20.    I've been told by other members that there are always some interest groups or lobbies in the House whose advice ought to be considered, whether they happen to be powerful or not. Could you name some of the groups you've run into here whom you feel would fall into this category? (What organizations do you have in mind?)

20a.   Could you tell me what it is about these organizations or persons that makes them worth listening to?

20b.   Are any of these groups particularly powerful in your own district? How is that (What do they do, sources of power, etc.)?

20c.    Any others?

20d.    Would you say that, on the whole, the House would operate better, worse, or what if no interest groups or lobbies were trying to influence legislation?

## IV. CAREER ASPIRATIONS

21.     Generally speaking, how do you view your future in politics?

21a.    What do you consider to be some of the more likely possibilities?

22a.    IF NOT COVERED: Did you have an opportunity to attend the American Political Science Association's program for new members when you arrived?

22b.    IF YES: What were your reactions to it?

22c.    IF NOT COVERED: Are there any changes you would suggest which would make it easier for future members to learn the ropes—both the formal and informal procedures?

22d.    Incidentally, how do you feel about four-year terms?

23.     Is there anything else about the operation of the House, and its relationship to new members, that you think I ought to pay attention to in this study?

# Bibliography

## I. Books

Acheson, Dean. *A Citizen Looks at Congress*. New York: McGraw-Hill, 1954.

Adamany, David. *Financing Politics*. Madison: University of Wisconsin Press, 1969.

Alford, Robert R. *Party and Society*. Chicago, Rand McNally, 1963.

Agger, Robert, et al. *The Rulers and the Ruled*. New York: Wiley, 1964.

Apter, David, ed. *Ideology and Discontent*. New York: Free Press, 1963.

Bachrach, Peter. *The Theory of Democratic Elitism*. Boston: Little, Brown, 1967.

————, and Baratz, Morton S. *Power and Poverty*. New York: Oxford University Press, 1970.

Barber, James D. *The Lawmakers*. New Haven: Yale University Press, 1965.

Baus, Herbert, and Ross, William. *Politics Battle-Plan*. New York: Macmillan, 1968.

Beck, Carl, et al. *A Survey of Elite Studies*. Washington, D.C.: Special Operations Research Office, 1965.

Bell, Wendell, et al. *Public Leaders*. San Francisco: Chandler, 1962.

Bem, Daryl. *Beliefs, Attitudes, and Human Affairs*. Belmont, Calif.: Wadsworth, 1970.

Berelson, Bernard, and Janowitz, Morris, eds. *Reader in Public Opinion and Mass Communications*. 2nd ed. New York: Free Press, 1966.

Bibby, John, and Davidson, Roger. *On Capitol Hill*. New York: Holt, 1966.

Bolling, Richard. *House Out of Order*. New York: Dutton, 1965.

Bullitt, Stimson. *To Be a Politician*. New York: Doubleday, 1956.

Bunzel, John. *Anti-Politics*. New York: Knopf, 1967.

Burnham, Walter D. *Critical Elections and the Mainsprings of American Politics*. New York: Norton, 1970.

Burns, James M. *The Deadlock of Democracy*. Englewood Cliffs, N.J.: Prentice-Hall, 1963.

Campbell, Angus, et al. *The American Voter*. New York: Wiley, 1960.

Chafee, Zechariah. *Free Speech in the United States*. Cambridge, Mass.: Harvard University Press, 1942.

Christie, Richard, and Jahoda, Marie, eds. *Studies in the Scope and Method of the Authoritarian Personality*. Glencoe, Ill.: Free Press, 1954.

Cohen, Arthur. *Attitude Change and Social Influence*. New York: Basic Books, 1966.

Connolly, William. *Political Science and Ideology*. Chicago: Atherton, 1967.

Coplin, William, ed. *Simulation in the Study of Politics*. Chicago: Markham, 1968.

Cotter, C. *Practical Politics in the United States*. Boston: Allyn & Bacon, 1969.

Cummings, Milton S., ed. *The National Elections of 1964*. Washington, D.C.: Brookings, 1965.

_____. *Congressmen and the Electorate: 1920–1964*. New York: Free Press, 1966.

Dahl, Robert A., ed. *Political Opposition in Western Democracies*. New Haven: Yale University Press, 1966.

_____. *Pluralist Democracy in the United States*. Chicago: Rand McNally, 1969.

David, Paul, et al. *The Politics of National Party Conventions*. Washington, D.C.: Brookings, 1960.

Davidson, Roger, et al. *Congress in Crisis: Politics and Congressional Reform*. Belmont, Calif.: Wadsworth, 1966.

Dawson, Richard, and Prewitt, Kenneth. *Political Socialization*. Boston: Little, Brown, 1968.

DeGrazia, Alfred. *Public and Republic*. New York: Knopf, 1951.

Dexter, Lewis A. *The Sociology and Politics of Congress*. Chicago: Rand McNally, 1969.

Dolbeare, Kenneth and Patricia. *American Political Ideologies*. Chicago: Markham, 1970.

Downs, Anthony. *An Economic Theory of Democracy*. Chicago: University of Chicago Press, 1954.

Duverger, Maurice. *Political Parties*. New York: Wiley, 1954.

Edinger, Lewis, ed. *Political Leadership in Industrial Societies*. New York: Wiley, 1967.

Eldersveld, Samuel J. *Political Parties: A Behavioral Analysis*. Chicago: Rand McNally, 1964.

Eulau, Heinz, and Sprague, John. *Lawyers in Politics*. Indianapolis: Bobbs-Merrill, 1965.

Fenno, Richard F. *The Power of the Purse*. Boston: Little, Brown, 1966.

Froman, Lewis. *Congressmen and Their Constituencies*. Chicago: Rand McNally, 1963.

Goldman, Ralph M. *The Democratic Party in American Politics.* New York: Macmillan, 1966.

Goodwin, George. *The Little Legislatures: Committees of Congress.* Amherst: University of Massachusetts Press, 1970.

Greenberg, Edward, ed. *Political Socialization.* Chicago: Atherton, 1970.

Greenstein, Fred. *Children and Politics.* New Haven: Yale University Press, 1965.

Hennessy, Bernard C. *Public Opinion.* 2nd ed. Belmont, Calif.: Wadsworth, 1971.

Herzberg, Donald, and Peltason, Jack. *A Student's Guide to Campaign Politics.* New York: McGraw-Hill, 1970.

Hinckley, Barbara. *The Seniority System in Congress.* Bloomington: Indiana University Press, 1971.

Hofstadter, Richard. *The Age of Reform.* New York: Doubleday, 1954.

———. *The Idea of a Party System.* Berkeley: University of California Press, 1969.

Holt, Robert, and Turner, John. *The Political Basis of Economic Development.* Princeton, N.J.: Van Nostrand, 1965.

Huckshorn, Robert, and Spencer, Robert. *The Politics of Defeat.* Amherst: University of Massachusetts Press, 1971.

Huitt, Ralph, and Peabody, Robert. *Congress: Two Decades of Analysis.* New York: Harper, 1969.

Jewell, Malcolm, and Patterson, Samuel. *The Legislative System in the United States.* New York: Random House, 1966.

Jones, Charles O. *The Republican Party in American Politics.* New York: Macmillan, 1965.

———. *The Minority Party in Congress.* Boston: Little, Brown, 1970.

Keech, William R. *The Impact of Negro Voting.* Chicago: Rand McNally, 1966.

Kessel, John H. *The Goldwater Coalition.* Indianapolis: Bobbs-Merrill, 1968.

Kingdon, John. *Candidates for Office.* New York: Random House, 1968.

Klapper, Joseph. *The Effects of Mass Communication.* New York: Free Press, 1963.

Kornberg, Allan. *Canadian Legislative Behavior.* New York: Holt, 1967.

———, ed. *Legislatures in Comparative Perspective.* New York: McKay, 1973.

Ladd, Everett, C. *American Political Parties: Social Change and Political Response.* New York: Norton, 1970.

Lamb, Karl, and Smith, Paul. *Campaign Decision-Making.* Belmont, Calif.: Wadsworth, 1968.

Lane, Robert. *Political Ideology.* New York: Free Press, 1965.

Lasch, Christopher. *The New Radicalism in America.* New York: Vintage, 1965.

Leuthold, David A. *Electioneering in a Democracy*. New York: Wiley, 1968.·

Lipset, S. M. *Political Man*. New York: Doubleday Anchor, 1960.

————, and Bendix, Reinhard. *Social Mobility in Industrial Society*. Berkeley: University of California Press, 1959.

————, and Altbach, Philip, eds. *Student Politics*. New York: Basic Books, 1967.

Lowi, Theodore. *The End of Liberalism*. New York: Norton, 1968.

MacRae, Duncan. *Dimensions of Congressional Voting*. Berkeley: University of California Press, 1959.

Manley, John F. *The Politics of Finance*. Boston: Little, Brown, 1969.

Marvick, Dwaine, ed. *Political Decision-Makers*. Glencoe, Ill.: Free Press, 1963.

Matthews, Donald R. *U.S. Senators and Their World*. New York: Vintage, 1963.

Mayhew, David R. *Party Loyalty Among Congressmen*. Cambridge, Mass.: Harvard University Press, 1967.

McFarland, Andrew. *Power and Leadership in Pluralist Societies*. Stanford: Stanford University Press, 1969.

McKeough, Kevin. *Financing Campaigns for Congress*. Princeton, N.J.: Citizen's Research Foundation, 1970.

Mendelson, Harold, and Crespi, Irving. *Polls, Television, and the New Politics*. San Francisco: Chandler, 1970.

Milbrath, Lester. *Political Participation*. Chicago: Rand McNally, 1965.

Miller, Clem. *Member of the House*. New York: Scribners, 1963.

Mills, C. Wright. *The Power Elite*. New York: Oxford University Press, 1956.

————. *The Sociological Imagination*. New York: Oxford University Press, 1959.

Nimmo, Dan. *The Political Persuaders*. Englewood Cliffs, N.J.: Prentice-Hall, 1970.

Peabody, Robert L., et al. *To Enact a Law: Congress and Campaign Finance*. New York: Praeger, 1972.

————, and Polsby, Nelson W., eds. *New Perspectives on the House of Representatives*. Rev. ed. Chicago: Rand McNally, 1969.

Pitkin, Hanna. *The Concept of Representation*. Berkeley: University of California Press, 1967.

Polsby, Nelson W. *Congress and the Presidency*. 2nd ed. New York: Macmillan, 1970.

Pomper, Gerald. *Elections in America*. New York: Dodd, Mead, 1968.

Prewitt, Kenneth. *The Recruitment of Citizen Politicians*. Indianapolis: Bobbs-Merrill, 1971.

Ranney, Austin. *Pathways to Parliament*. Madison: University of Wisconsin Press, 1965.

Rieselbach, Leroy N. *The Roots of Isolationism*. Indianapolis: Bobbs-Merrill, 1966.
_____, ed. *The Congressional System*. Belmont, Calif.: Wadsworth, 1970.
Ripley, Randall. *Party Leadership in the House of Representatives*. Washington, D.C.: Brookings, 1967.
_____. *Majority Party Leadership in Congress*. Boston: Little, Brown, 1969.
Rogin, Michael. *The Intellectuals and McCarthy*. Boston: MIT Press, 1966.
Saloma, Joseph, III. *Congress and the New Politics*. Boston: Little, Brown, 1968.
Schlesinger, Joseph. *Ambition and Politics*. Chicago: Rand McNally, 1966.
Scoble, Harry M. *Ideology and Electoral Action*. San Francisco: Chandler, 1967.
Smith, T. V. *The Legislative Way of Life*. Chicago: University of Chicago Press, 1940.
Sorauf, Frank. *Party and Representation*. Chicago: Atherton, 1963.
_____. *Party Politics in America*. 2nd ed. Boston: Little, Brown, 1972.
Truman, David. *The Congressional Party*. New York: Wiley, 1959.
_____, ed. *Congress and America's Future*. Englewood Cliffs, N.J.: Prentice-Hall, 1965.
Udall, Morris, and Tacheron, Donald. *The Job of the Congressman*. Indianapolis: Bobbs-Merrill, 1966.
Wahlke, John, and Eulau, Heinz, eds. *Legislative Behavior*. Glencoe, Ill.: Free Press, 1959.
_____, et al. *The Legislative System* New York: Wiley, 1963.
Wilson, James Q. *The Amateur Democrat*. Chicago: University of Chicago Press, 1960.
Wolfinger, Raymond, ed. *Readings on Congress*. Englewood Cliffs, N.J.: Prentice-Hall, 1971.
Zimbardo, Philip, and Ebbesen, E. *Influencing Attitudes and Changing Behavior*. New York: Addison-Wesley, 1969.

## II. Articles

Alford, Robert R., and Scoble, Harry M. "Sources of Local Political Involvement." *American Political Science Review*, December 1968: 1192–1207.
Bachrack, Stanley, and Scoble, Harry M. "Controlled Reduction of Non-Response." *Public Opinion Quarterly*, Summer 1967: 265–72.
Bowman, Lewis, and Boynton, George R. "Recruitment Patterns Among Local Party Officials." *American Political Science Review*, September 1966: 667–77.
Browning, Rufus. "The Interaction of Personality and Political System in Decisions to Run for Office." *Journal of Social Issues*, July 1968: 93–110.

————. "Hypotheses about Political Recruitment: A Partially Data-Based Computer Simulation." In *Simulation in the Study of Politics*. Edited by William D. Coplin. Chicago: Markham, 1968.

————, and Jacob, Herbert. "Power Motivation and the Political Personality." *Public Opinion Quarterly*, Spring 1964: 79–90.

Clark, Peter B., and Wilson, James Q. "Incentive Systems: A Theory of Organization." *Administrative Science Quarterly*, September 1961: 129–66.

Converse, Philip E., et al. "Electoral Myth and Reality: The 1964 Election." *American Political Science Review*, June 1965: 321–36.

————, and Schuman, Howard. "'Silent Majorities' and the Vietnam war." *Scientific American*, June 1970: 17–25.

Conway, M. Margaret, and Weigart, Frank. "Motivation, Incentive Systems, and the Political Party Organization." *American Political Science Review*, December 1968: 1159–74.

Costantini, Edmond, and Craik, Kenneth. "Competing Elites within a Political Party: California Delegates to the 1968 National Conventions." *Western Political Quarterly*, December 1969: 879–904.

Crotty, William. "Party Effort and Its Impact on the Vote." *American Political Science Review*, June 1971: 439–51.

————. "The Utilization of Mail Questionnaires." *Western Political Quarterly*, March 1966: 44–54.

Derge, David. "The Lawmaker as a Decision-Maker in American State Legislatures." *Journal of Politics*, August 1959: 408–33.

Erikson, Robert S. "The Electoral Impact of Congressional Roll Call Voting." *American Political Science Review*, December 1971: 1018–33.

————. "The Advantage of Incumbency in Congressional Elections." *Polity*, Spring 1971: 395–405.

Eulau, Heinz, and Hinckley, Katherine. "Legislative Institutions and Processes." In *Political Science Annual I*. Edited by James A. Robinson. Indianapolis: Bobbs-Merrill, 1966.

————, et al. "Latent Partisanship in Non-Partisan Elections." In *The Electoral Process*. Edited by M. Kent Jennings and L. Harmon Zeigler, Englewood Cliffs, N.J.: Prentice-Hall, 1965.

————, and Koff, David. "Occupational Mobility and the Political Career," *Western Political Quarterly*, September 1962: 508–22.

Fenno, Richard F. "The Freshmen Congressman: His View of the House." In *American Governmental Institutions*. Edited by Aaron Wildavsky and Nelson W. Polsby. Chicago: Rand McNally, 1969.

————. "The Internal Distribution of Influence: The House." In *Congress and America's Future*. Edited by David B. Truman. Englewood Cliffs, N.J.: Prentice-Hall, 1965.

————. "The House of Representatives and Federal Aid to Education." In *New Perspectives on the House of Representatives*. Edited by Robert L. Peabody and Nelson W. Polsby. Chicago: Rand McNally, 1963.

Field, John Osgood, and Anderson, Ronald A. "Ideology in the Public's Conception of the 1964 Election." *Public Opinion Quarterly*, Fall 1969: 380–98.

Fiellin, Alan. "Recruitment and Legislative Role Conceptions: A Conceptual Scheme and Case Study." *Western Political Quarterly*, June 1967: 271–88.

Friedman, Robert S. "The Urban-Rural Conflict Revisited." *Western Political Quarterly*, June 1961: 461–70.

Froman, Lewis A., "A Realistic Approach to Campaign Strategy and Tactics." In *The Electoral Process*. Edited by M. Kent Jennings and L. Harmon Zeigler. Englewood Cliffs, N.J.: Prentice-Hall, 1965.

Gregg, James. "Newspaper Editorial Endorsements and California Elections: 1948–1962." *Journalism Quarterly*, Autumn 1965: 532–38.

Gore, William, and Peabody, Robert L. "The Functions of the Political Campaign: A Case Study." *Western Political Quarterly*, March 1958: 55–70.

Greenstein, Fred I. "The Impact of Personality on Politics: An Attempt to Clear Away the Underbrush." *American Political Science Review*, September 1967: 629–43.

Hacker, Andrew. "The Elected and the Annointed." *American Political Science Review*, September 1961: 539–49.

Hahn, Harlan. "Correlates of Public Sentiment about War: Local Referenda on the Vietnam Issue." *American Political Science Review*, December 1970: 1186–98.

Hirschfield, Robert, et al. "A Profile of Political Activists in Manhattan." *Western Political Quarterly*, September 1962: 489–97.

Huntington, Samuel. "A Revised Theory of American Political Parties." *American Political Science Review*, September 1950: 669–77.

Jacob, Herbert. "Initial Recruitment of Elected Officials in the U.S.—A Model." *Journal of Politics*, November 1962: 701–16.

Jones, Charles O. "The Role of the Campaign in Congressional Politics." In *The Electoral Process*. Edited by M. Kent Jennings and L. Harmon Zeigler. Englewood Cliffs, N.J.: Prentice-Hall, 1965.

_____ . "Interparty Competition for Congressional Seats." *Western Political Quarterly*, September 1964: 461–76.

Joyner, Conrad. "Running a Congressional Campaign." In *Practical Politics in the United States*. Edited by C. Cotter. Boston: Allyn & Bacon, 1969.

King, Anthony. "Political Parties in Western Democracies." *Polity*, Winter 1969: 111–41.

King, Larry. "The Road to Power in Congress: The Education of Mo Udall—and What it Cost." *Harper's*, June 1971: 39–63.

Masters, Nicholas A. "Committee Assignments in the House of Representatives." *American Political Science Review*, June 1961: 345–57.

McClosky, Herbert. "Consensus and Ideology in American Politics." *American Political Science Review*, June 1964: 361–82.

――――, et al. "Issue Conflict and Consensus Among Party Leaders and Followers." *American Political Science Review*, June 1960: 406–27.

McKinney, Madge. "The Personnel of the Seventy-Seventh Congress." *American Political Science Review*, March 1942: 67–73.

Minar, David. "Ideology and Political Behavior." *Midwest Journal of Political Science*, November 1961: 317–31.

Mueller, John. "Trends in Popular Support for the Wars in Korea and Vietnam." *American Political Science Review*, June 1971: 358–76.

Murphy, Thomas P. "Political Ethics in a Coattail Congress." *Ethics*, April 1967: 291–96.

Murphy, William P. "Student Power in the 1970 Elections: A Preliminary Assessment." *P.S. (Political Science)*, Winter 1971: 27–33.

Nexon, David. "Asymmetry in the Political System: Occasional Activists in the Democratic and Republican Parties." *American Political Science Review*, September 1971: 704–16.

Paletz, David. "The Neglected Context of Congressional Campaigns." *Polity*, Winter 1971: 195–218.

Polsby, Nelson W. "Strengthening Congress in National Policy Making." *Yale Review*, Summer 1970: 481–97.

――――. "The Institutionalization of the U.S. House of Representatives." *American Political Science Review*, March 1968: 144–69.

――――, et al. "The Growth of the Seniority System in the U.S. House of Representatives." *American Political Science Review*, September 1969: 787–807.

Price, Charles M., and Bell, Charles G. "The Rules of the Game: Political Fact or Academic Fiction?" *Journal of Politics*, November 1970: 839–56.

Putnam, Robert. "Studying Political Elites: The Case of 'Ideology.'" *American Political Science Review*, September 1971:651–58.

Rieselbach, Leroy N. "Congressmen as 'Small Town Boys.'" *Midwest Journal of Political Science*, May 1970: 321–30.

Roeher, G. Allen. "Effective Techniques in Increasing Response to Mail Questionnaires." *Public Opinion Quarterly*, Summer 1963: 299–302.

Schlesinger, Joseph. "Political Careers and Party Leadership." In *Political Leadership in Industrialized Society*. Edited by Lewis Edinger. New York: Wiley, 1967.

Schoenberger, Robert. "Campaign Strategy and Party Loyalty." *American Political Science Review*, June 1969: 515–29.

Schubert, Glendon. "Ideological Distance: A Smallest Space Analysis Across Three Cultures." *Comparative Political Studies*, October 1968: 319–47.

Scoble, Harry M. "Political Money: A Study of Contributors to the National Committee for an Effective Congress." *Midwest Journal of Political Science*, August 1963: 229–53.

Seligman, Lester G. "Political Recruitment and Party Structure: A Case Study." *American Political Science Review*, March 1961: 77–86.

———. "Recruitment in Politics." *PROD*, 1958: 14–17.

Shannon, Wayne. "Electoral Margins and Voting Behavior in the House of Representatives." *Journal of Politics*, November 1968: 528–45.

Snowiss, Leo. "Congressional Recruitment and Representation." *American Political Science Review*, September 1966: 627–40.

Soule, John, and Clarke, James. "Issue Conflict and Consensus: A Comparative Study of Delegates to the 1968 Conventions." *Journal of Politics*, February 1971: 72–92.

Sullivan, John L., and O'Connor, Robert. "Electoral Choice and Popular Control of Public Policy: The Case of the 1966 House Elections." *American Political Science Review*, December 1972: 1256–68.

Warner, Emmy E. "Women in Congress: 1917–1964." *Western Political Quarterly*, March 1966: 16–31.

Wasby, Stephen. "National Party Contributions to Non-incumbent Candidates: the Democrats in 1964." *Social Science Quarterly*, March 1968: 573–85.

Weinbaum, Marvin E., and Judd, Dennis. "In Search of a Mandated Congress." *Midwest Journal of Political Science*, May 1970: 276–302.

Weisberg, Herbert F., and Rusk, Jerrold G. "Dimensions of Candidate Evaluation." *American Political Science Review*, December 1970: 1167–86.

Wolfinger, Raymond E., and Hollinger, Joan Heifetz. "Safe Seats, Seniority, and Power in Congress." *American Political Science Review*, 1965. Updated with new data in *Readings on Congress*. Edited by Raymond E. Wolfinger. Englewood Cliffs, N.J.: Prentice-Hall, 1971.

## III. Unpublished Materials

Bell, Charles G., and Price, Charles. "The Impact of Pre-Legislative Experience on Legislators' Role Orientations." Paper delivered to the 1969 annual meeting of the American Political Science Association.

Gertzog, Irwin. "Frustration and Adaptation: The Adjustment of Minority Freshmen to the Congressional Experience." Paper delivered to the 1966 annual meeting of the American Political Science Association.

———. "The Socialization of Freshmen Congressmen: Some Agents of Organizational Continuity." Paper delivered to the 1970 annual meeting of the American Political Science Association.

Oleszek, Walter J., ed. "The Freshman Legislator: Selected Articles." Washington, D.C.: Legislative Reference Service, 1968.

Price, H. Douglas. "The Congressional Career: Risks and Rewards." Harvard University, 1961.

Phillips, Harry. "The Relationship Between Party Regularity on Roll Calls and Subsequent Re-election Attempts." Ph.D. dissertation, Indiana University, 1972.

Schwartz, David. "Political Recruitment: An Essay in Theory and Research." Ph.D. dissertation, MIT, 1965.

# INDEX